D1231432

MedQuest
MCAT® FastPass
Study Guide

By
Elizabeth Malphrus and Conrad Fischer, MD

Copyright © 2016 Elizabeth Malphrus and Conrad Fischer, MD

ISBN: 978-1-63491-260-0

All rights reserved. No part of this publication may be reproduced, stored in a retrieval system, or transmitted in any form or by any means, electronic, mechanical, recording or otherwise, without the prior written permission of the author.

Published by BookLocker.com, Inc., Bradenton, Florida.

Printed on acid-free paper.

BookLocker.com, Inc.
2016

First Edition

MCAT FastPass Study Guide should be paired with MedQuest's FastPass video course and practice materials, available at www.MedQuestReviews.com.

Taught by Elizabeth Malphrus, Conrad Fischer, MD, and Austin Fischer, these collective offerings are designed from scratch for the new test and built to integrate with official AAMC materials.

A New Kind of Book for a New Kind of MCAT

The new MCAT, released in 2015, is different from the old test in three ways:
1. It covers a wider breadth of content, but at a shallower depth.
2. It is more about reasoning and less about knowledge.
3. It prioritizes content at the places where subjects intersect.

This should change how you study for the test, and the MedQuest *FastPass Study Guide*—together with the FastPass video course—will show you how.

We're not giving you a set of seven textbooks that are essentially a rewrite of the ones you already bought for your college classes. That's a waste of your time, and a waste of your money. Instead, we've taken all of that information, boiled it down to just the essentials, and put it all into a single, comprehensive volume. Have a friend's old MCAT review books? Your own class notes or textbooks from college? Access to the Internet? That—plus the *FastPass Study Guide*—is all you need to study effectively for the new MCAT.

That's because preparing for the bigger, wider, longer MCAT is all about efficiency. You have limited time to prepare, hundreds of topics to cover, and you still somehow have to make time to take a few seven-and-a-half-hour-long practice tests! The *FastPass Study Guide* is the key to keeping your MCAT prep organized and effective, so you don't waste a minute on your journey to medical school.

Acknowledgements

- This book was reviewed for accuracy and clarity by the inimitable genius librarian **Rebecca Morgan**.
- **Nick Russell and Charles Witherspoon** contributed immeasurably with creative vision, experience, cat wrangling, and thoughtful humoring of long conversations with the authors about every little decision along the way.
- Kidneys, amino acids, and more were made beautiful by designer **Ben Gabelman**.
- Copyeditor **John Sherman** transformed our word processor ramblings into a series of coherent, precise, and grammatically correct sentences.
- **Austin Fischer** was our guinea pig, contributing fact-checker, youth consultant, and enthusiasm generator.
- **Debbie Campbell** kept this whole operation organized and on track. She also coined the name "MCAT FastPass."

DISCLAIMER: This book includes broad statements and assertions about the nature of complex, nuanced theories and ideas. If you find your inner nerd saying, "Harrumph, I read in the latest issue of *Nature*…" or "Well, it's really more of a continuum…" don't freak out. MedQuest's inner nerd understands. But the truth is that the MCAT has a college-101 level of knowledge (with a 401 level of reasoning), so that is how we wrote the book.

Special extra disclaimer for social scientists: The Psychology/Sociology section of the MCAT was designed by a group of medical doctors and medical education experts. That's why it is the way that it is, and why we wrote it the way we wrote it. Googling "AAMC Behavioral and Social Science Expert Panel" may provide some useful context.

Table of Contents

Plan your study sessions. Never really got glycolysis? Before you dive into a textbook chapter or Wikipedia page, look at the *FastPass Study Guide*. It will give you an overview of what glycolysis is all about for the MCAT, and what topics, ideas, and/or formulas are most important for you to get a handle on. When you're done studying glycolysis, read through the section again to make sure it all clicks, and scribble notes in the margins if you need to. Then, the next day, the next week, the next month, you can reread the section again to make sure all that new knowledge is sticking.

Keep track of what you've covered. The *FastPass Study Guide* also works as a checklist for all of the topics covered on the MCAT. As you work through sections, check them off, so you'll have a clear record of what you've already covered, and won't let any topics fall through the cracks.

Refresh content that you haven't reviewed in a while. As you get toward the end of your MCAT studying journey, you will discover a frustrating truth about preparing for a test this big: By the time you've been through everything once, you start to forget the topics you reviewed early on! The *FastPass Study Guide* makes it easy to refresh your memory on important topics in just a few minutes. That way you can sneak some extra studying in throughout the day—whether you're commuting, working out, or just waiting for Netflix to autoplay the next episode.

Be confident that you're ready to take the MCAT. To do well on the MCAT, you need to know a little bit about every single topic in the AAMC outline, and a lot about the most important topics. This book will help you be confident that you know the most crucial ideas, facts, formulas, structures, and processes, so that you can make the most of your study time, and show medical schools that you have what it takes!

What This Book Is Not

This book does not include every single fact that could show up on an MCAT—that's actually not even possible. The AAMC provides detailed lists of the topics that will show up on the MCAT, but not the specific facts and ideas within those topics that are fair game to test. That means that even if you memorized every page of every one of your college textbooks, there are still going to be some surprises on test day. The best approach, then, to tackling the MCAT is to make sure you know *something* about every topic the MCAT covers, and spend most of your study time on the topics that are most important. Then, when you practice for the test, learn how to tackle the kinds of surprises that the MCAT is likely to throw at you.

This book is not going to teach you a topic if you haven't learned it before. It will, however, let you know right away whether you have a good grip on a subject or need to study more. That's because it's not a textbook—it's a study guide.

A lot of people try studying for the MCAT in the same way: linearly. They do content review first, studying chapter by chapter like you would for a regular class exam, and figure they'll start practicing later when they feel ready. This is not a winning strategy for MCAT prep, because the MCAT is different from any test you've ever taken before.

First of all, the content is so vast that if you just start reviewing at the beginning without a plan for how to get to the end, you're never going to make it in time. Second, practicing is how you learn what the test is all about, and how you know whether your studying is actually working—it doesn't make sense to leave it until the end.

Most importantly, though, **you are never going to feel ready to start practicing**. That's why so many people delay their MCAT dates—because they wait too long to start practicing, thinking that just a few more days, just a few more chapters, will make them feel ready.

The truth is, no matter how much you study, the answers are never going to become easy or obvious on the MCAT, because it is much more a test of your reasoning than a test of your knowledge. To start practicing for the MCAT is to acknowledge that no matter how much you study, you can never be confident that you're going to know every answer. That's a scary thought—but learning to accept it, and developing strategies to deal with it, are the first steps on the road to a great MCAT score.

Your plan to study for the MCAT should reflect the test itself. That means starting your practice early, gradually spending a larger and larger percentage of your time practicing, and reviewing your practice. It also means reviewing every single topic covered by the test, but doing so in parallel rather than one subject at a time. The MCAT prioritizes topics that integrate ideas from multiple different fields, so studying the subjects together, rather than compartmentalizing them, will help you get more comfortable transitioning between subjects, as well as recognizing those places where the subjects intersect.

On the next page is a sample FastPass Study Plan, based on a student who is planning to study for three months (that's 25 hours a week, for 300 hours total), using MedQuest FastPass alongside several official AAMC practice products (in this case: E-Book Mini-Test, Official Guide, Sample Test, Practice Test, and Question Packs). A study plan is a personal thing, so make sure to consider your own schedule, resources, strengths, weaknesses, and goals in making your plan. But whatever your plan is, stick to it! And be sure you give yourself time to come back to tricky and high-priority subjects, like we did with the "review weeks" in our plan.

Sample MedQuest FastPass Three-Month Study Plan
3 months, 3 full-length practice tests, 852 practice problems
(CP=chem/phys; BB=bio/biochem; PS=psych/soc)

Week	Study	Practice
1	*Watch: FastPass Introduction and Strategy* **CP:** Physical properties of matter **BB:** Proteins **PS:** The senses, the nervous system	AAMC E-Book Mini-Test: 12 Qs
2	*Watch: FastPass Chemistry/Physics* **CP:** Electrochemistry and circuits **BB:** Genes **PS:** Cognitive processes, behavior	AAMC Official Guide: 60 Qs
3	*Watch: FastPass Biology/Biochemistry* **CP:** Light and sound **BB:** Energy and metabolism **PS:** Social processes, psychological change	AAMC Official Guide: 60 Qs
4	*Watch: FastPass CARS and Psychology/Sociology* **CP:** Atoms and the periodic table, **BB:** Cells and molecules **PS:** The self, social thinking	**MedQuest MCAT Practice Test**
5	*Watch: FastPass Test Day* **CP:** Solutions **BB:** Cell and organism reproduction **PS:** Social interaction, social structure	AAMC Question packs: 120 Qs
6	**CP:** Classes of molecules **BB:** Human systems: reproductive, endocrine, respiratory, circulatory **PS:** Demographics, social inequality	AAMC Question packs: 120 Qs
7	**CP:** Chemical dynamics **BB:** Human systems: lymphatic, immune, digestive, excretory, musculoskeletal, skin	AAMC Question packs: 120 Qs
8	**CP review week:** Catch-up and revisit problem areas; re-watch CP videos	**AAMC Sample Test**
9	**BB review week:** Catch-up and revisit problem areas; re-watch BB videos	AAMC Question packs: 120 Qs
10	**PS review week:** Catch-up and revisit problem areas; re-watch CARS and CP videos	**AAMC Practice Test**
11	**Final review week:** Review problem areas from AAMC Practice Test; re-watch Test Day video	AAMC Question packs: 120 Qs

12	**Get ready week:** Read over everything one last time, plan for test day, and manage stress	AAMC Question packs: 120 Qs
	Rock the MCAT!	

FORMULAS TO MEMORIZE FOR THE MCAT

MCAT Formula List[§]	
$F = ma$	Force (N) = mass (kg) * acceleration (m/s^2)
$W = Fd\cos\Theta$	Work (J) = force (N) * distance (m) * cosine of angle between them
$KE = \left(\dfrac{1}{2}\right)mv^2$	Kinetic energy (J) = .5 * mass (kg) * velocity (m/s) squared
$PE = mgh$	Potential energy (J) = mass (kg) * gravity (m/s^2) * height (m)
$PE\ (spring) = \left(\dfrac{1}{2}\right)kx^2$	Potential energy (J) = .5 * spring constant * displacement squared
$P = \rho gh$	Hydrostatic pressure (Pa) = density (kg/m^3) * gravity (m/s^2) * height (m)
$P + (\dfrac{1}{2})pv^2 + pgh = constant$	Bernoulli's equation: atmospheric pressure + gauge pressure + hydrostatic pressure = constant
$AV=AV$	Continuity equation: area * volume = area * volume
$PV = nRT$	Ideal gas law: pressure (atm, torr, Pa, mmHg) * volume (L, m^3) = number of moles * gas constant * temperature (K) Boyle's law: PV = PV Charles' law: V/T = V/T Avogadro's law: V/n = V/n
$I = \Delta Q/\Delta T$	Current (A) = change in charge (C) over time (s)
$V = IR$	Ohm's law: voltage (volts) = current (A) * resistance (Ω)

$\rho = RA/L$	Resistivity ($\Omega * m$) = resistance(Ω) * cross-sectional area (m^2) /length (m)
$E = hf$	Photoelectric effect: Energy of a photon (J) = $6.6 * 10^{-34}$Js * frequency (Hz)
$n_1 \sin(\Theta_1) = n_2 \sin(\Theta_2)$	Snell's Law: index of refraction for incident material * sin(angle of incidence) = index of refraction for refractive material * sin(angle of refraction)
$\dfrac{1}{p} + \dfrac{1}{q} = \dfrac{1}{f}$	For thin lenses, 1/image distance + 1/object distance = 1/focal length
$K_w = [H^+][OH^-]$	Water ionization constant = concentration of H^+ * concentration of OH^- = 10^{-14}
$\Delta G = \Delta H - T\Delta S$	Gibb's free energy: change in free energy (kJ/mol) = change in enthalpy (kJ/mol) – temperature(K) * change in entropy (J/Kmol)
$k = Ae^{-\frac{E}{RT}}$	Arrhenius equation: rate constant = A (constant) * e^-activation energy (J)/gas constant * temperature (K)
$[P + a * \dfrac{n^2}{v^2}][(\dfrac{V}{n})\text{-}b] = RT$	Deviation of real gas behavior due to Van der Waals forces. Pressure (Pa) + constant (number of moles/volume)^2 * (Volume/number of moles – constant) = gas constant * temperature (K)
$Vo = \dfrac{Vmax[S]}{Km + [S]}$	Michaelis-Menten kinetics: Rx velocity = maximum reaction velocity * substrate concentration/substrate concentration at .5 V_{max} + substrate concentration

$$Keq = \frac{[C]^y[D]^z}{[A]^w[B]^x}$$	For wA + xB → yC + zD. The equilibrium constant (Keq) for a reaction is equal to the concentrations of products over the concentration of reactants, each raised to the power of its coefficient.
$C = kP_{gas}$	Henry's law: solubility of a gas at a fixed temperature (M) = Henry's constant (M/atm, unique to each solute) * Partial pressure of the gas (atm).
$E = E^o - (0.06/n) \ln(Q)$	Nernst Equation: voltage for non-standard conditions = standard voltage – (0.06/ number of moles of electrons transferred) * ln (reaction quotient)

§ *These are the formulas that the AAMC has explicitly indicated you should be able to recall for test day. There are additional equations throughout the book that may be useful to know, but these are the essential ones.*

PART I:
CHEMICAL AND PHYSICAL FOUNDATIONS OF BIOLOGICAL SYSTEMS

Physical Properties of Matter

- ☐ **Translational motion** is the movement of objects from one point in space to another.
  - **Speed** = distance/time (units: m/s)
  - **Scalar vs. vector:** Scalar quantities have magnitude, but no direction (speed, mass, time, volume, temperature, friction). Vector quantities have magnitude and direction (velocity, displacement, acceleration, force).
  - **Acceleration** is change in speed over time (m/s^2).
- ☐ **Periodic motion** describes the movement of waves.
  - **Velocity** = frequency * wavelength $(v=f\lambda)$
  - **Amplitude** is one half the distance from the crest to the trough.
  - **Wavelength** is the distance from peak to peak, or trough to trough.
  - **Frequency** is the number of wavelengths per unit time.
  - **Period** is the time it takes for one wavelength to occur, or the inverse of the frequency (period = 1/f).
  - **Transverse vs longitudinal waves:** In transverse waves, particles vibrate up and down in space, perpendicular to propagation of the wave (light, strings). In longitudinal waves, particles move back and forth in space, parallel to propagation of the wave (sound, springs).
- ☐ **Force** is an interaction that causes a mass to accelerate or deform.
  - Force = mass * acceleration (unit: Newton = $kg*m/s^2$).
  - **Newton's 1st Law** (inertia): An object at rest stays at rest and an object in motion stays in motion, unless acted on by an external force.
  - **Newton's 2nd Law:** The vector sum of forces on an object is equal to the mass of the object multiplied by the acceleration $(F_{net}=ma)$.
  - **Newton's 3rd Law:** When one object applies a force to a second object, the second object exerts an equal and opposite force on the first object.
  - **Static vs. kinetic friction:** Static friction is what resists a stationary object starting to move. Kinetic friction is what resists the motion of an object that is already moving.
    - Static friction is always higher than kinetic for the same materials, because it is harder to start an object moving than to keep it moving.

SI Unit Prefixes	
Tera-	10^{12}
Giga-	10^{9}
Mega-	10^{6}
Kilo-	10^{3}
Hecto-	10^{2}
Deka-	10^{1}
Deci-	10^{-1}
Centi-	10^{-2}
Milli-	10^{-3}
Micro-	10^{-6}
Nano-	10^{-9}
Pico-	10^{-12}

- **Center of mass** is used to simplify modeling of multiple forces acting on an object. An object's center of mass is the point where it could be balanced on your fingertip (ex: A pencil balances at a point halfway between the two ends, but a hammer would balance at a point much closer to the head).
- **Conservative force:** When the work done by a force is independent of the path taken. (ex: Gravity is conservative; gravity is doing the same work whether an object falls straight down or at an angle. Friction is non-conservative; if you push a box in a straight line, friction does a lot less work than if you were to push a box in a curvy path to the same end point.)
☐ **Equilibrium:** When the sum of forces acting on an object is zero, it remains at rest or at constant speed. Equilibrium in physics means the object has an acceleration of 0 m/s^2.
  - **Vector analysis:** To determine net force acting on an object, add the vectors.

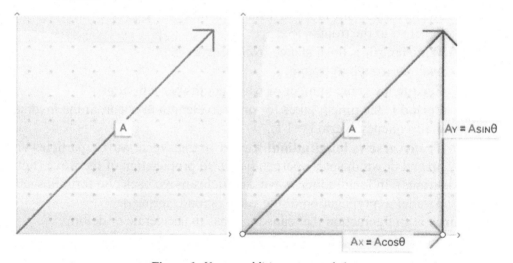

Figure 1: Vector addition approach 1.

- **Vector addition approach 1:** Break any diagonal forces into x and y components. Sum all the x components, sum all the y components. Hypotenuse is the resultant force vector ($A = \sqrt{A_y^2 + A_x^2}$).
- **Vector addition approach 2:** Put vectors tip to tail. Resultant is the distance between the start of the first vector and the end of the last vector.

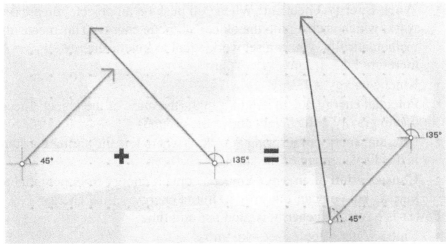

Figure 2: Vector addition approach 2.

☐ **Torque** is a force that causes an object to rotate some distance around an axis or pivot point (units: Joules = N*m, or $kg*m^2/s^2$).
- *MCAT application: muscle moving bone.*
- Torque = force * distance to fulcrum, or force * lever length
- Torque = radius * force * sin(theta)
- As the length of the lever arm increases, the force needed decreases, but the distance that the lever arm must be moved increases. (ex: That's why we put door knobs on the far side of doors, instead of in the center. It takes less force to open them that way.)
- W = F*d*cosΘ
- **Mechanical advantage** is the difference between the force needed to do work if you use a tool (lever or pulley), and the force needed to do work without the tool.

☐ **Kinetic and Potential Energy:** energy due to motion (kinetic) or position (potential)
- Units: Joules = N*m = $kg*m^2/s^2$

Relationship Between Physics Work and Energy Units

Force (mass*acceleration) = $kg*m/s^2$ = **Newton**
Torque (Force*distance) = N*m = $kg*m^2/s^2$ = **Joules**
Work (Force*distance) = N*m = $kg*m^2/s^2$ = **Joules**
Kinetic/potential energy (force*distance) = N*m = $kg*m^2/s^2$ = **Joules**
Power (work/time) = Joules/sec = $kg*m^2/s^3$ = **Watts**
Hydrostatic pressure (force/area) = N/m^2 = $kg/(m*s^2)$ = **Pascal**

- **Work Energy Theorem:** When you push on an object, you are doing work, which is changing the object's kinetic energy. This means that, mathematically, you can set work equal to kinetic energy ($W_{net} = \Delta KE$, therefore $Fd = 1/2\ mv_{final}^2 - 1/2 mv_{initial}^2$)
- Kinetic energy = $1/2mv^2$
- Potential energy due to height = mgh (the mass of the object * acceleration due to gravity * the height above the ground)
- Potential energy of a spring = $1/2kx^2$ (where k is the spring constant and x is the displacement of the spring)
- **Conservation of energy:** You can convert energy from potential to kinetic, but you can't destroy it. Initial energy = final energy
☐ **Power** is how much energy is used per unit time.
- Units: Watts = Joules/sec = $kg*m^2/s^3$
- While running a mile and walking a mile take the same amount of energy (Joules), you need more power (joules/second) to run a mile than to walk a mile.
☐ **Properties of fluids** describe the characterization and behavior of fluids.
- *MCAT application: circulatory system.*
- **Density** = mass / volume (units: kg/L, g/cm^3)

Know the Density of Water

$1\ g/ml = 1\ g/cm^3 = 1\ kg/L$

- **Specific gravity** is the ratio of the density of a substance to the density of water (unitless). If specific gravity is > 1, then the substance is denser than water. If specific gravity is < 1, then the substance is less dense than water.
- **Surface tension** is the attraction between fluid molecules, and between fluid molecules and their containers.
- Fluids take a form that reduces their surface area as much as possible. This causes the **meniscus** of fluids in containers, and beads of water on a windshield.
☐ **Fluid dynamics** describe how volume, velocity, and pressure change as blood moves through a closed system.
- **Archimedes' Principle** states that the buoyant force on an object is equal to the weight of the fluid displaced by the object.
- **Buoyant force** = weight of water displaced = mass displaced * gravity = density of fluid displaced * volume submerged * gravity (units: Newton = $kg*m/s^2$)
- When buoyant force is greater than the weight of an object, it rises. When buoyant force is less than the weight of an object, it sinks. When buoyant force = weight of object, it will float fully submerged.

- Change in gravity will not affect floating/sinking behavior. If buoyant force = weight of fluid displaced, then m(fluid)*g = m(object)*g, so g cancels from both sides.
- **Pascal's Law** states that pressure applied to a liquid is transmitted uniformly to all parts of the liquid. A small pressure on a small area can create a large pressure on a large area (ex: This is how brake fluid works.)
  - Force / area = force / area
- **Hydrostatic pressure** is the pressure a fluid exerts on an object at a given depth, due to the force of gravity acting on the fluid. As height of fluid increases, pressure increases.
  - Hydrostatic pressure = fluid density * gravity * height of fluid above point ($P = \rho gh$, units = Pascal = N/m^2 = $kg/(m*s^2)$)
- **Pouiselle Flow:** When a viscous fluid flows through a pipe (ex: blood through a blood vessel), its flow front is shaped parabolically, such that flow is fastest at the center, and slowest where it contacts the container. Viscosity causes the fluid to be dragged back at the edges.
- **Flow rate** = area * velocity for all points in a closed tube. This means that if the cross-sectional area of a blood vessel decreases, the velocity of blood moving through it must increase (ex: putting your thumb over the top of a garden hose).
  - Flow rate vs. velocity: the flow rate (units: m^3/s) of a fluid is constant for a given closed container, but the velocity (units: m/s) changes with variation in cross-sectional area
- **Venturi Effect:** As the velocity of a fluid through a constricted section of a tube increases, the pressure it exerts on the container decreases. Measured using a **pitot tube**.
- **Bernoulli's Equation:** Absolute pressure + pressure due to motion + gauge pressure = a constant value. $P + 1/2\rho v^2 + \rho gh$ = constant
- □ **Fluid dynamics in the circulatory system**: The circulatory system can be modeled as a closed series of pipes.
  - Pressure is highest as blood leaves the aorta, and lowest as it reenters the heart via the vena cava.
  - As blood goes from aorta →arteries →arterioles → capillaries, the total cross-sectional area of the vessel system is increasing, so pressure is decreasing, velocity is decreasing, and flow rate remains the same (A*V = A*V = flow rate)
  - As blood goes from capillaries → venules →veins → vena cava, the total cross-sectional area of the vessel system is decreasing, so velocity is increasing. Due to the resistance of the circulatory system, pressure continues to decrease as blood travels from capillaries back to the heart. Blood pressure is lowest as the vena cava reenters the heart.

- If you raise your arm above your head, the blood pressure in your arm decreases because you are decreasing the height of fluid that is above your arm ($P = \rho gh$).
- ☐ **Ideal gas** is a theoretical gas that meets the criteria described by the Kinetic Molecular Theory of Gases, which are:
  - o Molecules move in random motion.
  - o Molecules themselves have zero volume.
  - o No intermolecular forces exist between molecules.
  - o Collisions among molecules are perfectly elastic (e.g., kinetic energy is conserved).
  - o One mole of an ideal gas at STP has a volume of **22.4 Liters**.
- Unless otherwise stated, assume Standard Temperature and Pressure (STP):
  - o Temperature: 0° C = 273° K.
  - o Pressure: 1 atm = 760 mm Hg =100 kPa
  - o *MCAT application: gas exchange in the lungs*
- **Ideal Gas Law**: PV = nRT (P = pressure, V = volume, n=number of moles, R = universal gas constant (8 J/mol K), T = temperature in Kelvin)
  - o Boyle's Law: PV = PV
  - o Charles' Law: V/T = V/T
  - o Avogadro's Law: V/n = V/n
- **Boltzmann's Constant** relates temperature to energy. Essentially, it is the ideal gas constant per particle, rather than per mole. R/N_A (R = ideal gas constant, N_A = Avogadro's number)
- **Heat capacity** is a measure of the amount of heat required to raise the temperature of a given mass by 1° C.
- **Deviation from ideal gas behavior (real gasses):** Sometimes gases don't behave as ideal gases due to intermolecular forces, which cause collisions to become inelastic:
  - o At high pressure, actual volume is less than volume predicted by ideal gas law due to increased intermolecular attraction.
  - o At low temperature, actual volume is less than predicted by ideal gas law due to reduced velocity of collisions, which enhances influence of intermolecular forces.
- **The composition of gases** can be measured in several ways:
  - o **Mole fraction**: the number of moles of one gas in a mixture divided by the total moles of gas in the mixture (moles of gas of interest / total moles in gas mixture).
  - o **Partial pressure**: the contribution of a single gas in a mixture of gasses to the total pressure of that gas (pressure due to gas of interest / total pressure of gas mixture).

- o **Dalton's Law**: Total pressure of a gas mixture is the sum of the partial pressure of the individual gases. ($P_{total} = P_1 + P_2 \ldots$).

Electrochemistry, Circuits, and the Nervous System

- ☐ **Electrostatics:** Charge is a physical property of matter that can cause it to experience a force due to the presence of electromagnetic field.
  - Charge is a conservative property (it can't be created or destroyed).
  - **Insulators vs. conductors:** Conductors are materials that conduct electric charge; insulators are materials that do not conduct electric charge. The cytoplasm of a neuron is a conductor, the myelin sheath is an insulator.
  - **Coulomb's Law:** The magnitude of the electrostatic force between two charges is inversely proportional to the square of the distance between them ($F = k_e|q_1q_2|/r^2$). If the forces have the same sign, they move away from each other. If they have opposite signs, they move toward each other. K_e(Coulomb's Constant) is $9*10^9$.
  - **Electric field** (E): electric force per unit charge ($E = F/q$)
  - Electric field lines are drawn pointing outward from positive charges and inward for negative charges.

Distinguishing Between Related Electrostatic Concepts			
Concept	**Formula**	**Units**	**Definition**
Electric Force (F)	$F = k_e|q_1q_2|/r^2$	N	Amount of attraction between charged objects. Vector
Electric field (E)	$E = F/q$	N/C	electric force per charge
Electric potential energy (U)	$U = K_e\, q_1q_2/r$	J	Potential energy of a charged particle due to the presence of 1 or more additional charges nearby
Voltage or Electric potential (V)	$V = kQ/r$, or $V = U/q$	J/C = V	Same as voltage. Amount of electric potential energy that a point charge would have if it were moved from infinity to a certain point in space

- **Electric potential energy** (U) is the potential energy stored in a system of two or more charged particles.

- o $U = (K_e * q_1 * q_2)/r$ (unit: Joules), or the work that would be required to bring a group of points from an infinite distance apart into a given configuration.
- **Electric potential** (V) at a point in space can be calculated for a point in space by adding the voltage vectors of the individual charges that are acting on that point.
  - o $V = kq_1/r_1 + kq_2/r_2$ ... (k = Coulomb's Constant $9*10^9$)
- ☐ **Circuit basics:** characterizing the electrical behavior of simple physical or biological system.
  - *MCAT application: electrical activity of neurons and cardiac muscle.*
  - **Ohm's Law:** Voltage = Current * Resistance (V=IR)
  - **Current** (I) is the rate of flow of electric charge in a wire or neuron. I=Q/t, where Q is charge and t is time. (unit: Ampere = Coulomb/sec)
  - **Voltage or Electric Potential** (V) is the difference in electric potential energy between two points, per unit charge. It can also be thought of as the work done by an electric field if you were to move a point charge. $V = U/q_0$ or $(k_e * q)/r$ (unit: volts = Joules/Coulomb).
- ☐ **Resistance** (R) is a measure of the difficulty encountered by an electric current moving through a conducting wire or neuron. (unit = Ohm, Ω)
  - **Resistors in series:** current is the same in each resistor ($I_{total} = I_1 = I_2$ ...), voltage splits between resistors ($V_{total} = V1+V2...$), sum individual resistance to find total resistance ($R_{total} = R_1+R_2$ ...)
  - **Resistors in parallel:** current splits ($I_{total} = I_1 + I_2$ ...), voltage is the same in each resistor ($V_{total} = V1 = V2$), total resistance is the inverse of the sum of the inverse of the individual resistances ($1/R_{total} = 1/R_1+1/R_2$ ...)
  - **Resistivity** (ρ) is a measure of how much a material (wire, axon, etc.) resists the flow of current. $ρ = (R*A/L)$ where R is resistance, A is cross-sectional area, and L is length.
- ☐ **Capacitance** (C) is the magnitude of stored charge per applied voltage (C=Q/V), or a measure of the ability of an object, typically a parallel-plate capacitor, to store electrical charge.
  - **Parallel plate capacitor:** a circuit element consisting of two parallel surfaces, one of which accumulates positive charges, while the other accumulates negative charges
  - Capacitance can be increased by increasing the area of overlap between the plates, decreasing the distance between the plates, or by adding a **dielectric** between the plates
    - o A dielectric is an insulating material, typically glass.
  - **Capacitors in series:** voltage splits ($V_{total} = V1+V2$ ...), charge is equal ($Q_{total} = Q1 = Q2$ ...), total capacitance is the reciprocal of the inverse of the capacitance of each capacitor ($1/C_{total} = 1/C1+1/C2$ ...)

- **Capacitors in parallel:** voltage is equal ($V_{total} = V1 = V2...$), charge splits ($Q_{total} = Q1+Q2 ...$) (capacitance sums ($C_{total} = C1+C2...$)
- Energy of charged capacitor (U) = .5Q2/C
- If capacitance increases, energy decreases. If stored charge increases, energy of the charged capacitor increases, squared.
- ☐ **Conductivity** is a measure of the ability of a material to conduct electricity (electrical conductivity), or a measure of the electrical conductance per distance traveled in a solution (electrolytic).
  - Conductivity is the inverse of resistivity.
  - Pure, deionized water has low conductivity relative to a solution containing dissolved solids or ions. (ex: Sea water has higher conductivity than distilled water.)
  - Conductivity also increases as temperature decreases (improve conductivity by increasing ion concentration, and/or decreasing temperature).
- ☐ **Tools for measuring circuits: voltmeter** measures voltage, **ammeter** measures current. Remember that these tools for measuring circuit elements have resistance themselves, so for measuring voltage across a resistor, voltmeter must be placed in parallel (voltage is equal for resistors in parallel). For measuring current in a resistor, ammeter must be placed in series, immediately following the resistor of interest (current is equal for resistors in series).
- ☐ **Neurons**: Principles of electrical circuits can be applied to the electrophysiology of neurons.
  - **Membrane as a capacitor:** A parallel plate capacitor accumulates and separates charges, with one plate taking on a positive charge and the other taking on a negative charge. A non-conducting/insulator material, such as air or glass, separates the two plates. A neuron uses active transport to generate a separation of charges (resting potential). The membrane acts as an insulator between the two regions of charge (extracellular and intracellular).
  - **Resistance:** When ion channels open, they reduce the resistance (R) of the membrane to the flow (current, I) of that ion. Ion channels closing lead to increased resistance.
  - **Voltage:** Typical resting membrane potential is -70 mV. During an action potential, the cell depolarizes to approximately +30mV, and then repolarizes to approximately -90 mV. This hyperpolarization is called the refractory period, as no new action potentials can be generated until the neuron returns to its resting potential.

- **Nodes of Ranvier:** The speed of propagation along an axon is increased because of gaps in the myelin sheath. Depolarization moves from node to node, rather than from point to point, along uninsulated axons.
- ☐ **Magnetism** is the effect of nearby electric currents on the movement of charged particles.
  - **Magnetic field** (B) is the force experienced by a charge moving through space as a result of nearby electric currents. (Unit: tesla, or N*s/m*C).
  - **Force due to a magnetic field** is called the Lorentz Force (F) = qvB, or charge of the particle * velocity of the particle * magnitude of the magnetic field. Force is a vector quantity, so direction is also needed. The magnetic force is perpendicular to both the direction of the magnetic field and to the velocity of the particle (right-hand rule).
- ☐ **Electrochemistry** concerns electric properties and behaviors of solutions and biological systems.
  - *MCAT application: neurons and proton motive force.*
  - An **electrolytic cell** undergoes a redox reaction when electrical energy is applied to it.
  - An **electrolyte** is a solution that contains ions, increasing its ability to conduct electricity.
  - **Electrolysis** is a lab technique in which a current is applied to a solution in order to drive forward a nonspontaneous redox reaction. It requires voltage input, typically from a battery.
  - The **anode** is where oxidation occurs; the **cathode** is where reduction occurs. Electrons flow from the anode to the cathode (mnemonic: An Ox, and a Red Cat).
  - Ions move through solution or salt bridge, electrons move through wire.
  - **Faraday's Law** can be used to find what quantity of a product is deposited (or liberated, if a gas). IT = nF, current * time = number of moles of electrons * Faraday's Constant (95,000 C/mol). Solve for moles of electrons, then use half reaction to find moles of product (ex: $Ag^+ + e^-$ → Ag, if n = 2, then 2 moles of silver are deposited).
- ☐ **Galvanic/voltaic cells:** A spontaneous redox reaction is used to produce an electric current (no battery).
  - Galvanic/voltaic cells use a salt bridge to prevent charge buildup.
  - **Half-reactions:** The oxidation half-reaction happens at the anode (electrons as product); the reduction half-reaction happens at the cathode (electrons as reactant).
  - **Cell potential** is positive for galvanic/voltaic cells, so no energy input is needed. Cell potential is negative for electrolytic cells, so a battery must be added.

- **Electrons flow** from the anode to the cathode.
- A **concentration cell** is a form of galvanic cell that includes two half cells with the same electrodes, but different concentrations. Voltage is produced by movement toward equilibrium.
- **Nernst Equation** is used to calculate cell potential based on the concentration gradient of the redox reaction. $E = E^o - (0.06/n) \ln(Q)$. Voltage of a galvanic/voltaic/concentration cell (E) = standard voltage (E^o) – (0.06/ number of moles of electrons transferred) Ln (reaction quotient).
  - Reaction quotient is essentially the equilibrium expression (multiplied product concentrations over multipled reactant concentrations, all raised to the power of their coefficient), but for non-equilibrium conditions.
  - At equilibrium, Q=K, and E=0.
- *MCAT application: flow of ions across a membrane.*
☐ **Batteries** are used to store electrical energy.
- **Electromotive force** is what we call voltage when it is generated by a battery or magnetic field.
- **Lead-storage batteries** ($Pb+PbO_2+2SO_4^{2-}+4H^+ \rightarrow 2PbSO_4+2H_2O$) are voltaic cells in that they are driven by a spontaneous redox reaction. Their reactions are also reversible for "recharging."
- **Nickel-cadmium batteries** ($Cd+NiO(OH) \rightarrow Cd(OH)_2+Ni(OH)_2$) produce cadmium hydroxide and nickel hydroxide, both solid precipitates. This means the reaction can be easily reversed, and the battery recharged.

Light and Sound, Hearing and Sight

☐ **Sound** is longitudinal waves in a medium, detectable by the ear.
- **Sound moves faster as the medium gets denser** (opposite of light). Sound cannot travel in a vacuum.
  - **Intensity of sound** is measured in Decibels, on a logarithmic scale.
    - Intensity = power / area (Watts/m^2)
    - Sound level (Decibels) = 10 log (I/I_0), where I_0 represents the lower threshold of human hearing ($I_0 = 10^{-12}$ W/m^2 = 0 Db).
    - Measurement is logarithmic because a large increase in intensity results in a small increase in sound level, or in its perceived loudness.
  - **Attenuation** (damping) is the capacity of a material to dissipate energy.
  - **Pitch** refers to the frequency of sound waves. Waves with higher frequency are perceived to have a higher pitch.

- **Resonance** occurs when the vibration of one system matches the natural frequency of another system, causing it to vibrate with a greater amplitude.
- **Standing waves vs. traveling waves:** Traveling waves are produced when one end of the wave is fixed, but the other moves up and down (ex: moving your arm up and down to make a wave in a string that is bolted to a wall at one end). Traveling waves appear to be propagating forward. Standing waves occur when both ends are fixed, such that the wave appears to be stationary (ex: plucking a guitar string).
  - Wavelength of standing wave for string or open pipe = 2L/n
  - Wavelength of standing wave in a closed pipe = 4L/n
- **Ultrasound** is medical imaging made possible by devices that emit ultrasound waves (soundwaves at frequency too high for human perception), which reflect off of surfaces back to a detector in order to form an image. Ultrasound can show both structures and movement (due to the Doppler effect).
- **Shock waves** occur when a wave moves faster than the speed of sound in a medium. A shock wave is characterized by an abrupt change in pressure, temperature, and density of a medium that dissipates quickly.

☐ **Doppler effect**: When the source of a sound and the perceiver of a sound are in motion relative to one another, the perceived frequency of the sound differs from the actual frequency in a predictable way.
- Perceived frequency will be higher if source and perceiver are moving toward each other.
- Perceived frequency will be lower if source and perceiver are moving away from each other.
- $F_{perceived} = F_{emitted} ((V \pm V_{observer}) / (V \pm V_{source}))$

☐ **Light** is electromagnetic radiation. Electromagnetic radiation consists of perpendicularly oscillating electric and magnetic fields, where the direction of propagation is perpendicular to both.

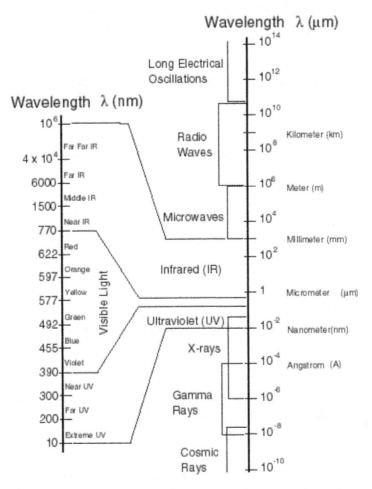

Figure 3: *Electromagnetic Spectrum. Visible light is 400-700 nm, from violet to red (Image credit: NFejza).*

- **Interference:** Waves out of phase by 180 degrees (half a wavelength) produce destructive interference (a.k.a. "cancelling out").
- The **Young double-slit experiment** demonstrates that light has properties of a both a particle and a wave: A laser beam is shone on a plate with two thin, parallel slits, so that the light passes through the slits and is projected on a screen behind.
  - **Wave property**: When light passes through the two slits, the slightly different paths taken by the two sets of light waves causes them to be out of phase, such that they create an interference pattern that can be observed on the screen (alternating bright bars, which indicate **constructive interference**, and dark bars, which indicate **destructive interference**).

- o **Particle property**: If photon detectors are used on each slit, they will show that each photon goes only through one slit or the other, whereas a typical wave would be expected to pass through both slits.
- ☐ **Thin film interference** occurs when light waves are reflected from both the top and the bottom boundary of a thin film of oil on the surface of a fluid.
  - When light hits a thin film, some of it is reflected off the top layer, and some is transmitted through and then reflected off the bottom layer. This causes the waves reflected off the top layer to be out of phase with waves reflected off the bottom layer, such that they form an interference pattern, like what can be seen when you see iridescent patterns of oil on the road.
- ☐ **Diffraction grating:** When a laser is shined on a series of slits, the light spreads out as it passes through the slits, creating interference patterns on a screen behind.
- ☐ **Single-slit diffraction:** If a laser is shown through a single slit, it creates a bright central band on the screen behind, with a series of smaller and smaller bands on either side.
  - When the light passes through the slit, its wave fronts take on a rounded form. Every point of this rounded wave front also acts as a secondary source of spherical waves. The central bright band indicates the highest intensity, where all of the secondary spherical waves interfere constructively, while the alternating dark and light bands represent alternating destructive and constructive interference at lower levels of intensity (that is, between some but not all of the secondary waves).
- ☐ **Pinhole diffraction:** The same diffraction concepts apply for light shone through pin holes, rather than slits, such that there will be alternating bright and dark rings on the screen.
- ☐ **X-ray diffraction**, also known as x-ray crystallography, involves projecting x-rays onto a crystalline substance and analyzing the diffraction pattern to identify the molecular structure of the crystal.
- ☐ **Polarization of light:** Unpolarized light propagates along any plane with equal probability.
  - Linearly polarized light consists of waves that travel along a single plane.
  - Circularly polarized light travels along two planes at a $90°$ angle from each other.
- ☐ **Properties** of electromagnetic radiation:
  - **Speed of light**, c, is constant at $3*10^8$ meters/second in a vacuum.

- **V=fλ:** Velocity (m/s) = frequency (hertz)* wavelength (meters)
- Photon energy (E) = hf (photon energy = Planck's Constant ($6.6*10^{-34}$ J*s) * frequency)

☐ **The visual spectrum** of light is 400-700 nanometers.
  - Violet: 400 nm
  - Blue: 480 nm
  - Green: 540 nm
  - Yellow: 580 nm
  - Orange: 590 nm
  - Red: 700 nm

☐ **Molecular structure and absorption spectra**: Absorption patterns can be used to identify compounds and functional groups or to elucidate chemical structures.

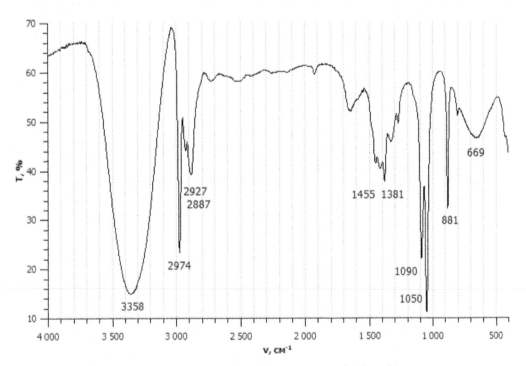

***Figure 4:** Infrared Spectroscopy of Ethanol.*

☐ **Infrared region spectroscopy** (wavelength: 700 nanometers to 1 millimeter) can be used to assess intramolecular vibrations and rotations.
  - Shining infrared waves on a chemical sample causes bonds (modeled as springs) to stretch and compress. Only vibrations that alter the dipole or polarity will absorb in the infrared region.
  - No polarity in bond (ex: diatomic elements), then no infrared absorption

- Fingerprint region: 500 to 1500 cm^{-1}. Patterns in fingerprint region are unique for every individual compound, but are difficult to read/interpret.
- Diagnostic region: 1500 to 4000 cm^{-1}. Patterns are not unique, but can tell you about what functional groups are in the molecule.
- In general, for common characteristic group absorptions in the diagnostic region:
  - Higher frequency indicates bond stretching, and therefore high-energy bonds; lower frequency indicates bond vibration and therefore low-energy bonds.
  - More s character in a bond (ex: sp) leads to a higher frequency; less s character (ex: sp3) leads to lower absorption frequency.
  - A larger dipole moment means a stronger, more intense signal. (ex: A C-C double bond would produce "weak" signal, while carbonyl would produce stronger signal.)
  - Look around 1500-1800 for double bonds.
  - Look around 3000 for different types of C-H bonds (sp, sp2, sp3).
  - If there's no dipole moment, there will be no signal in the double bond region (ex: symmetrical alkane).
  - Broad peaks are due to hydrogen bonding that can spread/weaken adjacent bonds (alcohols).

Characteristic IR Absorption Spectra	
Structure	**Absorption region (cm^{-1})**
H—C≡C—H	• 3300 for the C-H bonds (sp hybridization) • 2200 for the C-C triple bond
H C=C H / H H (ethene structure)	• 3100 for C-H bonds (sp2 hybridization) • 1600 for C-C double bond (low intensity relative to C-O double bond)
H—C—C—H with H H / H H (ethane structure)	• 2900 for C-H bonds (sp3 hybridization) • 1200 for C-C single bond
R—O—H	• 3300 (broad peak) for O-H bond

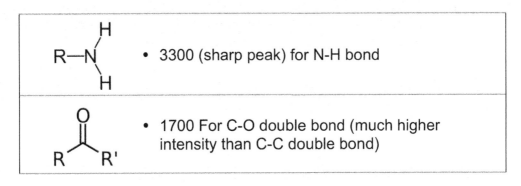

- ☐ **Visible region spectroscopy**: When light hits a compound, energy from absorbed photons can promote electrons from bonding or non-bonding orbitals into available anti-bonding orbitals. Molecules that absorb light in the visible region tend to have conjugated double bonds or aromatic rings.
  - Absorption in the visible region gives the complementary color. Ex: Carotene (from carrots) has 11 conjugated bonds, which is enough conjugation to enter the visible spectrum. The absorbance max is about 500, which is blue/green, so what is perceived is the complementary color: orange.
  - If there is 100 percent transmittance, no absorption occurred, so no bonds were stretching or vibrating.
  - Color-change indicators take advantage of visible light absorption properties. If you have an indicator that is one color when in ion form, and another color when bonded to a hydrogen, you can use its color change to assess pH of the substance.
- ☐ **Ultraviolet region spectroscopy** is used to observe pi electrons and non-bonding electron transitions
  - Only double bonds absorb UV radiation because pi electrons can transition with relative ease from bonding/non-bonding orbitals to anti-bonding orbitals.
  - The more conjugated a system is, the longer the wavelengths of electromagnetic radiation absorbed. Highly conjugated systems can have long enough wavelengths to enter the visible spectrum.
- ☐ **NMR spectroscopy** (nuclear magnetic resonance) involves shooting a bunch of electrons at a sample of ionized gas, which enables the analysis of their relative mass and charge through manipulating electric and magnetic fields in the detector.
  - **Equivalent protons**: The number of signals seen on an NMR spectrum indicates how many different kinds of protons are present.
  - **Spin-spin splitting**: When you see a cluster of peaks in one area, that indicates that you have a group of protons with slightly different magnetic

environments due to the presence of other protons (and therefore positive charges) nearby. If a proton has n neighbors, it will split into n+1 lines.

Ethanol

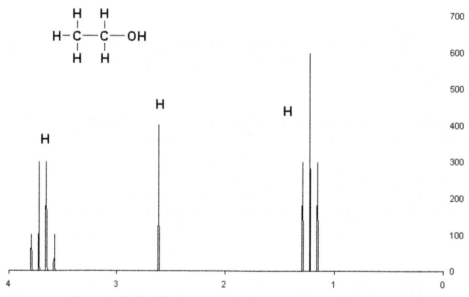

Figure 5: NMR Spectroscopy of Ethanol (Image credit: T.vanschaik).

☐ **Geometric optics** describes how the path of light is altered when it encounters different media.
  • **Reflection** of light from a plane surface: the angle of incidence equals the angle of reflection.
  • **Refraction** is when light bends as it passes through different media.

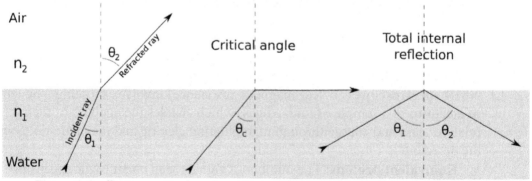

Figure 6: Snell's Law, critical angle, and total internal reflection (Image credit: Josell7).

- Refractive index (n) is a number specific to a medium that describes how light is refracted through it: $n = c/v$, or the speed of light in a vacuum divided by the velocity of light in the medium; $n = 1$ for a vacuum.
- **Snell's Law**: $n_1 \sin\theta = n_2 \sin\theta$, where n is index of refraction, and θ is the angle formed by the ray and normal (an imaginary line perpendicular to the surface between the two mediums)
- For many transparent media, the index of refraction is higher for light with shorter wavelengths and lower for light with longer wavelengths (ex: Violet light (400 nm) is refracted/bent more than red light (700 nm), as illustrated by a dispersion prism.)
- **Dispersion:** Media with wavelength-dependent refraction indices can cause white light to be split into component colors, due to the unequal refraction of light of different wavelengths.
- **Total internal reflection** occurs when a light wave passing through transparent media is completely reflected at the media boundary, rather than passing through. Two conditions are required:
  - The wave is moving from a media with a higher refractive index to a lower refractive index (ex: glass to air); and
  - The angle of incidence is greater than some critical angle.
- ☐ **Spherical mirrors** come in two types: converging/concave mirrors, which bend light inward, and Diverging/convex mirrors, which bend light outward.
  - The **center of curvature** is the radius of the circle created by completing the sphere of a plane mirror
  - **Focal length** is one half the radius of curvature. Focal length is positive for converging mirrors, negative for diverging mirrors.
  - **Real** images are on the same side of the mirror as the object.
  - **Virtual** images are on the back side of the mirror. (ex: When you look in a regular mirror, you see a virtual image of yourself.)
  - Diverging mirrors can only form virtual images.
- ☐ **Thin lenses** can be converging (thicker in the middle and tapering at the edges) or diverging (thinner in the middles and flared out at the edges).

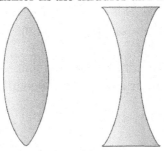

Figure 7: *Convex/converging lens (left) and concave/diverging lens (right).*

- **Image formation equation: $(1/p) + (1/q) = (1/f),$** or, 1/object distance + 1/image distance = 1/focal length.
- Sign conventions:
  - o p is always positive.
  - o q is positive for real images and negative for virtual images. For lenses, real images are on opposite side of lens from the object; for mirrors, real images are on the same side of the lens as the object.
  - o f is positive for converging lenses and mirrors, negative for diverging lenses and mirrors.
- **Ray diagrams:**
  - o Draw one line from the top of the object, straight across through the lens (this ray will be bent either out or in);
  - o Draw a second line from the top of the object through the center of the lens (rays through center of any lens are not diffracted).
- **Lens strength**, or power, is equal to the inverse of the focal length (meters). Unit: **diopters**, or m^{-1}. As the focal length gets smaller (and therefore the lens gets more curved), the lens becomes more powerful because it refracts light to a greater extent. As focal length gets larger, lens strength goes down ($P = 1/f$).
- **Combination of lenses**: If one lens forms a real image, that real image can be used as the object for a second lens (and so on). Magnification of a series of lenses is the product of the individual magnifications.
- Lens aberrations come in two types:
  - o **Spherical:** light rays toward the edges of a lens are refracted more than those at the center, which leads to imperfect focusing (blurry).
  - o **Chromatic:** different wavelengths of light get refracted differently (color fringing).
- ☐ **Optical instruments:**
  - **Optical microscope:** uses a series of lenses to increase total lens power (magnification) while controlling for aberrations.
  - **Eye:** the crystalline lens is a converging lens, and focuses light on the retina (diverging lenses correct near-sightedness, converging lenses correct far-sightedness).
  - **Magnifying glass:** a converging lens that, at distances smaller than the focal length, creates virtual, upright, magnified images.

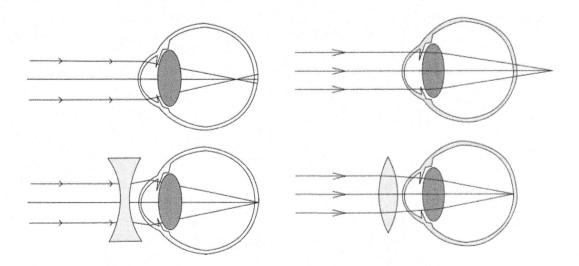

Figure 8: *Myopia corrected with a concave lens (left), and hyperopia corrected with a convex lens (right).*

Atoms and the Periodic Table

☐ **Atoms** are the smallest sub-units of all matter that still exhibit the chemical and physical properties of their element.
- **Neutrons**: uncharged particles in the nucleus
- **Protons**: positively charged particles in the nucleus
- **Electrons**: negatively charged particles that move around the nucleus
- **Atomic number**: the number of protons in the nucleus. This defines the element, and is the same across isotopes.
- **Atomic weight**: weight of a mole of atoms of that element (g/mol). Isotopes of the same element can have different atomic weights.
- **Isotopes**: variations of a single element that have the same number of proton and electrons, but a different number of neutrons (same atomic number, different atomic weight). Most elements exist as a mix of 2 or more isotopes.
  - o Tools: a **mass spectrometer** measures the ratio of mass to charge in a sample by bombarding a sample with electrons. Different isotopes appear as a cluster of peaks; the taller the peak, the more abundant the isotope.
- **Nuclear forces** are the forces that govern the interactions among protons and neutrons in a nucleus.

- o **Strong force**: extremely strong, but works over extremely short distances. Overcomes the repulsive forces between protons to bind the nucleus together.
- o **Electrostatic force**: repulsive force among protons in the nucleus. Weaker than the strong force.
- **Binding energy** is the energy that would be required to disassemble a nucleus, or the energy released when a nucleus is created.

☐ **Radioactive decay** occurs when a nucleus releases energy by emitting radiation in various forms.
- α decay: release of an alpha particle (He^{2+}); changes the element by removing 2 protons and 2 neutrons
- β decay: release of a beta particle (1 electron)
- γ decay: release of an electromagnetic wave (no atomic number, no mass number)
- **Half-life**: the time it takes for an element to decay to half its original mass; with successive half-lives, exponential decay occurs (1st half-life, sample is 50% of original. 2nd half-life, 25% of original, etc.)

☐ **Electron structure** is modeled in two primary ways:
- Electrons orbit the nucleus, like planets around the sun (Bohr atom model)
- Electrons are found in "probability clouds," or orbitals, around the nucleus (quantum mechanics model)
- **Heisenberg uncertainty principle:** You can measure the position or the momentum of an electron, but you can't know both simultaneously.

☐ **Principal quantum number** (n) indicates what shell an electron is in (1, 2, 3…). Higher n indicates higher energy electrons.
- Each shell has n^2 orbitals. Each orbital has 2 electrons with opposite spins.
- Each shell can hold $2n^2$ electrons (2 in shell 1, 8 in shell 2, etc.).
- **Orbital structure of hydrogen atom:** hydrogen has one electron in an s (spherical) orbital in shell n=1.

☐ **Ground state vs. excited state:** Electrons are normally found in their ground, or lowest, energy state, unless they absorb additional energy, which can cause them to enter an excited state, or a higher energy level. Excited electrons return to their ground state by releasing energy.

☐ **Absorption and emission line spectra**: light absorption/emission spectra, or patterns, are unique to each element or compound, and can therefore be used to identify unknowns. Specific wavelengths are associated with a specific transition between energy levels (ex: 656 nm indicates a transition from N = 3 to N = 2).

- **Absorption line spectra** show wavelengths of absorbed photons, as electrons are excited into a higher energy level. Looks like black bars against a rainbow background.
- **Emission line spectra** show wavelengths of emitted photons, as electrons fall from higher to lower energy levels. Looks like colored lines against a black background.
☐ **Pauli exclusion principle:** No two electrons can have identical quantum numbers. Electrons in the same orbital have opposite spins.
☐ **Paramagnetism and diamagnetism:** Each electron has a spin (+ and –, or up and down). If two electrons spin in the same direction (parallel), their magnetic fields add. If two electrons spin in opposite directions (antiparallel), their magnetic fields cancel each other out.
- Paramagnetic materials have one or more unpaired electrons, and therefore the magnetic fields of their individual electrons do not fully cancel each other out. Paramagnetic materials are attracted to external magnetic fields.
- Diamagnetic materials have no unpaired electrons, and therefore the magnetic fields of their individual electrons cancel each other out (no net magnetic field). Paramagnetic materials are not attracted (or are weakly repelled) by external magnetic fields.
- To determine whether an element is paramagnetic or diamagnetic, write electron configuration to determine whether it has unpaired electrons.
☐ **Conventional notation for electronic structure** comes in two varieties: energy level notation, which identifies the number of electrons in each shell; and orbital diagrams, which identify the energy level, the orbital, and the spin for each electron.
- **Energy level notation:** the energy level (principle quantum number, n); the orbital (s, p, d, f); and the number of electrons in that orbital as an exponent
  - Ex: Helium is $1s^2$
  - Ex: Phosphorous is $1s^2\,2s^2\,2p^6\,3s^2\,3p^3$
  - Energy level notation is often abbreviated to only the last shell, as the configuration of lower shells is standardized across all elements.
- **Orbital diagrams:** Draw each electron as an arrow, one pointing up and one pointing down in each individual orbital (Pauli exclusion principle and Hund's Rule apply).
  - Lithium: 1s[↑↓] 2s[↑_]
  - Beryllium: 1s[↑↓] 2s[↑↓]
  - Boron: 1s[↑↓] 2s[↑↓] 2p[↑_] [_ _] [_ _]
  - Carbon: 1s[↑↓] 2s[↑↓] 2p[↑_] [↑_] [_ _]
  - Nitrogen: 1s[↑↓] 2s[↑↓] 2p[↑_] [↑_] [↑_]

2 (2

- ☐ **Photoelectric effect:** Light striking a metallic surface can cause electrons to be emitted, if the frequency of the light is able to overcome the binding energy of the electron.
  - **e=hf:** energy of a photon = Planck's Constant ($6.6*10^{-34}$) * frequency
  - **Light as wave:** The photoelectric effect depends on light of a certain frequency.
  - **Light as particle:** One photon striking one electron causes it to be ejected as a photoelectron. The energy of the photon is transferred to the photoelectron (conservation of energy).
- ☐ **The Periodic Table** organizes the elements by their characteristics. *A periodic table is provided for you on the MCAT, but is only helpful if you know how to read it. A periodic table is also printed inside the back cover of this book, for reference.*
  - **Periods** all have the same highest energy level, but different number of electrons in that energy level.
  - **Groups** are columns of the periodic table. Elements in the same group have similar properties because they have the same number of electrons in their outermost shells.
    - **Alkali metals** (group 1): shiny and soft metals; highly reactive; found only in salts; likely to have +1 charge
    - **Alkaline earth metals** (group 2): shiny and silvery-white metals; somewhat reactive; full s orbital
    - **Transition metals** (groups 3-12): filling up the d orbitals as you move across the D block; have multiple oxidation states; conduct electricity
    - **Metals:** shiny; good conductors; form alloys; malleable
    - **Metalloids:** semiconductors; share properties with metals and nonmetals
    - **Non-metals:** the stuff people are made of; brittle; good insulators
    - **Halogens** (group 17): "salt-makers"; highly reactive; colorful; diatomic
    - **Noble gases** (group 18): stable/inert; colorless; full octets
  - **Blocks:** Groups 1 and 2, plus helium, are the s-block (last electron was added to an s orbital); groups 3-12 are the d block (last electron was added to a d orbital); and groups 13-18, except for helium, are the p block (last electron was added to a p orbital).
  - **Diatomic elements:** all halogens plus hydrogen, nitrogen, and oxygen
  - **Valence electrons:** electrons in the outer shell(s) of an atom that participate in bonding and give the atom its physical/chemical character
  - **Electron love:** Ionization energy, electron affinity, and electronegativity are different ways to define how much atoms love their electrons.

- o **Ionization energy** is the energy required to remove an electron from an atom (form a cation). It increases L to R across the periodic table, and decreases top to bottom.
- o **Second ionization energy** (removing a second electron to form a 2+ cation) follows the same trend as first ionization energy. Second ionization energy is always higher than first ionization energy for a given element.
- o **Electron affinity** is a measure of the energy released when an electron is added to a neutral atom.
- o **Electronegativity** is a measure of how hard an atom pulls on electrons in a bond.
- o Ionization energy, electron affinity, and electronegativity increase L to R across the periodic table, and decrease top to bottom.
- **Atom size** increases as you go down a group (addition of shells), and decreases L to R across a period.
- **Ion size:** Cations (+ charge) of a given element are smaller than neutral atoms; anions (- charge) are larger than neutral atoms.
- ☐ **Stoichiometry** measures the composition of elements and compounds.
  - **Empirical vs. molecular formula:** Empirical formula is the simplest ratio of elements in a compound; the molecular formula represents the actual number of atoms in a molecule in its natural state. These can be the same (ex: H_2O) or different (ex: butane's empirical formula is CH_2 and its molecular formula is C_4H_8). Change a molecular formula to an empirical formula by dividing by the largest common factor.
    - o The atomic mass of a compound is the sum of the masses of the individual elements.
  - **Mole** = $6*10^{23}$ atoms or molecules = Avogadro's Number (N_A)
  - **Density** = mass/volume = kg/L = g/ml = kg/m^3 = g/cm^3
  - **Oxidation number** is the theoretical charge an atom would have if all of its bonds were purely ionic (no sharing—each electron is "owned" by only one atom). Ex: For CO2, C is +4 and oxygen is -2. For CO, carbon is +2 and oxygen is -2. For KMnO4, K is +1, Mn is +7, and O is -2.
    - o Pure elements and diatomics have an oxidation number of 0.
    - o For monoatomic ions, oxidation number is equal to charge.
    - o For charged and uncharged molecules, oxidation numbers of individual atoms sum to the charge of the whole molecule.
    - o For elements in s and p blocks, oxidation numbers are found by counting the smallest number of electrons that need to be added or removed to achieve an octet (ex: oxygen is -2, because it achieves an octet by adding two electrons; H is +1, because it achieves an octet by losing one electron).

- o Transition metals can take on multiple oxidation states.
- **Oxidizing agents** enable the oxidation of another species, and become reduced in the process. They generally contain oxygen. Ex: ozone (O_3), peroxide (H_2O_2), permanganate (MnO_4-)
- **Reducing agents** enable the reduction of another species, and become oxidized in the process. They generally contain hydrogen. Ex: sodium (Na), zinc (Zn), $NaBH_4$, PCC
- **Disproportionation reactions** are a special category of redox reactions, in which a single reactant is both oxidized and reduced, forming two different products. Ex: $2H_2O_2 \rightarrow 2H_2O + O_2$ (Oxygen has a -1 oxidation number in hydrogen peroxide. It is then reduced to -2 in water, and oxidized to 0 in diatomic oxygen.)

☐ **Conventions for writing chemical equations**
- **Phase:** solid (s), liquid (l), aqueous (aq), or gas (g)
- Liquid (l) refers to a pure substance in liquid form; aqueous (aq) refers to a substance that is in liquid form because it is dissolved in water
- **Charge:** if no charge is shown, assume it is neutral
- **Direction**: unidirectional arrow means that the reaction proceeds to completion in one direction; bidirectional arrow means that the reaction proceeds in either direction to achieve equilibrium.
- **Coefficient:** whole number multipliers added to ensure that the same number of atoms of each element appear on each side of the equation
- *Equations are often presented unbalanced on the MCAT. Always balance equations before using them to answer questions.*

☐ **Balancing equations:** One element at a time, and starting with the simplest to balance, count the number of atoms on each side of the equation. If there are different numbers of atoms on each side, add the smallest possible whole number coefficients to one or both sides to balance. An equation is balanced when it has the same number of each kind of atom on each side.

☐ **Balancing redox equations:**
- Use oxidation numbers to find the oxidant and the reductant.
- Write the two half-reactions: oxidation and reduction. Exclude any spectator ions.
- Balance each half-reaction for number of atoms, and then for charge
  - o Add water, and then hydrogen molecules if needed to balance hydrogen and oxygen. Add electrons to balance charge.
  - o If there are the same number of electrons on each side, add the two equations together. If there are different numbers of electrons, multiply the half-reactions by whole number coefficients so that you will be left with no free electrons.

- o Add spectator ions back in.
- The **limiting reactant/reagent** is the reactant that gets used up first in a reaction. Determine how many moles of each reactant you have, and then divide the number of moles of each reactant by its coefficient. The reactant with the smallest value is the limiting reactant, because its atoms will get used up first as the reaction proceeds.

☐ **Theoretical yield** is how much of each product should be produced by a reaction, as determined by its stoichiometry. In determining theoretical yield, always start with the limiting reactant. Based on the number of moles of the limiting reactant, determine the number of moles of products that would be produced.

- Experimental yields are almost always slightly higher or lower than theoretical yields.

☐ **Covalent bonds** share electrons equally between two atoms, enabling the atoms to achieve a more stable state than they could independently. Lewis structures are written assuming equal sharing of electrons.

- **Lewis Electron Dot formulas** are written with the element symbol (He, Na, etc.) in the center, and dots representing individual valence electrons drawn around the symbol in pairs. To form compounds, draw lines connecting the element symbols, with each line representing two electrons.

Lewis Dot Structure Examples		
Water	Methane	Nitrate

- **Resonance structures** occur when an electron is delocalized within a molecule, such that the electron participates in bonding in more than one area of the molecule. Resonance is illustrated by drawing Lewis structures for each possible form, with double-headed (equilibrium) arrows between them.
  - o Ex: carbonate (CO_3^{2-}) has 3 resonance structures, because the double bond is delocalized across three different C-O bonds.

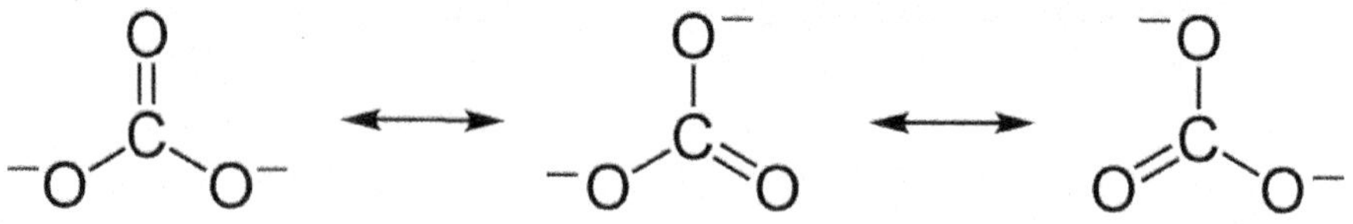

Figure 9: *Carbonate ion resonance structures.*

- **Formal charge** is the charge of an atom within a molecule, assuming that the electrons are all shared equally. Found by comparing the number of valence electrons the atom has in isolation with the number of electrons it is assigned in a Lewis structure.
- **Lewis acids and bases** are defined by their ability to accept or donate electrons.
  o A Lewis acid is an electron-pair acceptor.
  o A Lewis base is an electron-pair donor.
□ **Partial ionic character** occurs when there is a difference in the electronegativity of atoms in a molecule, resulting in electrons being shared unevenly (spending more time around one nucleus than the other), but without forming a fully ionic bond.
- **Electronegativity determines charge distribution**, such that the more electronegative nucleus "pulls" more electrons toward it.
- **Dipole moment** is a measure of the polarity of a molecule or bond, determined by electronegativity differences among atoms. The larger the difference, the larger the dipole moment.
  o **Permanent dipoles** are persistent, and due entirely to electronegativity differences.
  o **Induced dipoles** occur when a molecule comes into close contact with a concentration of charge on another molecule, which causes a temporary dipole, or polarity of charge, in a molecule.
□ **Sigma (σ) vs pi (π) bonds:** Sigma bonds are single bonds, or the first bond in a double or triple bond. Pi bonds are the second and third bonds of double and triple bonds.
- **Hybrid orbitals** occur when two or more orbitals mix, or hybridize, to take on geometries that place electron pairs as far apart from each other as possible, thereby minimizing the repulsive forces among them.
  o sp: 1 s and 1 p orbital, linear geometry
  o sp^2: 1 s and 2 p orbitals, trigonal planar geometry
  o sp^3: 1 s and 3 p orbitals, tetrahedral geometry

- **Valence shell electron pairs repel** each other (VSEPR theory). The number and orbital location of these pairs can be used to predict the shapes of molecules.
  - NH_3 has a trigonal pyramidal molecular geometry
  - H_2O has a bent molecular geometry
  - CO_2 has a linear geometry
- ☐ **Structures and common names** for molecules involving H, C, N, O, F, S, P, Si, Cl
  - **Silicon** (Si) can sometimes behave like carbon in biological systems, because it is in the same group in the periodic table.
  - **Ammonia** is NH_3
  - **Ammonium** is NH_4^+
  - **Cyanide** is CN^-
  - **Permanganate** is MNO_4^-
  - **Phosphate** is PO_4^{3-}
  - **Phosphoric acid** is H_3PO_4
  - **Chromate** is CrO_4^{2-}
  - **Dichromate** is $Cr_2O_7^{2-}$
  - **Halogens + oxygen:** suffixes are the same for all halogens
    - **Chlorate** is ClO_3^-
    - **Perchlorate** is ClO_4^-
    - **Chlorite** is ClO_2^-
    - **Hypochlorite** is ClO^-
- ☐ **Multiple bonds**, relative to single bonds, are shorter in length, higher energy, and more rigid (single bonds can rotate freely, multiple bonds cannot).
- ☐ **Stereochemistry** of covalently bonded molecules:
  - **Isomers** have the same chemical formula, but different molecular structures.
  - **Structural/constitutional isomers** have different connectivity of their atoms (Ex: 2-methylhexane and 3-methylhexane, or glucose and fructose).
  - **Stereoisomers** have the same connectivity, but differ in terms of 3-D shape and/or orientation.
    - **Diastereomers** are stereoisomers that differ at one or more, but not all, stereocenters. This creates two stereoisomers that are not mirror images.
    - **Enantiomers** are stereoisomers that are non-superimposable mirror images of each other.
    - **Cis/trans isomers** are stereoisomers that differ only in the relative orientation of functional groups. This typically occurs because of a

multiple bond in a molecule, which prevents free rotation, and therefore locks the molecule into a cis or trans form.

Examples of Special Isomer Types	
Diastereomers	
Enantiomers	
Cis/trans isomers	

- **Conformational isomers** occur when two isomers can be interconverted by rotation around single bonds.
  - This is the only form of stereoisomer in which no bond-breaking is required to interconvert.
  - Different conformational isomers (or conformers) can have different levels of energy or strain, based on the relative position of functional groups.
  - **Fully or partially eclipsed** conformers have high torsional strain, and are therefore less stable.

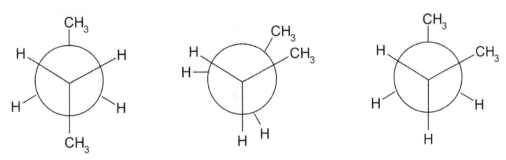

Figure 10: *Conformational stability of butane: Left and right are staggered, middle is eclipsed. Left is more stable than right because it has methyl groups in anti-position (Image credit: Dissolution).*

- o **Staggered** conformers have low torsional strain, and are therefore more stable.
- ☐ **Polarized light** is light that has been filtered such that all waves are traveling in the same direction. It can be used to assess stereochemical properties of molecules.
  - **Specific rotation** is a measurable property of chiral compounds. If polarized light hits a sample of a single enantiomer, it will rotate the plane of light either to the left (levorotatory), which gives a negative value for specific rotation, or to the right (dextrorotatory), which gives a positive value for specific rotation.
- ☐ **Absolute vs. relative configuration**: Absolute configuration of chiral centers is notated as R or S, while relative configuration is defined relative to another chiral center.
  - Ex: Cis/trans isomers and D/L or +/- notation indicate relative configuration
  - **R and S notation** indicates the absolute configuration of a chiral center.
    - o The four functional groups attached to the carbon are ranked in order of priority, and then you figure out whether these functional groups are arranged clockwise (R) or counterclockwise (S).
    - o Determine the lowest-priority functional group (often a hydrogen), and imagine that you are holding the molecule with that functional group pointing straight back. Then determine whether the other three functional groups are ordered clockwise or counterclockwise.
  - **E and Z notation** is used to notate how functional groups are arranged around a rigid double bond.
    - o **E** means that the highest-priority functional groups are on opposite sides (one above and one below the double bond). In German, entgegen = opposite.

- o **Z** means that the highest-priority functional groups are on the same side (both above or both below the double bond). In German, zusammen = together.

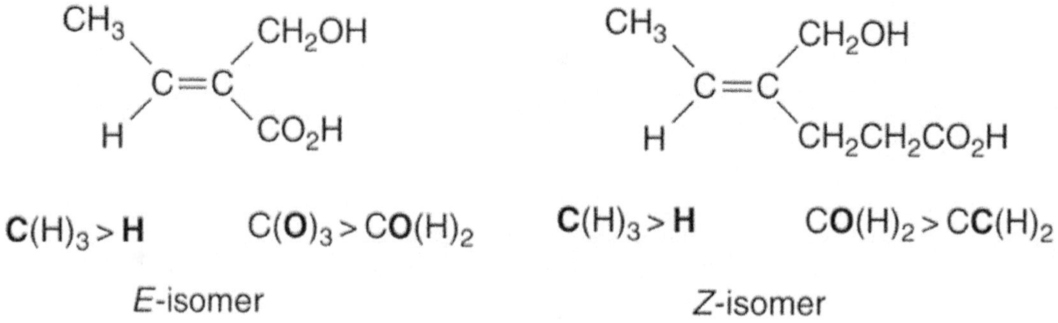

$C(H)_3 > H$ $C(O)_3 > CO(H)_2$ $C(H)_3 > H$ $CO(H)_2 > CC(H)_2$

E-isomer   *Z*-isomer

Figure 11: E and Z isomers.

- ☐ **Intermolecular forces** are the interactions between molecules. These forces are weaker than covalent or ionic bonds, but play a significant role in influencing the properties of elements and compounds, particularly in the liquid phase.
  - **Hydrogen bonding** is a specific type of dipole interaction that occurs when hydrogen is bonded to an electronegative atom, often oxygen. The hydrogen atom takes on a partial positive charge, while the electronegative atom takes on a partial negative charge. This leads to attractive forces between the positive and negative ends of adjacent molecules.
    - o The greater the electronegativity difference, the stronger the hydrogen bonding becomes.
  - **Dipole interactions** are seen in all polar molecules. Molecules will arrange themselves so that partial positive charges on one molecule are adjacent to partial negative charges on another molecule.
  - **Van der Waals/London dispersion forces** are the result of induced and instantaneous dipoles, which occur in all molecules, whether or not they are polar.
    - o Dispersion forces become more significant as molecules are packed more tightly together.

Solutions

- ☐ **Acid/Base Equilibria**
  - **Bronsted-Lowry definitions** of acids and bases are based on the exchange of hydrogen ions.
    - o A Bronsted-Lowry acid is a proton donor.
    - o A Bronsted-Lowry base is a proton acceptor.

- **pH** is a measure of acidity or basicity of a substance, on a scale of 0 to 14. A pH of 7 is neutral.
  - $pH = -\log[H+]$
  - $pOH = -\log[OH-]$
  - $pH + pOH = 14$
- **Ionization of water** into H_3O+ and $OH-$ occurs in a continuous equilibrium with H_2O
  - Kw, or the auto-ionization of water $= [H+][OH-] = (10^{-7}*10^{-7}) = 10^{-14}$ at 25°C, 1 atm
  - pH of pure water is $-\log[10^{-7}] = 7$
- **Conjugate acids and bases** are acidic and basic forms of a molecule that can be created through the loss or gain of a proton.
  - NH_4^+ is the conjugate acid of NH_3; NH_3 is the conjugate base of NH_4^+
- **Strong acids and bases** dissociate, or ionize, completely in solution.
  - Ex: nitric acid (HNO_3), sulfuric acid (H_2SO_4), hydrochloric acid (HCl)
- **Weak acids and bases** dissociate partially in solution.
  - Ex: acetic acid (CH_3COOH), benzoic acid (C_6H_5COOH), hydrofluoric acid (HF)
  - Weak acids and bases dissociate less when the salt of that acid or base is also in the solution. The salt is hydrolyzed, forming additional molecules of the conjugate acid or base. Because of **Le Chatelier's Principle**, this drives equilibrium in the opposite direction, decreasing dissociation. (Ex: CH_3COOH dissociates less when CH_3COONa is added.)
  - Calculation of pH of solutions of salts of weak acids requires determining the extent to which the weak acid or base dissociates.
- **K_a and K_b** are the equilibrium constants for acids and base, respectively. They are also called **dissociation constants**, because they measure the extent of dissociation of the acid or base in solution.
  - The larger the K_a or K_b (and therefore the more that it dissociates in solution), the stronger the acid or base.
  - $K_a = [H_3O+][A-]/[HA]$
  - $K_b = [BH+][OH-]/[B]$
  - $K_a*K_b = K_w = 1*10^{-14}$
- **pK_a and pK_b** are just a different way of expressing K_a and K_b
  - $pK_a = -\log[K_a]$; $pK_b = -\log[K_b]$
- **Buffers** are solutions that resist changes in pH because they contain an equilibrium between an acidic and basic species.
  - The acidic species is able to donate protons to resist a shift toward basic pH, while basic species are able to accept protons to resist a shift toward acidic pH.

- o Buffers are often salts of weak acids or bases (ex: CH_3COOH + CH_3COONa).
- o Titration curves show "flattening" of the curve when buffering is taking place, because the pH is changing relatively little in spite of more and more acid or base being added.
- ☐ **Ions in Solution:** Anions are negatively charged ions, cations are positively charged ions.
  - • Common names, formulas, and charges for familiar ions:
    - o **Carbon**: CO_3^{2-} is carbonate; HCO_3^- is hydrocarbonate (bicarbonate); CH_3COO^- is acetate; CN^- is cyanide
    - o **Nitrogen**: NH_4^+ is ammonium; NO_3^- is nitrate; NO_2^- is nitrite
    - o **Phosphorous**: PO_4^{3-} is phosphate; PO_4^{3-} is phosphate; HPO_4^{2-} is hydrogen phosphate; $H_2PO_4^{2-}$ is dihydrogen phosphate
    - o **Sulfur**: SO_4^{2-} is sulfate; SO_3^{2-} is sulfite; HSO_4^- is hydrogen sulfate (bisulfate)
  - • **Solvation** is the process by which solvents interact with the ions of a solute. We call solvation **hydration** when the solvent is water. Because ions are charged and water molecules are polar, water molecules will form a "solvation layer," in which the water molecules are all oriented in the same direction, around an ion.
    - o **Anions** (-) have solvation layers with the hydrogens (+) of water molecules pointing toward them.
    - o **Cations** (+) have solvation layers with oxygens (-) of water molecules pointing toward them.
    - o Although solvation is typically a spontaneous and exothermic process, it results in a decrease in entropy because of the regular, patterned nature of the solvent-solute interactions.

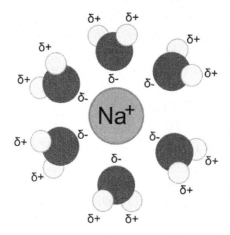

Figure 12: Solvation layer

- **Hydronium ion** (H_3O^+): though water is often described as splitting into H+ and OH-, in reality, H+ exists as the hydronium ion (a water molecule with an extra proton) rather than a free proton.
- ☐ **Solubility** is the ability of some substances to form solutions when dissolved in a solvent (usually water for the MCAT).
  - Concentration of solutions can be expressed in different units:
    - ○ **Molarity (M)** is moles of solute per liters of solution (mol/L).
    - ○ **Molality (m)** is moles of solute per kilograms of solvent (mol/kg).
    - ○ **Mole fraction (x)** is moles of solute per total moles (mol/mol, or unitless).
  - The **equilibrium constant (K_{eq})** is an expression used to indicate the position of equilibrium for a given reaction.
    - ○ Calculate K_{eq} by multiplying the concentrations of the products, raised to the power of their coefficients, and then dividing by the product of the concentrations of the reactants, raised to the power of their coefficients.
    - ○ Higher K_{eq} means that the reaction favors products; lower K_{eq} means that the reaction favors reactants.
  - **Solubility product constant (K_{sp})** is the K_{eq} for the dissolution, or solubility of a substance. The higher the K_{sp}, the more soluble it is, or the larger the proportion of it exists in dissociated form at a given time.
  - **Common ion effect** is a specific case of Le Chatelier's Principle, in which a reaction involves two sources of the same ion. For example, if you had a solution of NaCl, which dissociates into Na^+ and Cl^-, and then you added extra Cl^-.
    - ○ **In separations**, if you want to drive the equilibrium of a soluble compound (say NaCl) back toward the reactants (in this case, solid NaCl), you can do so by adding a compound with a common ion, such as AgCl.
    - ○ **Complex ions**, which consist of a metal ion bonded to one or more other ions, are called ligands. Ligands act as Lewis bases, or electron pair donors.
    - ○ **Complex ion formation increases solubility** because it is essentially the opposite of the common ion effect. The formation of complex ions effectively removes some of the ions that are dissolved in the solution, driving the equilibrium toward dissociation.
  - **pH and solubility:** If an ion of a soluble compound is acidic, it will increase the solubility of that compound in basic solution. If an ion of a soluble compound is basic, it will increase the solubility of that compound in acidic solution (Le Chatelier's Principle).

- o Strong acids and strong bases dissociate completely in solution, while weak acids and weak bases only partially dissociate.
- ☐ **Titration** is a technique for determining the concentration and/or composition of an unknown solution. You slowly add a solution of known concentration to the solution of unknown concentration and monitor changes in pH.
  - **Indicators** for pH change are typically weak acids or bases, because they change form based on the pH of the solution (ex: HA dissociates to H+ and A- in high pH; is in HA form at low pH).
    - o Blue litmus turns red in acid; red litmus turns blue in base.
  - **Neutralization**: acid + base → salt + water. The pH at which neutralization occurs is also an equivalence point of titration.
    - o Strong acid + strong base → neutralized at pH of 7
    - o Strong acid + weak base → neutralized at pH below 7
    - o Weak acid + strong base → neutralized at pH above 7
  - **Interpretation** of the titration curve:
    - o **Flattening** indicates buffering, and therefore a transitional state between species (ex: protonated → deprotonated form).
    - o The **isoelectric point** is the pH at which the molecule has a 0 net charge. For amino acids, this is often a zwitterionic form.
    - o **Equivalence points** indicate the pH at which two different species exist in equal proportion (ex: concentration of acid = concentration of base).
  - **Redox titration** can be used to determine the concentration of a charged species.
    - o A charged species of known concentration is added to a charged species of unknown concentration, often with a color change indicator.
    - o The molar concentration at which the color change occurs (indicating the endpoint of the redox reaction) is used to determine the unknown concentration.
    - o **Iodine** is often used as an indicator, because it is colorless in ionic form (I-) and dark blue in diatomic form (I_2).
- ☐ **Separation and Purification** techniques are used to separate substances in solution, or to remove impurities from a sample.
- ☐ **Extraction** is achieved via distribution of a solute between two immiscible solvents.
  - Two immiscible phases (typically one aqueous and one organic) form two layers in a separation funnel, with the less-dense phase on the top and the more-dense phase on the bottom.
  - The separation into two layers allows them to be removed from the container in sequence by opening the bottom stopcock and slowly draining.

- **Solutions** can be separated with this technique. A solute present in this mixture of solvents will preferentially dissolve in one layer or the other (ex: polar solutes tend to dissolve in polar solvents; organic solutes tend to dissolve in organic solvents). This allows a solute to be removed from one solvent into another.
☐ **Distillation** uses differences in boiling point to separate liquids.
  - Slowly heat the liquid sample, and the substances with the lowest boiling point will begin to vaporize first.
  - A fractioning column can make the distillation more precise, by providing hundreds of intermediate surfaces where the substances can condense, and then revaporize, until it reaches the top and can exit into the collecting flask
  - Vacuum distillation can be used for substances with very high boiling points, so that they will boil at lower temperature.
☐ **Chromatography** uses size, charge, or hydrophobicity to separate samples.
  - **General principles:** Chromatography involves a mobile phase and a stationary phase. If a substance is attracted to the stationary phase, it will move more slowly or not at all; if a substance is attracted to the mobile phase, it will move more quickly. This enables separation based on whether a substance is attracted to the mobile or stationary phase
☐ **Column chromatography** uses a solid stationary phase in a glass column, which is then coated with a liquid mobile phase. The sample is then poured into the top of the column.
  - The substance in the mobile phase will exit the bottom of the tube, and the one in the stationary phase will remain in the column.
  - **Gas-liquid chromatography**: Gas is the mobile phase, liquid is the stationary phase. Liquid coats the inside of the column, gas moves through the middle.
  - **High-pressure liquid chromatography**: A liquid sample in solution is forced through a column at high pressure. The solvent is the mobile phase, and an absorbent material inside the tube is the stationary phase.
☐ **Paper chromatography** uses a solid stationary phase (paper) and a solvent as the mobile phase.
  - One end of a strip of paper is put into a container with the sample and solvent. Capillary action drives the liquid up the paper.
  - Substances with the greatest affinity for the paper move the shortest distance; those with low affinity for the paper move the farthest distance
☐ **Thin layer chromatography** is an advanced form of paper chromatography
  - A glass or plastic plate is coated with an absorbent (stationary phase). The sample of interest is loaded onto one end of the plate, and then that end is inserted into a shallow container of solvent (mobile phase).

- Capillary action moves the solvent up the paper, sweeping the sample up along with it.
- Farther travel = more attracted to mobile phase; shorter travel = more attracted to stationary phase

☐ **Separation and purification of peptides and proteins**
- **Electrophoresis** is used to separate and identify charged particles, including proteins and nucleic acids, by how they move in response to an electric field.
- **Gel electrophoresis** occurs when charged particles are added to an agarose gel.
  - o DNA/RNA fragments are separated by length. Shorter molecules move faster through the porous gel and longer molecules move more slowly.
    - ▪ All DNA/RNA is negatively charged, so the sample would be added at the anode end (-) and migrate toward the cathode end (+).
  - o Amino acids can be separated by isoelectric points. The charged gel sets up a pH gradient. Amino acids will travel through the gel until they reach the part of the gel where the pH matches their isoelectric point.
  - o Proteins are treated with a detergent (SDS) and then separated by size.
    - ▪ Proteins have complex shapes and varying charges. Treatment with a detergent denatures the protein and gives it a uniform negative charge.
    - ▪ SDS-treated protein is placed at the anode (-) and will migrate to the cathode (+) more quickly if it is small, and more slowly if it is large.
- **Retention factors** (Rfs) are used to report separations/purifications for quantitative analysis.
  - o Rf = distance traveled by solute/distance traveled by solvent

☐ **Size-exclusion chromatography** is used to separate by size or molecular weight.
- Column contains porous beads. Larger molecules can't enter these pores, so they move through the column quickly. Smaller molecules travel through the pores, so they take a longer path to reach the bottom and therefore a longer time.

☐ **Ion-exchange chromatography** is used to separate based on charge.
- Beads are coated with a charged substance. This substance will hold oppositely-charged particles in the column, while particles will the same charge will be repelled and travel out of the column.

☐ **Affinity chromatography** is used to separate based on specific binding properties (ex: enzyme and substrate, antigen and antibody).

- If you want to separate a specific molecule from a mixture, and then be able to reuse it, affinity chromatography is the most precise approach.
- The stationary phase is a material that will bind specifically to the substance of interest (receptor, antibody, etc.).
- When poured through the column, the molecule of interest will be bound to the stationary phase, while the rest will pass through.
- A wash can then be used to release the substance of interest from the stationary phase so that it can be further analyzed or reused.

☐ **Racemic mixtures**, or equal mixtures of two enantiomers, can be separated based on optical activity.

- Use a stationary phase that will bind only one enantiomer. The other enantiomer will flow through, and then the first enantiomer can be washed out. Confirm separation by assessing rotation of polarized light.

Classes of Molecules

☐ **Aldehydes** are a class of molecules that contain a carbonyl carbon (double bonded to oxygen) with one hydrogen and one R group.
- **Formaldehyde** is the simplest ketone, in which the R group is a hydrogen.
- **Suffix –al** is used to name aldehydes. (ex: Butanal is butane with an aldehyde group at one end.)

☐ **Ketones** are a class of molecules that contain a carbonyl carbon (double bonded to oxygen) with two R groups.
- **Acetone** is the simplest ketone, in which both Rs are methyl groups
- **Suffix –one** is used to name ketones. (ex: Butanone is butane with a ketone group at one end.)

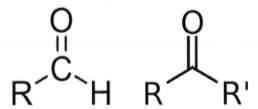

Figure 13: Aldehyde (left) and Ketone (right).

☐ **Physical properties of aldehydes and ketones:** The carbonyl group makes these molecules more polar than alkanes, but less polar than molecules with -OH or -Halide groups.
- **Infrared absorption** of carbonyl: 1700 cm^{-1}
☐ **Important reactions** of aldehydes and ketones:

- **Nucleophilic addition reaction** at C=O bond occurs when the positive carbon is attacked by a more electronegative group (generally an alcohol). These reactions can create:
- **Carbonyl + alcohol** yields:
  - ○ **Hemiacetals,** in which the carbonyl double bond is replaced by two separate bonds: one to an oxygen and one to a hydroxyl group.
  - ○ **Acetals,** in which the carbonyl double bond is replaced by two separate bonds to oxygens.

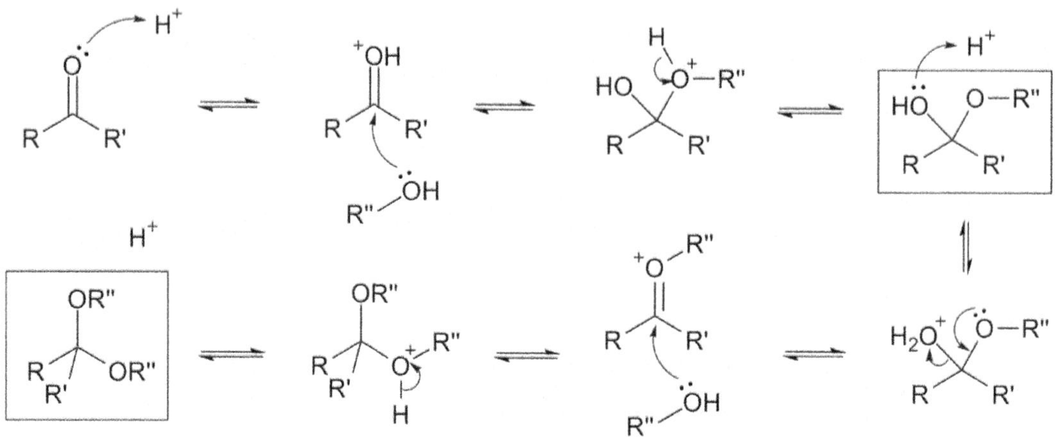

Figure 14: Ketone becomes hemiacetal, hemiacetal becomes acetal.

- **Carbonyl + amine** yields:
  - ○ **Imines** form from the reaction of a primary amine with an aldehyde or ketone. An imine includes a carbon-nitrogen double bond. (Hemiaminal intermediate)
  - ○ **Enamines** form from the reaction of a secondary amine with an aldehyde or ketone. An enamine includes a carbon-carbon double bond, with one of the carbons single-bonded to nitrogen. (Hemiaminal intermediate)

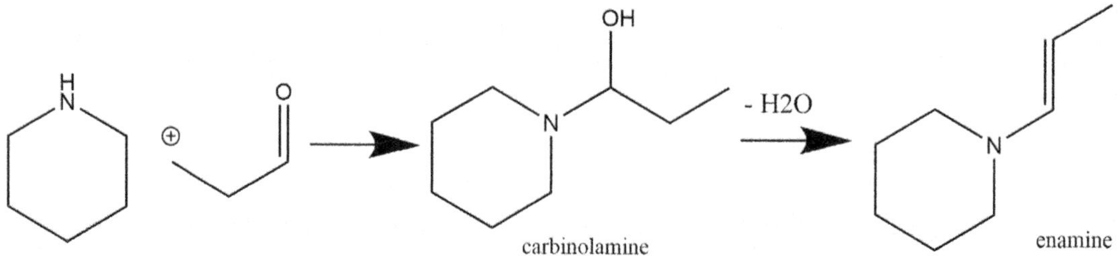

Figure 15: amine and aldehyde yield enamine, via a hemiaminal intermediate (Image credit: Akhitun).

- o **Hydride reagents** (ex: NaBH₄) are used to transform an aldehyde or ketone into an alcohol.
- **Carbonyl + cyanide** yields:
  - o **Cyanohydrin** (functional group with cyano and hydroxyl groups on the same carbon) is produced when an aldehyde or ketone reacts with a cyanide ion.
- **Oxidation of aldehydes** (not ketones) with a strong oxidizing agent (ex: KMnO₄, Ag₂O) yields carboxylic acids.
- **Reaction at adjacent (alpha) carbon** to a carbonyl can produces enolates (negatively charged oxygen adjacent to a C=C double bond).
  - o Alpha carbon has slightly more acidic hydrogens, and therefore enhanced reactivity.
  - o Ketone + hydroxyl → enolate
- **Aldol condensation**: Carbonyl reacts with enol or enolate to form an aldol (β-hydroxyaldehyde or β-hydroxyketone), followed by a dehydration, which yields a conjugated enone.

Base catalyzed aldol reaction (shown using ⁻OCH₃ as base)

Base catalyzed dehydration (sometimes written as a single step)

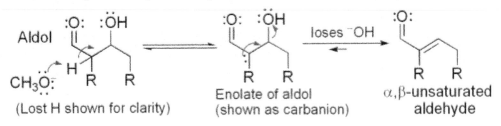

Figure 16: Aldol condensation

- **Retro-aldol** is the reverse of the aldol condensation, and reproduces the reactants.
- **Thermodynamic vs. kinetic enolate**: Thermodynamic enolates form a double bond with the more substituted alpha carbon. Kinetic enolates form a double bond with the less substituted alpha carbon.
  - Thermodynamic enolates are more stable (higher degree of substitution around double bond), but thermodynamic enolates are formed more quickly (less steric hindrance to deprotanation).
- General principles for predicting mechanics of reactions with aldehydes and ketones:
  - **Steric hindrance:** Bulky substituents can shield the central carbon from attack. Carbonyl carbons with bulky substituents are less reactive.
  - **Acidity of alpha-H** arises from the resonance-stabilization of the carbanions.
- ☐ **Alcohols** are a class of organic molecules that have hydroxyl (-OH) groups.
  - **Nomenclature**: Prefix: hydroxy, hydroxyl; Suffix: ol, alcohol
  - **Physical properties**: Alcohols experience hydrogen bonding, and have relatively high polarity due to the -OH group, which leads to high boiling points and high solubility.

- ☐ **Important reactions** of alcohols:
  - **Oxidation** of alcohols to carboxylic acids:
    - $KMnO_4$, and CrO_3 will oxidize primary alcohol to carboxylic acids.
    - PCC will oxidize primary alcohols only to aldehydes.
    - Secondary alcohols always oxidize to ketones.
    - Tertiary alcohols do not oxidize.
  - **Substitution reactions:** S_N1 (nucleophilic substitution with 1 molecule involved in the transition state) or S_N2 (nucleophilic substitution with 2 molecules involved in the transition state).
    - S_N1 is favored when there is a stable carbocation intermediate, a tertiary carbon center, and/or a protic solvent.
    - S_N2 is favored when there is an unstable carbocation, a primary carbon center, and/or an aprotic solvent.

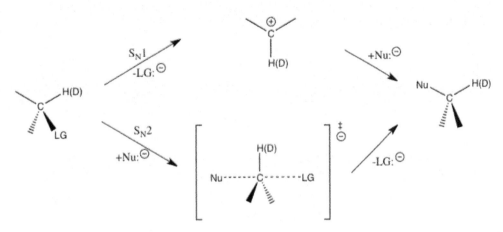

Figure 17: *S$_N$1 vs. S$_N$2 reaction mechanism. LG is leaving group, Nu is nucleophile. D is deuterium.*

- **Protect alcohols** by adding a bulky trialkylsilyl group (bond between Si and O), which prevents the alcohol from reacting while a reaction is occurring elsewhere in the molecule.
  - o Ex: tert-butyldimethylsilyl. The silicon acts as an electrophile, pulling some electrons away from the oxygen.
  - o Deprotect with fluoride ions (F-).
- **Preparation of mesylates and tosylates:**
  - o Mesylates come from reacting an alcohol with mesyl chloride (MsCl).
  - o Tosylates come from reacting an alcohol with tosyl chloride (TsCl).

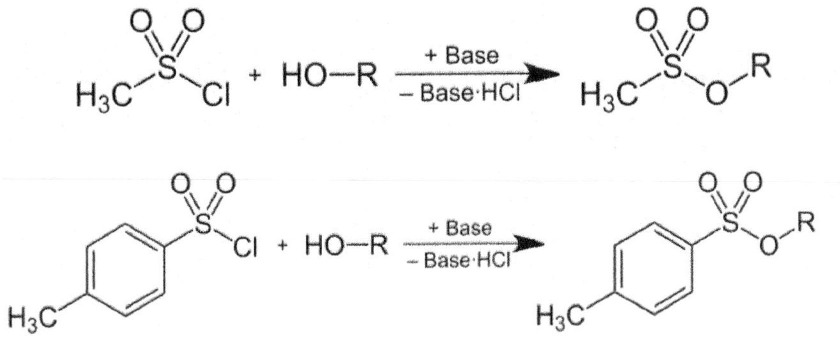

Figure 18: *Mesylate synthesis (top) and tosylate synthesis (bottom).*

- ☐ **Carboxylic acids** are a class of molecules with a carboxyl group (a carbonyl and a hydroxyl on the same carbon).
  - **Nomenclature:** –oic acid suffix
  - **Physical properties:** polar and acidic; capable of both donating and accepting hydrogen bonds; high boiling point and solubility
  - Infrared absorption: C=O at 1700 cm^{-1} and OH at 3100 cm^{-1}

☐ **Important reactions** of carboxylic acids:

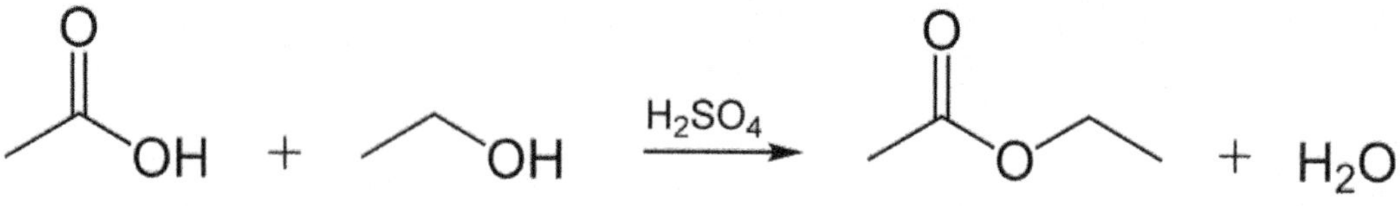

Figure 19: Formation of ester linkage.

- **Amides** are formed from reaction of a carboxylic acid with an amine, forming a carbonyl adjacent to a nitrogen.
- **Lactams** are cyclic amides, formed from the reaction of the amino group and the carboxylic acid group within a single molecule.
- **Esters** (-oate) are formed when a carboxylic acid reacts with an alcohol.
- **Lactones** are cyclic esters, formed from the reaction of a carboxylic acid group and a hydroxyl group within the same molecules, forming an ester linkage.

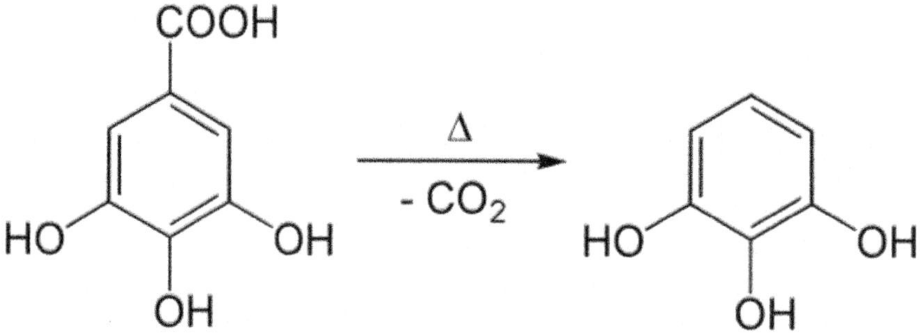

Figure 20: Example decarboxylation.

- **Anhydrides** are formed by condensation of two carboxylic acids, forming a single molecule with two carbonyls connected by an ester linkage.

Key reactions with carboxylic acids (RCOOH)
RCOOH + Base → deprotonation (RCOO-)
RCOOH + LiAlH$_4$ → alcohol (RCOH)
RCOOH + R'OH → ester (RCOOR')
RCOOH + SOCl$_2$ → acid chloride (RCOCl)
RCOOH + R'COCl → acid anhydride (RCOOCOR')
RCOOH + Amine (R'NHR") → Amide (RCONR'R")
RCOOH + R'SH → thioester (RCOSR')

- **Reduction:** $COOH + LiAlH_4 \rightarrow$ alcohol.
- **Decarboxylation** is the removal of a carboxyl group, forming CO_2.
- **Reactions at 2-position**: substitution of -OH group for alternate electrophile (typically a halide).
- ☐ **Acid derivatives** include anhydrides, amides, and esters.
  - **Anhydrides** (-oic anhydride) are formed from the reaction of two carboxylic acids.
  - **Amides** (-amide) are formed from the reaction of an acid chloride and an amine.
  - **Esters** (-oate) are formed from the reaction of an acid chloride and an alcohol.
- ☐ **Important reactions** of acid derivatives:
  - **Nucleophilic substitution**: nucleophile attacks central carbon
  - **Transesterification**: ester + alcohol yields a new ester
  - **Hydrolysis of amides**: hydroxyl attacks carbonyl carbon, replacing amine
  - General principles for predicting reaction mechanics:
    - o **Relative reactivity** of acid derivatives (Most to least reactive): acid chloride > anhydrides > esters > amides
    - o **Steric effects**: bulky groups can protect carbonyl carbon from attack
    - o **Electronic effects**: resonance can enhance stability of intermediates
    - o **Strain** (beta-lactams): Because C-N bond has partial double-bond character, it cannot rotate. This creates ring strain in lactams.

Acid Derivative Reactions with Nucleophiles

Acid chloride (ROCl) + R'OO- $\rightarrow$ anhydride (R'OOOR)

Acid chloride (ROCl) + RO- $\rightarrow$ ester (ROOR')

Acid chloride (ROCl) + OH- $\rightarrow$ carboxylic acid (ROOH)

Anhydride (ROOOR) + R'O- $\rightarrow$ ester (ROOR')

Anhydride (ROOOR') + OH- $\rightarrow$ carboxylic acid (ROOH)

Ester (ROOR) + R'O- $\rightarrow$ ester (ROOR')

Ester (ROOR) +OH- $\rightarrow$ carboxylic acid (ROOH)

Amide (RONR$_2$) + OH- $\rightarrow$ carboxylic acid (ROOH)

- ☐ **Phenols** (carbolic acids) consist of a phenyl group ($-C_6H_5$) and an alcohol (-OH) functional groups.
  - The resonance stabilization of the phenol makes the hydroxyl group especially acidic.

- Oxidation and reduction (hydroquinones, ubiquinones): biological two-electron redox centers
- Phenol + oxidizing agent → quinones (fully conjugated cyclic or heterocyclic diones)
- Hydroxyquinones have the ring and carbonyl structures of quinones, but have one or more extra hydroxyl groups.
- Ubiquinone/coenzyme Q is a type of quinone that acts as an electron carrier in the ETC.

Me
HO
Me
Ag_2CO_3/celite
benzene, 0.5h, ref
O
Me
Me
O
Me
Me

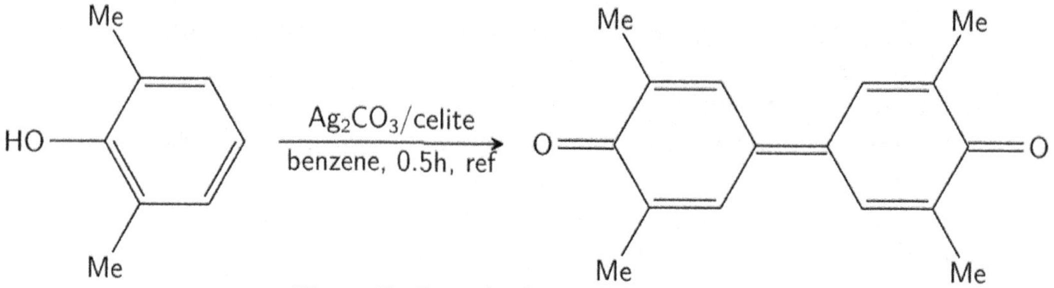

***Figure 21**: Example phenol oxidized to quinone.*

☐ **Polycyclic and heterocyclic aromatic compounds** have aromaticity and two or more ring structures.

- **Huckel's Rules** are used to determine whether a cyclic molecule is aromatic. In order to be aromatic, the molecule must: be planar, be fully conjugated (alternating single and double bonds; overlapping p orbitals), and have 4n+2 π electrons, where n is any positive integer.
- **Purines and pyrimidines** are aromatic heterocycles, both of which are found in DNA. A and G are purines; C, T, and U are pyrimidines.

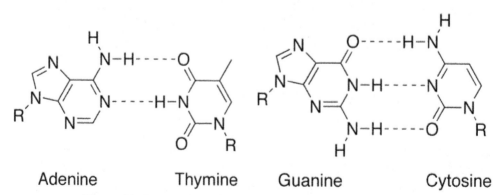

Adenine
Thymine
Guanine
Cytosine

***Figure 22:** Purines (A and G) bonded with pyrimidines (T and C).*

Chemical Dynamics

☐ **Thermodynamics** describe how heat relates to work and energy.
- **State Function:** Thermodynamic properties (energy, enthalpy, entropy) are considered state functions/quantities, meaning that their properties depend only on starting and ending states, not the path taken to move between them.
- **Zeroth Law:** If two objects are in thermal equilibrium with a third object, then they are also in thermal equilibrium with each other (meaning that measuring temperature is possible).
- **First Law**: Energy is conserved in thermodynamic processes.
- **Second Law**: The entropy of the universe is increasing. The entropy (a measure of "disorder") of a system generally increases over time.
  - ○ Highest to lowest entropy: gas > liquid > solids/crystal states
- **PV diagram:** Pressure on the y axis, volume on the x axis. Work done = area under or enclosed by the curve.

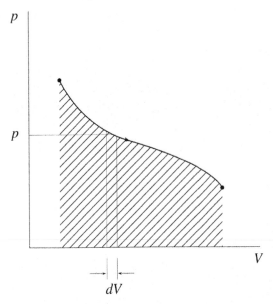

Figure 23: PV diagram showing work done by a closed system.

☐ **Calorimetry** is used to measure heat and state changes, by gradually increasing the temperature of a sample in an insulated container and plotting heat absorbed (q) versus change in temperature.
- Phase changes can be seen on the graph as "flattening," because a phase change requires significant absorption of energy without an increase in temperature.

- **Q = mc(ΔT),** or, heat absorbed is equal to the mass of the object (m) * specific heat (c) * change in temperature. Applies only within a single phase state.
- **Heat capacity** is the amount of heat required to raise the temperature of something by 1°C.
- **Specific heat** is the amount of heat *per unit mass* required to raise the temperature of something by 1°C.

☐ **Heat transfer** occurs in several forms:
- **Conduction** is energy transfer by direct contact between objects.
- **Convection** is energy transfer by the motion of fluids/gasses.
- **Radiation** is energy transfer by electromagnetic radiation.

☐ **Endo- and exothermic:** Endothermic reactions absorb heat (+ΔH), and exothermic reactions produce heat (-ΔH).
- **Enthalpy**, H (in joules), is the heat of a reaction (or "formation," which is just a reaction producing a new product). H is constant for a given reaction.
- **Hess's Law** of heat summation: Total heat of formation = sum of the heat of formation of products – sum of heat of formation of the reactants

☐ **Bond dissociation energy** is the energy required to break a bond.
- **Heat of formation** of a reaction = bond dissociation energy of bonds in the reactants – bond dissociation energy of all the product
- **Free energy** (G) is a measure of the amount of energy available to perform work in a system.

☐ **Spontaneous reactions and delta G**: $\Delta G = \Delta H - T\Delta S$
- Free energy is a state function.
- If ΔG is negative, then the reaction is spontaneous.
- If ΔG is positive, then the reaction is not spontaneous.
- Endothermic reactions can be spontaneous if delta S is positive and sufficiently large.
- Exothermic reactions can be non-spontaneous if delta S is negative and sufficiently large.

☐ **Coefficient of expansion** is a constant used to determine the change in the length, volume, or area of an object due to change in temperature.
- In general, increase in temperature leads to expansion, and decrease in temperature leads to contraction. (Exception: water → ice)
- L_0 is constant for a given material.
- $\Delta L = \alpha L_0 \Delta T$. The change in length of an object is equal to the object's coefficient of linear expansion (α) times the initial length (L_0) times the change in temperature.

☐ **Phase change** among gas, liquid, and solid forms requires some input or release of energy without an increase or decrease in temperature.
- Heat of fusion is the energy needed for fusion (phase change from solid to liquid) with no change in temperature.
- Heat of vaporization is the energy needed for vaporization (phase change from liquid to gas) with no change in temperature.

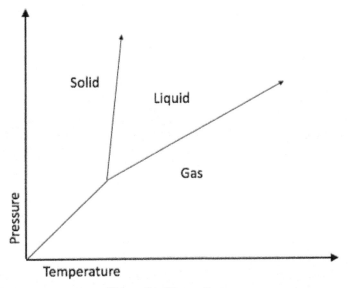

Figure 24: *Phase diagram.*

- **Phase diagrams** are used to illustrate the influence of temperature and pressure on the physical state of a substance. Pressure on the y axis, temperature on the x axis. Curve divides the graph into 3 sections. Solid is on the far left (low temp), gas is on the far left (high temp) and liquid is in the middle.

PART II:
BIOLOGICAL AND BIOCHEMICAL
FOUNDATIONS OF LIVING SYSTEMS

Amino Acids

□ **Amino acids** are the building blocks of proteins. *Amino acid names, structures, and special properties are the most important things to memorize for the MCAT. A summary of amino acid structures is provided on the inside front cover for quick reference.*

- **Structure**: All amino acids have the same backbone, consisting of an amino group, a carboxyl group, and an alpha carbon connecting the two. Each amino acid has a unique R group, also attached to the alpha carbon, which gives rise to its individual characteristics and properties.
  - **Dipolar/zwitterion**: Amino acids are dipolar, meaning that at certain pHs, they contain both positive and negative charges, but have a net charge of zero. When an amino acid (or other molecule) is in a dipolar form, it is called a zwitterion.
  - **Isoelectric point**: pH at which amino acid has a neutral net charge. For neutral amino acids, it is approximately 6. The isoelectric point is higher for basic side chains and lower for acidic side chains.
- **Function**: Amino acids form long chains, called polypeptides, by forming peptide linkages. These polypeptides, or proteins, perform a range of functions in cells, including structural support, catalysis, signaling, etc.
- **Peptide linkages** are formed in a dehydration reaction, such that a hydroxyl group is lost from the carboxyl group of one amino acid, and a hydrogen is lost from the amino group of a second amino acid. The hydroxyl and hydrogen form a water molecule, and a new bond is formed between the carboxyl carbon and the amino nitrogen.
- **Naming convention**: Polypeptides are written from left to right, from the N terminus (amino group) to the C terminus (carboxyl group).

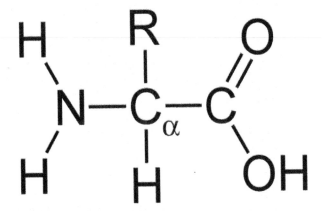

Figure 25: Basic structure of amino acids.

- **Classifications** of amino acids (see inside front cover for 1- and 3-letter codes, structures, and properties):
  - **Acidic**: aspartic acid/aspartate, glutamic acid/glutamate
  - **Basic**: histidine, arginine, lysine
  - **Hydrophobic**: alanine, cysteine, phenylalanine, isoleucine, leucine, methionine, proline, valine, tryptophan
  - **Hydrophilic**: aspartic acid/aspartate, glutamic acid/glutamate, histidine, lysine, asparagine, glutamine, arginine, serine, threonine, tyrosine.
  - **Aliphatic/non-aromatic**: alanine, cysteine, aspartic acid/aspartate, glutamic acid/glutamate, glycine, isoleucine, lysine, leucine, methionine, proline, glutamine, arginine, serine, threonine, asparagine, valine
  - **Aromatic**: phenylalanine, histidine, tryptophan, tyrosine
- **Special properties** of amino acids:
  - **Cysteine**: forms disulfide bridges in oxidizing conditions. Cysteine is called cystine when oxidized. Cysteine is also the only R configuration amino acid.
  - **Histidine**: pKa of sidechain is near physiological pH, so that histidine exists with both a protonated and deprotonated sidechain in near equal proportions at physiological pH.
  - **Glycine**: only achiral amino acid. Found in both hydrophobic and hydrophilic regions due to small side chain.
  - **Proline**: found at the fold in beta sheets, and make a kink in an alpha helix.
- **Synthesis of alpha-amino acids:**
  - **Strecker synthesis**: An aldehyde or ketone is reacted with ammonia in acid, yielding an imine. The imine then reacts with cyanide in acid, and is then hydrolyzed to form an amino acid.
    - Aldehyde or ketone becomes the carbon backbone.
    - Ammonia gives the amino group.
    - Cyanide carbon (hydrolyzed) forms the carboxylic acid group.
  - **Gabriel synthesis**: Phthalimidomalonic ester (basically, a resonance-stabilized bicyclic that contains the amino acid backbone structure) reacts with an alkyl halide in base, then hydrolyzes in acid, and then decarboxylates with heat.
    - Amine nitrogen, alpha carbon, and COO- all come from phthalimidomalonic ester.
  - Strecker is generally preferred because it is the simpler approach.

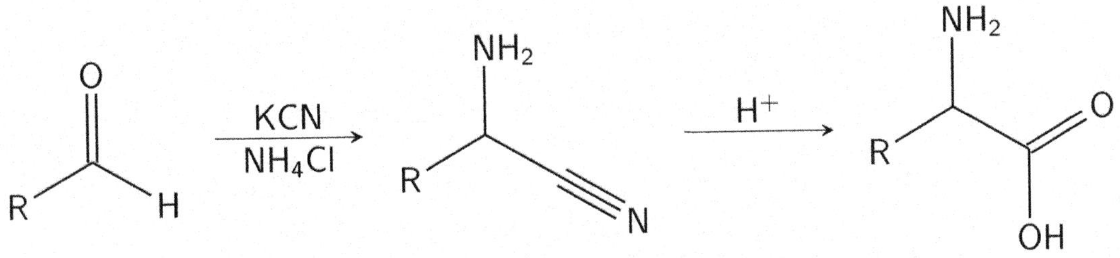

Figure 26: Strecker synthesis of amino acids.

☐ **Amino acid linkage** reactions:
  - **Sulfur linkages**: cysteine → cystine + 2e- + 2H+ in oxidizing conditions. Hooks together two different peptide chains by creating bonds between sidechains, or two different sections of a single chain.

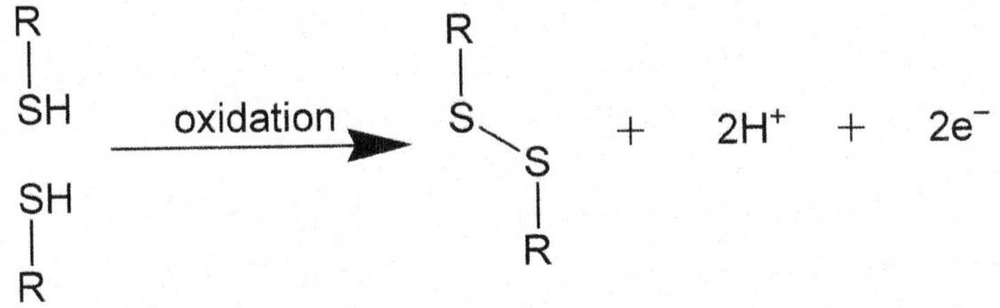

Figure 27: Disulfide bond formation.

  - **Peptide linkages**: dehydration reaction between the amino group of one amino acid and the carboxyl group of another
    o Naming convention: always N-terminus to C-terminus
    o Hydrolysis: add water to break a peptide bond

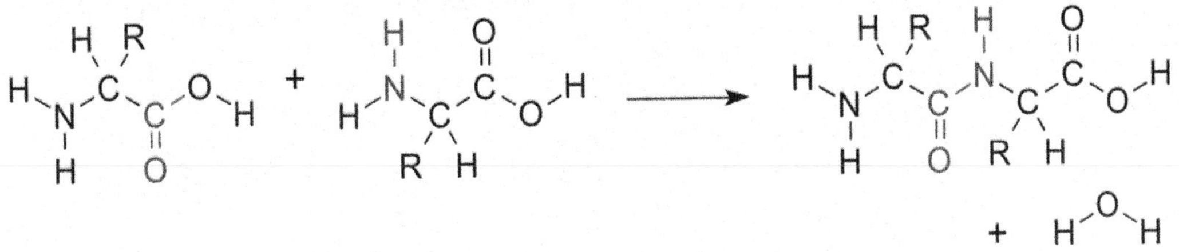

Figure 28: Peptide bond formation.

☐ **Proteins** consist of one or more amino acid chains folded into complex structures.
  - **Primary structure** is the amino acid sequence. By convention, primary structure reads N-terminus to C-terminus.
  - **Secondary structure** is formed by patterned hydrogen bonding of the backbone of a single chain with itself.

- An **alpha helix** is a uniform spiral or twist of amino acids, like a barbershop pole.
  - Proline is rarely found, except for at the ends, because it will create a kink.
- A **beta sheet** is a series of stacked, flat strands with sharp turns, connected laterally, like a blanket woven on a loom.
  - Proline forms the fold of the pleated beta sheet.
- **Tertiary structure** is additional folding into complex, 3-D shapes due to sidechain interactions, driven by hydrophobic interactions, and "locked" in place by bonds between distant sidechains, especially disulfide bonds.
  - Hydrophobic sidechains tend to end up on the interior, hydrophilic sidechains on the exterior.
  - Cysteine bonds to cysteine to form cystine (oxidized form) and create loops in the protein chain.
  - Tertiary structure creates the active site of an enzyme.
- **Quaternary structure** is when two or more folded polypeptide chains, or protein subunits, are bound together.
  - Monomers have no quaternary structure.
- **Conformational stability**: The 3-D folded structure of a protein is essential for its function, and can be disrupted by environmental factors.
  - **Denaturing and folding** of proteins:
    - Heat, pH, and other physical/chemical changes can cause denaturation, or unfolding, of a protein. This does not alter primary structure.
    - In some cases, proteins can regain their 3-D structure after heat has been removed, or pH restored (ex: melted butter becomes solid again when cooled).
  - **Solvation layer** (entropy): When a solute surrounds a solvent (ex: water around a protein molecule), the solute molecules take on a regular orientation around the solvent (ex: water molecules lined up with all + charges facing protein, all – charges on the outside).
    - Although a protein has greater entropy when unfolded, and less entropy when folded, the water surrounding the protein has greater entropy when the protein is folded, because of the regular order of the solvation layer, and less entropy when the protein is unfolded.
- ☐ **Separation techniques for proteins** are experimental approaches for segregation and identifications of proteins and other molecules in a sample.
  - **Isoelectric point** is the pH at which a molecule has a net charge of zero. It can be used to separate proteins through electrophoresis.

- **Electrophoresis** is a technique for separating molecules by applying an electric field that will cause molecules to migrate in different directions and/or at different rates based on their properties.
  - **Isoelectric focusing:** Proteins are loaded onto a gel with an electric field applied to it such that a pH gradient is established (cathode = low pH; anode = high pH). Proteins travel through the gel until they reach the pH associated with their isoelectric point.
  - **SDS-PAGE** separates molecules based on size. The sample is treated with SDS (detergent), which denatures the protein and gives it a uniform negative charge. Gel is full of tunnels and pockets, such that smaller molecules are able to move forward more quickly than larger molecules.
    - The farther a DNA fragment travels down the gel, the shorter it is. Since DNA is synthesized from 5 to 3 prime, the shortest fragments (those that travel the farthest down) are those at the 5 end of the gel. So, when looking at gel electrophoresis results, you read the sequence 5 to 3 prime from bottom (+) to top (-).
- ☐ **Non-enzymatic protein function**: Proteins are also membrane proteins, motors, antibodies, etc.
  - **Binding**: Proteins are responsible for binding, transporting, and/or sequestering biologically relevant molecules (ex: hemoglobin transports oxygen, calcium-binding proteins, transcription factors).
  - **Immune system**: Immunoglobulins (a.k.a. antibodies) bind to foreign antigens to label them for destruction.
  - **Motors:** Proteins are involved in generating movement of molecules, tissues, and organs.
    - **Myosin** uses ATP to drive muscle contraction in sarcomere.
    - **Kinesin and dynein** are motor proteins that "walk" along microtubules. Kinesin = anterograde transport (toward + end of microtubule); dynein = retrograde transport (toward – end of microtubule).
    - **Cilia and flagella** are tentacle-like structures that beat in waves to drive movement. Cilia line the fallopian tubes, in order to sweep the egg into the uterus; sperm each have a single flagellum to swim toward the egg.
- ☐ **Enzymes** are proteins that catalyze chemical reactions in biological systems.
  - Catalyze: to increase the rate of a reaction by lowering its activation energy (no change in K_{eq} or delta G)
  - Enzyme classification by reaction type (suffix –ase means enzyme):
    - **Oxioreductases** catalyze the transfer of an electron from one molecule (so that it is reduced) to another (so that it is oxidized).

Handwritten margin notes: BCHM '94; BCHM 85-86, 95; BCHM 85, 95

- o **Transferases** catalyze the transfer of a functional group (ex: methyl) from one molecule to another.
- o **Hydrolases** catalyze hydrolysis (breaking of a bond by addition of water) of a molecule.
- o **Lyases** catalyze the breaking of a bond, but not through hydrolysis or oxidation/reduction: one substrate, two products.
- o **Isomerases** catalyze the transformation between isomeric forms of molecules.
- o **Ligases** catalyze the formation of a new bond between two molecules.
- Reduction of activation energy is often achieved by making an intermediate of a reaction, or the transition state, more stable.
- Enzymes lower the activation energy of forward and reverse reactions simultaneously.
- Almost all enzymes are made of protein; a small subset are made of RNA.
- □ **Mechanisms of enzyme catalysis**: Enzymes bind specific substrates, sometimes with the assistance of cofactors or coenzymes.
  - **Substrates** and enzyme specificity: Enzymes are structurally optimized to bind a specific substrate, or a small number of very similar substrates.
    - o **Active site model:** Enzymes have a groove that is shaped to allow a specific substrate to bind. The groove does not change shape when bound and unbound by substrate. Binding sites often contain hydrogen bonds, as well as hydrophobic interactions and van der Waals interactions, which increase the stability of the bound substrate.
    - o **Induced-fit model:** The active site of an enzyme changes shape when it encounters a substrate. The substrate induces a change in shape of the active site, and then the site returns to its original shape when unbound.
  - **Cofactors** are enzyme helpers: inorganic molecules, typically ions, that some enzymes need for catalysis, and that increase the rate of the reaction further for some enzymes. Cofactors stabilize substrate intermediates.
  - **Coenzymes** are organic molecules that some enzymes need for catalysis. They bind the active site of the enzyme, acting as intermediate functional group or electron carriers for the substrate in transition, but are not considered reaction substrates (ex: NADH, CoA).
    - o **Water soluble vitamins** can function as coenzymes. B group and C vitamins are water soluble (D, E, K, and A are fat soluble, and do not act as coenzymes).
  - Changes in local conditions (pH, temperature, osmolality, etc.) can influence the function and/or efficiency of enzymes. Many enzymes work optimally at a specific temperature and pH range.

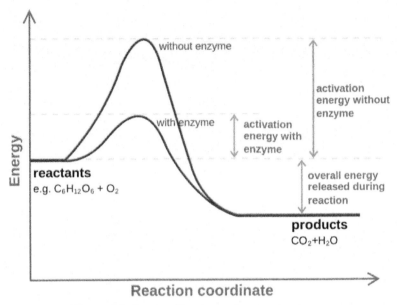

***Figure 29:** Enzyme kinetics and activation energy.*

- □ **Control of enzyme activity** is generally described in terms of chemical kinetics.
  - • General (catalysis): $E + S \longleftrightarrow ES \longleftrightarrow EP \longleftrightarrow E + P$
    - ○ Enzymes can be single-substrate or multi-substrate
  - • **Michaelis-Menten kinetics** is a model of enzyme kinetics that relates substrate concentration to reaction velocity.
    - ○ $V = (Vmax[S])/(Km + [S])$: reaction velocity = maximum velocity * substrate concentration / Michaelis constant + substrate concentration
    - ○ Km (Michaelis constant) represents the substrate concentration at which the reaction rate is half of Vmax.
    - ○ Km does not vary with concentration; Vmax is dependent on concentration. Therefore Km is an indicator of enzyme affinity.
  - • **Cooperativity**: For some enzymes with multiple active sites, once one substrate is bound to one site, it increases the affinity of other active sites on the molecule (ex: hemoglobin).
  - • **Feedback regulation:** Enzyme activity can be either enhanced or diminished by the products and/or substrates of the enzyme.

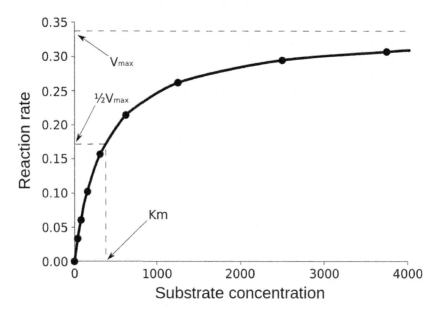

Figure 30: *Michaelis-Menten kinetics.*

- **Inhibition:** Enzymes can be inhibited by the binding of inhibitor molecules. There are 4 types of enzyme inhibition:
  - **Competitive:** The inhibitor competes with the substrate by binding with the active site, so that it is unavailable to be bound by the substrate.
    - Competitive inhibition raises the Km, but does not change Vmax, because it can be overcome by increasing substrate concentration.
  - **Non-competitive:** The inhibitor binds the enzyme at an allosteric site (not the active site). This changes the conformation of the enzyme so that it can no longer bond with the substrate.
    - Km is unchanged, but Vmax is lowered because the inhibition cannot be overcome by adding more substrate.
  - **Mixed:** The inhibitor binds an allosteric site, but the binding of the inhibitor affects affinity for the substrate, and vice versa.
    - Km increases or decreases (change in affinity); Vmax decreases.
  - **Uncompetitive:** The inhibitor binds the enzyme at an allosteric site only when the enzyme has already bound the substrate (inhibitor binds the enzyme-substrate complex).
    - Km and Vmax are both lowered.

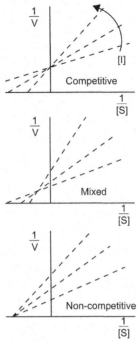

Figure 31: *Lineweaver-Burk plots for inhibition types (slope = Km/Vmax).*

- **Regulatory enzymes** are enzymes involved in the regulation of biochemical pathways, including metabolism. These enzymes typically exhibit cooperative behavior and/or covalent modification.
  - o **Allosteric enzymes** are enzymes with multiple substrate and allosteric binding sites that exhibit cooperative properties. Binding of a molecule to an allosteric site can either increase or decrease affinity at the substrate binding sites.
    - ▪ Michaelis-Menten kinetics do not apply to an enzyme with cooperative binding properties, because the binding of one active site affects the affinity of the others.
  - o **Covalently modified enzymes** modulate enzyme activity through the covalent bonding of functional groups (ex: phosphorylated and de-phosphorylated forms).
- **Zymogen** is the inactive form of an enzyme (ex: enzymes excreted in mouth as zymogens, but activated by pH changes in the digestive tract).

Genes

- ☐ **Nucleic acids** are polymers of nucleotides that are responsible for encoding the information needed for growth, maintenance, and reproduction of living things.
  - **Nucleosides** are monomers of nucleic acids containing a nitrogenous base and a 5-carbon sugar (ribose for RNA, deoxyribose for DNA).
  - **Nucleotides** are nucleosides with a phosphate group added to them.
    - ○ Sugar phosphate backbone: In a DNA or RNA molecule, all component nucleotides have the same "backbone" of sugars and phosphates, which are linked together in long chains.
    - ○ Nucleotides in DNA and RNA are either purines or pyrimidines.
      - ▪ Purines: adenine and guanine
      - ▪ Pyrimidine: thymine, cytosine, and uracil
- ☐ **Deoxyribonucleic acid** (DNA) comprises two polymers of nucleotides forming a double helix, also called the Watson and Crick model.
  - **Base pairing specificity:**
    - ○ In DNA, A forms two bonds with T.
    - ○ In RNA, A forms two bonds with U.
    - ○ In DNA and RNA, G forms three bonds with C.
  - By convention, DNA sequences are written 5'→3'.
  - **DNA transmits genetic information** from parents to offspring, and contains all of the information needed to build and maintain an organism.
  - **DNA denaturation** is a technique used to separate a DNA double helix into two separate strands by disrupting the hydrogen bonds and base pairing that hold the strands together, but without breaking any covalent bonds.
    - ○ Heat, increasing pH, and some chemicals can be used to denature DNA.
  - **Reannealing** is the process of reforming the helical structure of denatured DNA. If covalent bonding has not been disrupted, DNA will reanneal to its original form.
  - **Hybridization** occurs when complementary single-strand nucleic acids bind each other. This occurs in DNA reannealing, but can also be used in lab techniques such as polymerase chain reaction (PCR).
- ☐ **DNA replication** is the reproduction of DNA.
  - **Mechanism** of replication:
    - ○ Strands are separated at several points called origins of replication.
      - ▪ Eukaryotes have multiple origins, prokaryotes have one.
    - ○ **RNA polymerase** adds a primer.
    - ○ **DNA polymerase** binds and initiates replication.

- o Replication of both strands proceeds in both directions through the specific coupling of free nucleic acids to exposed bases. In each direction, there are two new strands being formed:
  - Leading strand: synthesized continuously, 5'→3'
  - Lagging strand: synthesized discontinuously, 5'→3', creating **Okazaki fragments**
- **Semi-conservative nature of replication:** When DNA replicates, each of the parental DNA strands serves as a template for the synthesis of a new daughter strand. Therefore, each new DNA molecule contains one old strand and one new strand.
- **Enzymes involved in replication:**
  - o **Replisome** is the complex of proteins that bind to the origin and carry out replication.
    - **Helicase** creates the replication fork and unwinds parent strands.
    - **Primase** synthesizes RNA primers, which allow DNA polymerase to bind.
    - **DNA polymerase III complex** synthesizes the new DNA by reading the parent strand 3→5, and synthesizing the daughter strand 5→3.
    - **DNA ligase** joins Okazaki fragments.
    - **DNA topoisomerase** removes positive supercoils to stabilize DNA for replication.
- Replicating the ends of DNA molecules: DNA polymerase cannot synthesize the 5' end of DNA. Therefore, DNA gets a little shorter each time it replicates.
  - o Telomeres are non-coding sequences at the ends of chromosomes. They protect coding DNA from degradation.
    - Telomeres are mostly C-G, making for stronger binding (3 bonds each).
- ☐ **Repair of DNA** occurs both during replication and after replication.
  - **Repair during replication:** Repairs can be fixed immediately by the "proofreader" function of DNA polymerase.
    - o Polymerase detects errors, cuts out the incorrect daughter base pair, and replaces it with the correct one.
    - o Polymerase can distinguish between parent and daughter strands because the parental strand is methylated and daughter strand is not.
  - **Repair of mutations** also occurs after replication is complete.
    - o Nucleotide excision: A damaged nucleotide is cut out and polymerase replaces it (ex: UV light can cause adjacent thymines to bind to each other, creating a kink that can interfere with replication).

- o Base pair excision: Some damage can cause one base pair to be converted to another base pair. Incorrect bases are detected and removed, then replaced by DNA polymerase and ligase.
- ☐ **Genetic code** contains all of the information needed to grow and maintain an organism.
  - Central dogma: DNA makes RNA and RNA makes protein.
  - Triplet code: The genetic code is read in three letter "words." Each of these words is matched to an amino acid. The amino acids are linked together into proteins.
  - **Codon-anticodon relationship**: For every 3-letter codon of an mRNA, there is a 3-letter anticodon (the sequence that would bind the codon) on a tRNA.
    - o ex: Codon 5'-UCG-3' pairs with anticodon 5'-CGA-3'.
  - **DNA code is degenerate**, meaning that each amino acid is coded for by more than one possible codon. This protects against errors, as a change of one letter of a codon will often still code for the intended amino acid.
    - o ex: CGU, CGC, CGA, and CGG all code for arginine.
  - **Wobble pairing:** There is not a different tRNA (and therefore an exact anticodon) for every possible codon. Therefore, some tRNA are able to bind to more than one codon due to wobble pairing, in which the 5' base of a codon has "wobble," meaning that it can be an imperfect match but still work fine.
  - **Point mutations** are mutations resulting from a change of a single nucleotide.
    - o **Missense mutation:** a change in one nucleotide creates a codon that codes for a different amino acid
    - o **Nonsense mutation:** a change in one nucleotide creates a stop codon
  - **Initiation and termination** codons signal the start and end of translation activity.
    - o Start codon: AUG
    - o Stop codons: UGA, UAA, UAG
  - **Messenger RNA** (mRNA) is a single-stranded transcript of DNA that is able to leave the nucleus, where it is used to synthesize protein.
    - o mRNA has a 5' cap and a 3' poly-A tail to protect it from degradation (eukaryotes only).
- ☐ **Transcription** is the process of creating RNA from a DNA template.
  - Mechanism:
    - o Transcription takes place in the nucleus.
    - o **Initiation factors** bind to a promoter (a sequence signaling a starting point for transcription) on the DNA, and build a protein complex that includes RNA polymerase.

- o **RNA polymerase** separates the DNA strands, and transcribes one strand of the DNA by reading 3'→5' and synthesizing 5'→3'.
  - Template strand (antisense) is transcribed.
  - Coding strand (sense strand) is not transcribed, but its sequence will be identical to that of the mRNA except for the replacement of T with U.
  - o RNA polymerase reaches a termination sequences, triggering it to uncouple from the DNA.
  - o mRNA travels to the cytoplasm to initiate translation.
- **Transfer RNA (tRNA) and ribosomal RNA (rRNA)** are produced through transcription, in addition to mRNA, but do not become templates for protein synthesis.
  - o tRNA binds to amino acids and brings the correct amino acids to the correct codons in translation.
  - o rRNA becomes part of the ribosome.
- Eukaryotic mRNA requires additional processing before leaving the nucleus:
  - o Introns are removed from the RNA and remain in the nucleus.
  - o Exons are hooked together after introns are removed, and exit the nucleus as processed mRNA.
- **Ribozymes** are RNA molecules that act as catalysts. They are found in ribosomes.
- **Spliceosomes** are RNA-protein complexes in the nucleus that remove introns and reassemble exons into processed mRNA.
  - o **Small nuclear ribonucleoproteins** (snRNPs) are the RNA-protein complexes of the spliceosome.
    - Small nuclear RNAs (snRNA) are the RNA strands in snRNPs.
- **Importance of introns:**
  - o Introns regulate gene expression.
  - o Some introns become functional RNAs.
  - o Introns enable multiple proteins to be created from a single gene (alternative splicing).
- ☐ **Translation** is the process of using an mRNA transcript to form a protein.
  - Mechanism:
    - o mRNA brings a transcript from DNA into the cytoplasm so that it can be translated into an amino acid sequence.
    - o Initiation complex forms around the start codon, and translation begins at the N-terminus.
    - o **Elongation**: tRNA brings the right amino acids to the ribosome by matching the tRNA anticodon to the mRNA codon.

- o **Translocation:** rRNA catalyzes the formation of peptide bonds between amino acids.
- o **Termination** occurs when the ribosome reaches a stop codon, the peptide chain is cleaved, and the translation complex disassembles.
- **Post-translational modification** of proteins enable alterations and fine-tuning of the final protein structure:
  - o Ex: add functional groups, phosphorylation

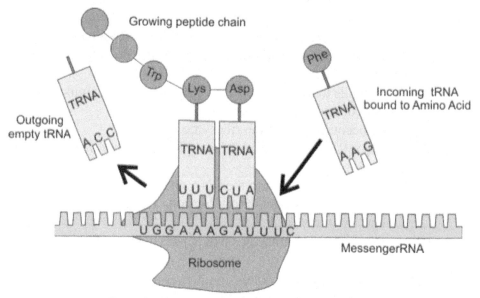

Figure 32: *Protein synthesis from mRNA transcript.*

- ☐ **Eukaryotic chromosome organization:**
  - **Histones** are chromosomal proteins. DNA is wound around them and packed tightly into units called nucleosomes. Histones also participate in gene regulation.
  - Single copy vs. repetitive DNA:
    - o Single copy DNA is the important DNA that you need most for survival. It is therefore better protected and has a low mutation rate. It is non-repetitive.
    - o Repetitive DNA is generally not transcribed or translated, is often found near the centromeres, and has a high mutation rate.
      - ▪ Telomeres are an example of repetitive RNA.
  - **Supercoiling** is the tight packing of DNA. If DNA is too tightly packed, it can interfere with replication and transcription.
  - **Heterochromatin vs. euchromatin:** heterochromatin is tightly packed and inactive DNA; euchromatin is loosely packed, and therefore accessible for transcription and/or replication.

- **Centromere** is the central part of the chromosome that links sister chromatids. Contains heterochromatin.
- ☐ **Control of gene expression in prokaryotes** (Jacob-Monod Model):
  - An **operon** is a functional unit of gene expression control. It consists of an operator, promoter, and genes associated with a single mRNA. Operons are found primarily in prokaryotes.
    - ○ The **promoter** is the binding site for RNA polymerase, which initiates transcription.
    - ○ The **operator** can be bound by a repressor protein, which will stop RNA polymerase from advancing.
    - ○ An inducer can bind to and disable a repressor protein, or can bind to an activator site upstream of the operon
    - ○ Ex: **lac operon** regulates transport and metabolism of lactose in E. coli. If no lactose is present, the bound repressor prevents production of enzymes for lactose digestion. If lactose is present, it binds the repressor, allowing production of the enzymes needed to digest lactose.

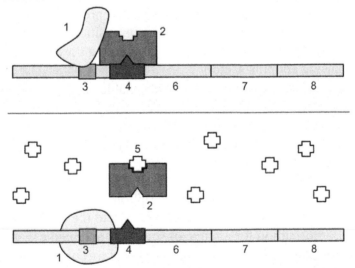

Figure 33: *1: RNA Polymerase, 2: Repressor, 3: Promoter, 4: Operator, 5: Lactose, 6: lacZ, 7: lacY, 8: lacA. Top is repressed, bottom is active.*

- **Positive control** in bacteria: For many bacterial operons, the operon is turned off (repressed) in normal conditions, and only becomes activated when an activator (positive control) is present.
- ☐ **Control of gene expression in eukaryotes** occurs at multiple levels, including transcription, translation, and post-translation.

- **Transcriptional regulation**: Transcription factors bind to enhancers to increase transcription, or to silencers to halt transcription. Enhancers and silencers can be located anywhere (unlike prokaryote operons).
- **Gene amplification/duplication** can occur naturally as a result of unequal crossing over in meiosis, genetic mutations, or genetic replication errors. Duplication of the whole genome occurs in polyploidy, which results from nondisjunction in meiosis.
- **Post-transcriptional control** includes the removal (splicing) of introns and rejoining of exons, as well as the addition of the 5' cap and the poly-A tail to mRNA.
- **Cancer** represents a failure of the controls that prevent runaway cell growth and mitosis. This typically involves disruption of gene expression.
  - **Oncogenes** are genes that have the potential to cause cancer because they are involved in the regulation of the cell cycle. They exist in normal organisms as proto-oncogenes, and can become oncogenes as a result of mutations that disrupt their function resulting in uncontrolled growth.
  - Tumor suppressor genes are genes that protect against the development of cancer by imposing additional controls on the progression of the cell cycle. (ex: slowing down the mitotic cycle, causing apoptosis, etc.)
- **Regulation of chromatin structure** enables control over access to different genes by cellular machinery, as well as protection of DNA when it is not in use. Examples include:
  - **Histone acetylation**, adding an acetyl group, loosens DNA wrapping (including gene expression)
  - **DNA methylation**, adding a methyl group to DNA, reduces expression by repressing transcription
- ☐ **Recombinant DNA and biotechnology** refer to the use and/or manipulation of genetic information for a range of scientific and medical applications.
  - **Gene cloning** is used to produce copies of a gene of interest from the mRNA transcript of that gene.
    - Reverse transcriptase is used to create complementary DNA(cDNA) from mRNA.
      - Remember: exons only
    - Transform cDNA into a plasmid, and add it to a bacterial sample. Bacteria will replicate the plasmid, producing many copies.
  - **Restriction enzymes** are able to cut DNA sequences at specific locations. They are found in bacteria, where their function is to destroy foreign DNA, but they can also be used in research applications because they can break DNA into predictable pieces.

- **DNA libraries** are collections of DNA fragments, perpetuated by gene cloning, that can be used for research.
- **Hybridization**: Single strands of nucleic acid will spontaneously stick together, or hybridize, wherever complementary sequences are present. This makes it possible to identify an unknown sequence by observing how it binds to a known sequence.
- **Polymerase chain reaction** (PCR) is a faster way to clone a gene, or to amplify a small section of DNA.
  - The DNA sample is mixed with DNA primers and heated until denatured. When it cools off again, the primers will hybridize to complementary sequences in the DNA of interest. Heat-resistant polymerase is then added along with free nucleotides, leading to the synthesis of new copies of the DNA sections tagged by the primers.
  - N cycles produces 2^n daughter strands.
  - Thermostable polymerase is used, as high temps are required to separate strands.
- **Gel electrophoresis and Southern blotting** can be used to test for the presence of a specific DNA fragment using fluorescent phosphorous.
  - DNA is cleaved into fragments, which are then sorted by size using gel electrophoresis.
  - pH is increased to denature the fragments.
  - Denatured strands are treated with a labeled probe, which will hybridize to its complementary sequence (if present), identifying its location.
- **DNA sequencing** uses PCR and dideoxynucleotides to determine the sequence of bases in a sample of DNA.
  - PCR is carried out normally, except that when the nucleotides are added to feed into the polymerase, one of the nucleotides (A, G, T, or C) will be a modified version called a dideoxynucleotide instead of a normal deoxynucleotide.
  - This modification causes elongation to be terminated as soon as a dideoxynucleotide is incorporated. Therefore, you know that the end of each resulting strand is associated with a particular base.
  - The process can be repeated for each base, or different tags can be used for each base in a single experiment, so that in the end, you can compare the individual fragments to determine the sequence.
- **Determining gene function** can be approached in a variety of ways. For example, removing the gene from a biological system and observing the effects, assessing the activity of a protein product, or comparing the sequence of an unknown gene to known genes.

- **Induced pluripotent stem cells** are pluripotent stem cells that have been produced from adult cells using biotechnology. These cells have significant potential for medical treatment, as they could enable the regeneration or replacement of lost or damaged tissues.
- **Practical applications** of DNA technology include medical applications such as human gene therapy, the synthesis of biologic pharmaceuticals, forensic DNA evidence, environmental cleanup or restoration, agricultural disease, or pesticide resistance.
- DNA technology includes **safety risks and ethical concerns**.
  - Ex: creation or transfer of harmful genes, creation of modified, unpredictable organisms, potential to modify genes of embryos, ethics of modifying our own genes or those of others, privacy of genetic information, etc.
- ☐ **Evidence that DNA is genetic material** includes observations of cell division and experiments with bacteriophages.
  - When cells divide, the nucleus is divided in an organized, exact process, while other cell components are split haphazardly. This suggests that the nucleus contains genetic material. However, the nucleus contains both protein and nucleic acid.
  - We know from experiments with bacteriophages, which are viruses consisting of nucleic acid surrounded by a protein cap, that the nucleic acid of the nucleus, and not the protein of the nucleus, is genetic material.
  - If either the protein cap or the nucleic acid is labeled (ex: radioactively labeled sulfur, which is found in amino acids but not nucleic acids), and the bacteriophage infects a bacterium, analysis will show that the labeled protein remains outside the bacterium, and is not incorporated into newly produced viruses, and/or that the labeled nucleic acid is found inside the bacterium, and incorporated into new viruses.
- ☐ **Mendelian concepts** for transmission of genetic information among generations:
  - **Phenotype vs. genotype:** Phenotype is the observed trait, while genotype is the genetic information underlying that trait.
    - Ex: Phenotype X could indicate genotype XX, or genotype Xx.
  - **Gene**: a section of DNA that codes for a certain product or trait
  - **Locus**: the position of a gene on a chromosome
  - **Allele**: a variant of a gene
    - A given gene can have multiple alleles, which are located at the same locus.
    - **Single-allele trait:** Only two alleles are present, dominant and recessive. If the dominant is present, it will always be expressed (DD

or Dr). The recessive trait will only be expressed if the dominant allele is absent (rr).

- Ex: If flower color is a single-allele trait, with red (R) as dominant and white (w) as recessive, then genotypes "RR" and "Rw" will both have a red phenotype, while "ww" will have a white phenotype.

o **Multiple allele trait**: More than two alleles interact to produce a trait. Incomplete dominance and co-dominance often lead to more than two phenotypes.

- Ex: Blood type has three alleles — I^A, I^B, and I — which interact to create six genotypes and four phenotypes: A, B, AB, and O.

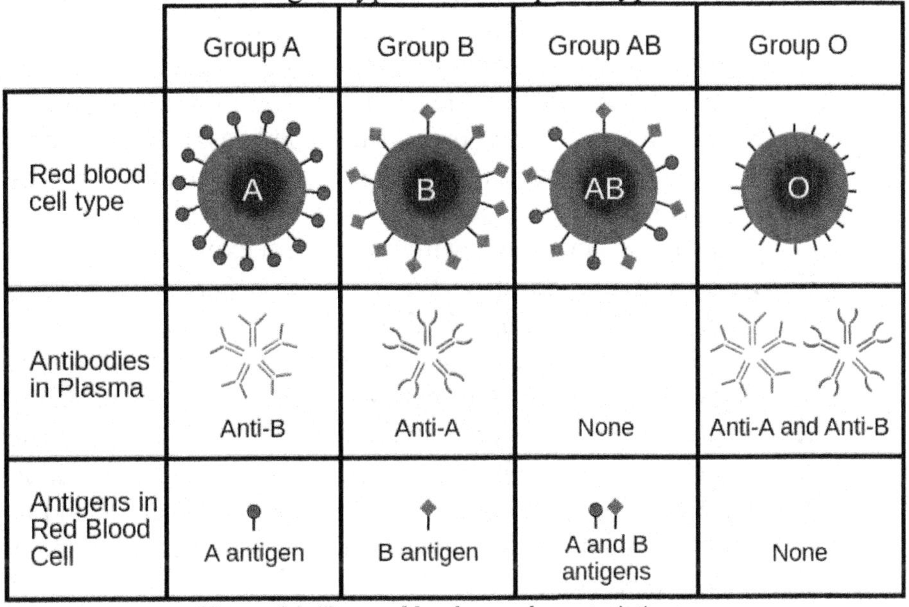

	Group A	Group B	Group AB	Group O
Red blood cell type	A	B	AB	O
Antibodies in Plasma	Anti-B	Anti-A	None	Anti-A and Anti-B
Antigens in Red Blood Cell	A antigen	B antigen	A and B antigens	None

Figure 34: Human blood type characteristics.

- **Homozygosity vs. heterozygosity:** A cell is homozygous for a gene if it has identical alleles on homologous chromosomes. It is heterozygous if it has different alleles on homologous chromosomes.
- **Wild-type** is the phenotype of the typical or dominant form of a certain species. Wild-type (WT) organisms are often used as the control groups in genetic experiments.
- **Recessiveness:** If a trait is recessive, its effect is completely masked when the dominant allele is present (Xx). Recessive traits are expressed only in the absence of a dominant allele (xx).
- **Complete dominance:** The effect of one allele completely hides the effect of the other allele. The phenotypes of the homozygous and heterozygous dominant forms are identical.

- **Co-dominance**: A heterozygous phenotype shows contributions from both alleles (ex: A cat that is heterozygous for white and black coat color (BW) has a phenotype of black and white patches).
- **Incomplete dominance:** A heterozygous phenotype is a mixture or midpoint between the dominant and recessive traits (ex: a red flower and a white flower produce pink offspring).
  - **Leakage** is when a gene transfers from one species to another, similar species.
  - **Penetrance** is the probability that a given genotype will result in a given phenotype. If penetrance is 100 percent, all organisms with the genotype will have the phenotype. Anything less than 100 percent, and some organisms with the genotype will not express the phenotype.
  - **Expressivity** is the extent to which a gene is expressed phenotypically in a population (ex: A gene for red flower color might have different expressivity in different organisms, visible as different shades of red).
    - For a binary phenotype with complete dominance, expressivity and penetrance are the same. For a non-binary phenotype, there can be complete penetrance without uniform expressivity.
- **Hybridization and viability:** When mating occurs between two different species or breeds, the dramatic differences between alleles often lead to failure of the offspring to mature at the zygotic or embryonic stage. In the rare cases when a hybrid does mature, it is often weak and infertile. This genetic mechanism helps prevent the flow of genes among species.
- A **gene pool** comprises all of the genes within a given population or species. A larger gene pool means higher genetic diversity and therefore better fitness. A smaller gene pool means less diversity and therefore higher risk of extinction.
- **Meiosis** contributes significantly to genetic diversity because it is the only opportunity for genetic recombination in eukaryotes, through independent assortment and crossing over.
  - In **prophase I**, homologous chromosomes line up next to each other, and can exchange sequences of DNA in a process called crossing over.
  - A **tetrad** is a pair of homologous chromosomes (four chromatids) in position to undergo crossing over. Tetrads are characteristic of meiosis.
  - Segregation of genes:
    - **Law of Independent Assortment**: Alleles are passed from parent to offspring independent of one another. Inheriting one allele for one trait does not influence which alleles are inherited for other traits.
    - **Linkage** is an exception to the law of independent assortment. Genes that are located close together on the same chromosome are more likely to be inherited together.

- There are degrees of linkage: All genes located on the same chromosome are somewhat linked, while the closer they are together, the more linked they are.
  - o **Recombination** is the creation of offspring with new combinations of traits not seen in either parent.
    - **Single crossovers** exchange one section of one chromosome with the same section from the other parent's homologous chromosome. This always results in recombination.
    - **Double crossovers**, in which two crossover events occur in the same section of a chromosome, do not always result in recombination. If the same section crosses over one, and then again, the original segments have been returned and no recombination has occurred. However, if slightly different sections crossover the second time, some recombination has occurred.
    - A **synaptonemal complex** is a complex of proteins that forms between homologous chromosomes to mediate recombination.
  - o **Sex determination**: XX is female, XY is male
  - o **Sex-linked characteristics** are carried on the sex chromosomes.
    - Very few genes exist on the Y chromosome, so the vast majority of sex-linked characteristics are carried on the X.
  - o **Cytoplasmic/extranuclear inheritance**: All cytoplasmic material, including mitochondria, is inherited from the mother. As a result, mitochondrial DNA in offspring is identical to that of the mother.
- ☐ **Mutations** are errors in a DNA sequence. Several types are possible:
  - o **Random mutation:** all mutations are random, in that they are not intended to result in any particular outcome, and do not occur according to predictable patterns
  - o **Transcription error:** mutations that result from errors in the creation of an RNA transcript from DNA
  - o **Translation error:** mutations that result from errors in the translation from mRNA to protein
  - o **Base substitution:** one base is replaced with another
  - o **Inversion**: a genetic sequence is reversed
  - o **Addition**: a genetic sequence is inserted
  - o **Deletion**: a genetic sequence is deleted
  - o **Translocation**: a sequence is moved from one region to another
  - o **Mispairing**: an error in base pairing
- • **Advantageous vs. deleterious mutation:** Sometimes mutations result in traits that benefit an organism (advantageous), while other times, mutations can harm an organism (deleterious).

- **Inborn errors of metabolism** are a class of genetic disorders that affect an organism's ability to metabolize certain substances properly, often resulting in the buildup of reactants or products due to a faulty enzyme.
- **Mutagens as carcinogens**: Because some mutations can cause cancer, many mutagens are also likely carcinogens. However, not all carcinogens are mutagens.
- **Genetic drift** refers to changes in the frequency of an allele in a population due to random effects, such that some alleles may disappear, or become more dominant, not because they represent a fitness advantage, but simply due to random variation in the rate at which different alleles were reproduced in a population.
  - Like a jar of marbles: If you have a jar of marbles and you randomly draw out 20 of them, that subset will not necessarily have a statistical distribution identical to the larger jar. It is also possible that a certain color of marble randomly wouldn't be picked at all, and therefore would not be carried forward into the next marble jar generation.
- ☐ **Analytic methods** for assessing genetic traits in a population:
  - **Hardy-Weinberg Principle:** Allele and genotype frequencies in a population remain constant from generation to generation in the absence of other evolutionary influences.
    - $P^2 + 2pq + Q^2 = 1$, where p and q are frequencies of alleles. Pq is a heterozygote, p-squared and q-squared are homozygotes.
    - Hardy-Weinberg equilibrium occurs when there is:
      - No natural selection
      - A large population
      - Random mating
      - No mutations
      - No migration
  - **Testcross:** Heterozygous (Aa) and homozygous (AA) dominant traits have the same phenotype. To determine whether it is heterozygous or homozygous, cross the unknown with a known homozygous recessive and assess the offspring. If it was AA, there won't be any recessive phenotypes. If there are recessive phenotypes, it must be Aa.
    - **Naming generations:** P (parental) is the one you start with, F1 is the offspring of the P generation. F2 is the offspring of the F1 generation, etc.
  - **Backcross:** If you want to get offspring that are as similar as possible to the parents, you can backcross, which means crossing the offspring with one of the parents, or an organism with genes very similar to the parents. This process is used in the development of knockout organisms.

- **Gene mapping using crossover frequencies**: The rate of recombination between two genes can be used to estimate the distance between them on a chromosome. The higher the rate of recombination, the further apart the genes are.
- **Biometry** is using statistics to analyze biological data.
  - o Probability of two events occurring (AND): multiply
    - If there is a 25 percent chance a plant will be pink and a 25 percent chance it will be tall, there is a .25*.25 = 6.25 percent chance that it will be pink and tall.
  - o Probability of one of two events occurring (OR): add
    - If there is a 10 percent chance you will get an A and a 20 percent chance you will get a B, there is a .1+.2 = 30 percent chance you will get an A or a B.
- ☐ **Evolution** is change in the traits of a population over successive generations.
  - **Natural selection** is an evolutionary process in which differences in survival and reproduction of organisms due to phenotype leads to differences in genetic composition of future generations and populations.
  - **Fitness concept** refers to how good an organism is at passing its genes to the next generation (reproducing).
  - **Selection by differential reproduction**: Traits that confer survival/reproduction advantages are more likely to be passed on than traits that do not.
  - **Concepts of natural and group selection**: Survival of the fittest individual; survival of the fittest group. Social factors can contribute to group selection (ex: herd behaviors).
  - **Evolutionary success** is defined as an increase in percent representation in the gene pool of the next generation
  - **Speciation** is the evolutionary process through which species are created. Organisms in a species are adapted for their environment through selection of advantageous traits over successive generations.
  - **Polymorphism** is when a single species has multiple distinct phenotypes, or "morphs." Polymorphism allows the maintenance of genetic diversity within a single species.
  - **Sexual dimorphism** refers to phenotypic differences between the genders of a species.
  - **Adaptation and specialization**: Species "specialize" in their environment through the development of advantageous traits or features over successive generations.
    - o Ex: Hummingbirds with longer beaks are better able to get nectar from flowers, so over time, hummingbirds with longer beaks were better able to survive and reproduce than hummingbirds with shorter beaks.

- **Inbreeding** is mating between individuals who are closely related genetically, which increases the likelihood of homozygosity, and therefore the appearance of recessive or harmful traits.
- **Outbreeding** is the opposite of inbreeding. Mating between individuals who are not closely related genetically increases heterozygosity.
- A **bottleneck** is a dramatic reduction in the size of a population due to a natural disaster, disease, etc. Bottlenecks reduce genetic diversity of the population, and can lead to adaptive changes (ex: survivors of a disaster may share certain advantageous traits).
- **Evolutionary time** as measured by gradual random changes in genome:
  - Because random genetic mutations occur at a constant rate, time can be measured based on the significance of the genetic differences between organisms/groups/species. This approach is used to determine how long ago species diverged from each other.

Energy and Metabolism

- ☐ **Bioenergetics** is the application of thermodynamic, electrochemical, and kinetic principles to energy flow in biological systems.
  - **Free energy** (G) measures how much energy is available to do work.
    - Negative ΔG means the reaction is spontaneous; positive ΔG means the reaction is nonspontaneous
  - **Equilibrium constant** (Keq) is a ratio of the concentration of products to the concentration of reactants at equilibrium. Each concentration is raised to the power of its coefficient.
    - If Keq > 0, then there are more products than reactants at equilibrium.
    - If Keq = 0, then there are equal concentrations of reactants and products at equilibrium.
    - If Keq < 0, then there are more reactants than products at equilibrium.
  - Relating delta G and Keq: $\Delta G^o = -RT*\ln(Keq)$
  - **Le Chatelier's Principle**: when a system in equilibrium experiences a change (concentration, pressure, volume, etc.), it will readjust to counteract the effect of the change until equilibrium is reestablished.
    - Ex: An increase in concentration of substrates will tend to push a reaction toward products. An increase in concentration of products tends to push a reaction toward substrates.
- ☐ **Adenosine triphosphate** (ATP) is the primary energy-carrying molecule.
  - ATP has three bulky, negatively charged phosphate groups close together, making it a high-energy molecule.
  - **ATP hydrolysis** (delta G < <0) reacts ATP with water to yield ADP and P.

- Phosphate group transfers enable transfer of energy from one molecule to another.
- Adding a phosphate group to ADP reproduces ATP.

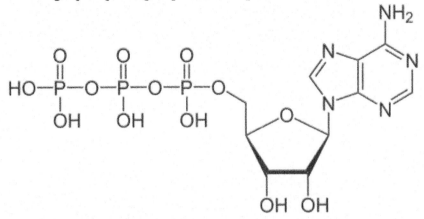

Figure 10. *Adenosine Triphosphate structure*

- ☐ **Oxidation and reduction** are critical in biological energy production, especially in the electron transport chain (ETC).
    - **Soluble electron carriers** in the ETC collect the electrons lost in the breakdown of glucose and use their energy to pump protons into the mitochondrial matrix. These protons, in turn, are used to power ATP synthase, which generates ATP from ADP.
        - ○ NADH, NADPH, $FADH_2$, and ubiquinone are all soluble electron carriers.
    - **Flavoproteins** are nucleic acid–derived electron carriers. They participate in the ETC, as well as in the oxidation of fatty acids.
- ☐ **Metabolism** refers to the chemical reactions involved in the synthesis of molecules for energy storage (anabolism) and the breakdown of molecules for energy release (catabolism).
    - Polysaccharides are broken down into monosaccharides; proteins are broken down into amino acids; and lipids are broken down into fatty acids and glycerol. These basic molecules then begin aerobic or anaerobic metabolism.
    - **Aerobic metabolism:** glycolysis → oxidative decarboxylation → citric acid cycle → electron transport chain
        - ○ Overall reaction: $C_6H_{12}O_6 + 6O_2 \rightarrow 6CO_2 + 6H_2O + $ energy
        - ○ For each molecule of glucose, 30 ATPs are produced.
    - **Anaerobic metabolism:** glycolysis → fermentation

- ☐ **Glycolysis** converts one glucose molecule into two pyruvate molecules, producing 2 ATP and 2 NADH in the process. It is the first step in both aerobic and anaerobic metabolism.
  - Net reaction of glycolysis: $C_6H_{12}O_6 + 2NAD^+ + 2ADP + 2P \rightarrow 2CH_3COCOO- + 2NADH + 2ATP + 2H_2O + 2H^+$
  - Glycolysis happens in the cytoplasm.
  - **2 ATP used, 4 produced, for net 2 ATP:** 2 ATP are consumed in the process of splitting dihydroxyacetone phosphate into two molecules of glyceraldehyde 3-phosphate. Each glyceraldehyde 3-phosphate is then broken down to pyruvate, producing 2 ATP each.
  - Glycolysis starts with 6 carbons (glucose), and ends with two 3-carbon pyruvates.
  - **Glucose gets trapped in the cell.** The first step of glycolysis uses one ATP to convert glucose into glucose 6-phosphate, which cannot diffuse through the cellular membrane. This reaction is irreversible.
  - **G-6-P is isomerized** into fructose-6-phosphate. This reaction is reversible.
  - **F-6-P commits to glycolysis.** F-6-P gets another phosphate group from ATP, becoming fructose 1, 6-bisphosphate. This is the primary rate-limiting step of glycolysis.
    - o The enzyme (Phosphofructokinase-1) is inhibited by ATP and citrate, so that glycolysis is downregulated when energy is abundant.
    - o In hepatocytes, phosphofructokinase-1 is stimulated by insulin and inhibited by glucagon.
  - **F-1,6-BP is split into two** molecules of glyceraldehyde-3-phosphate.
  - **Each GA-3-P gets another phosphate**, producing two molecules of 1, 3-bisphosphoglycerate. NAD+ is reduced to NADH in the process.
  - **Each 1,3-BPG undergoes substrate-level phosphorylation,** producing one pyruvate and two ATPs each (4 total ATPs produced, 2 consumed, for 2 net ATPs from glycolysis).
    - o *There are a lot of molecular steps here but they are unlikely to be tested on the MCAT.*
  - **Aerobic respiration:** products of glycolysis proceed to oxidative decarboxylation and the citric acid cycle
  - **Anaerobic respiration:** products of glycolysis proceed to fermentation

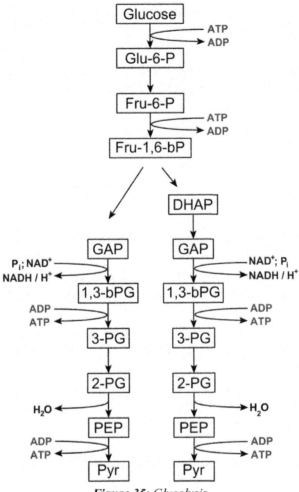

Figure 35: *Glycolysis.*

- ☐ **Fermentation** happens in anaerobic organisms, and in aerobic organisms when oxygen is scarce.
  - • Pyruvate is reduced to ethanol (yeast) or lactic acid (muscle), oxidizing NADH to NAD+ in the process.
  - • Ethanol: 2 pyruvates (6 carbons; 3 each) yield 2 CO_2 (2 carbons; 1 each) and 2 ethanol (4 carbons; 2 each). 2NADH is oxidized to 2NAD+.
  - • Lactic acid: 2 pyruvates (6 carbons; 3 each) yield 2 lactic acid (6 carbons, 3 each). 2NADH is oxidized to 2NAD+.
- ☐ **Gluconeogenesis** uses glycerol (from fatty acids), lactate (from fermentation), and amino acids (alanine and glutamine) to create glucose, which can then be metabolized. This is, generally speaking, the reverse of glycolysis.
  - • Gluconeogenesis happens in the liver, and helps maintain blood glucose levels in fasting states.

- Gluconeogenesis is promoted by glucagon and inhibited by insulin.
- Lactate becomes pyruvate.
- Amino acids are deaminated, forming pyruvate or oxaloacetate.
- Glycerol becomes fructose 1, 6-bisphosphate.
- ☐ **Pentose Phosphate Pathway** (PPP) produces NADPH, needed for fatty acid synthesis, as well as ribose 5-phosphate, which is used to synthesize nucleotides.
  - Pentose phosphate pathway happens in the cytoplasm.
  - **Glucose-6-phosphate becomes ribulose-5-phosphate**, reducing 2 NADP+ to 2NADPH in the process.
    - o The enzyme Glucose-6-phosphate dehydrogenase is the rate-limiting step and main control point of the PPP.
    - o G-6-PDH is activated by insulin (promoting fatty acid synthesis).
    - o G-6-PDH is activated by NADP+ and inhibited by NADPH.
  - **R-5-P can then become fructose-6-phosphate or glyceraldehyde-3-phosphate**, intermediates of glycolysis, or ribose-5-phosphate for nucleotide synthesis.
- ☐ **Citric Acid Cycle** (CAC) is a continuous cycle of reactions in aerobic respiration that produce energy by oxidizing acetyl-CoA.
  - The citric acid cycle happens in the mitochondrial matrix.
  - Acetyl-CoA, which feeds into the citric acid cycle, is produced from several precursor molecules:
    - o **Carbohydrates:** Pyruvate from glycolysis is transported into the mitochondrial matrix, where it is converted into Acetyl CoA in a reaction that also yields 1 CO_2 and reduces 1 NAD+ to NADH
    - o **Fatty acids** are transported into the intermembrane space, where they are converted to Acyl CoA in a reaction that uses 1 ATP. Acyl CoA is then transported into the mitochondrial matrix, where it reduces 1 NAD+ to NADH 1 one FAD to $FADH_2$ to produce Acetyl CoA.
    - o **Proteins:** Amino acids, after they are deaminated in the liver, are converted to pyruvate (and therefore enter via the carbohydrate path) or Acetyl CoA, which can enter the citric acid cycle directly.
  - **One turn of the citric acid cycle:** Acetyl CoA + $3NAD^+$ + FAD + GDP + $2H_2O \rightarrow 2CO_2 + 3NADH + FADH_2 + GTP + 2H^+ + CoA$
    - o **Per pyruvate,** you get 1 ATP, 3 NADH, 1 FADH.
    - o **Per glucose** (two pyruvate), you get 2 ATP, 6 NADH, and 2 FADH.
  - **Total ATP yield:** 12.5 ATP/pyruvate; 25 ATP/glucose. 1 NADH $\rightarrow$ 2.5 ATP, 1 $FADH_2 \rightarrow$ 1.5 ATP

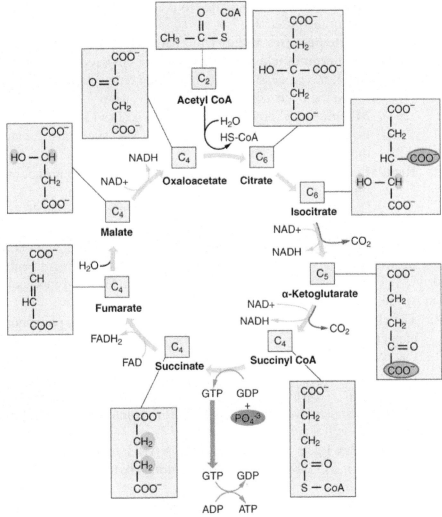

Figure 36*: Citric acid cycle.*

- Citric Acid Cycle reactions:
  - **Acetyl CoA (two carbons) enters the cycle** through a condensation reaction with oxaloacetate (four carbons) yielding citrate (six carbons).
  - **Citrate is isomerized,** forming isocitrate (six carbons).
  - **Isocitrate loses a carbon** as CO_2, yielding alpha-ketoglutarate (five carbons). In the process, 1 NAD^+ is reduced to NADH.
  - **Alpha-ketogluterate loses 1 carbon** as CO2, yielding succinyl-CoA (four carbons). In the process, 1 NAD^+ is reduced to NADH.
  - **Succinyl-CoA becomes succinate** (four carbons), producing 1 GTP from GDP in the process (this GTP then goes on to produce 1 ATP).

- Succinate becomes fumarate (four carbons), and 1 FAD becomes $FADH_2$ in the process.
- Fumarate becomes malate (four carbons).
- Malate becomes oxaloacetate (four carbons), reducing 1 NAD^+ to NADH in the process. Oxaloacetate then reacts with a new Acetyl-CoA, and the cycle continues.
  - Mnemonic: Cindy Is Kinky, So She Fucks More Often (citrate, isocitrate, α-ketogluterate, succinyl-CoA, succinate, fumarate, malate, oxaloacetate)
- **Regulation of the cycle:** In general, accumulation of a product inhibits the cycle, and accumulation of a reactant activates the cycle.
  - NADH and $FADH_2$ inhibit the cycle via negative feedback.
  - Acetyl CoA inhibits its own synthesis via negative feedback.
- □ **Oxidative phosphorylation** is the aerobic process by which mitochondria use the flow of electrons to create a proton gradient. That proton gradient then drives ATP synthase, which synthesizes ATP from ADP and inorganic phosphate.
  - The **electron transport chain** (ETC) is where oxidative phosphorylation happens. It is a series of proteins on the inner mitochondrial membrane that carry electrons, with oxygen acting as the final electron carrier.
    - Electron transport is exergonic, while ATP synthesis is endergonic.
  - **Steps of the electron transport chain:** Each step involves oxidation and reduction, and each step pumps some protons into the mitochondrial matrix.
    - **Complex I** gets two electrons from NADH, and passes them to coenzyme Q (ubiquinone). Four protons are transferred into the matrix.
    - **Complex II** gets electrons from succinate (CAC intermediate), and passes them to the same coenzyme Q as complex I. No protons transferred across the membrane.
      - $FADH_2$ enters the ETC at complex II. This explains why each $FADH_2$ yields fewer ATP than NADH
    - **Coenzyme Q passes electrons to complex III**, which then passes them to cytochrome c. Complex III transfers four protons.
    - **Cytochrome C uses oxygen**, electrons, and protons to make water (oxygen is reduced). Cytochrome C can carry one electron at a time.
    - Moving protons into the mitochondrial matrix both lowers the pH inside the matrix, and builds up an electrochemical gradient across the membrane.

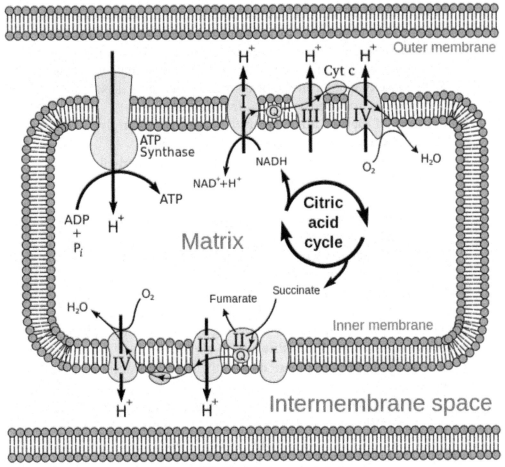

Figure 37: *Electron transport chain.*

- **ATP synthase is powered by chemiosmotic coupling**. Protons flowing across the membrane, down their concentration gradient, are used to power ATP synthase, which makes ATP from ADP and inorganic phosphate.
- **Proton motive force**, or the pumping of protons across a membrane, is created by the ETC.
- **Regulation of oxidative phosphorylation**: In general, the ETC is regulated by the availability of products from the citric acid cycle, as well as availability of oxygen.
  - The oxidative phosphorylation rate decreases when oxygen levels decrease.
  - If oxygen decreases, NADH starts to accumulate, which in turn inhibits the citric acid cycle.

- **Apoptosis**: Programmed cell death involves the release of proteins, especially cytochrome C, from the inner mitochondrial membrane.
- **Oxidative stress**: Sometimes electrons in the ETC reduce oxygen before they reach the end of the chain, creating reactive oxygen species (ROS). ROS cause oxidative stress, or damage, to proteins, DNA, and other cell components from peroxides and free radicals.

☐ **Metabolism of dietary fats**: Dietary fats are made of triglycerides, which can be broken down into monoglycerides and fatty acids.
- **Fatty acids** are carboxylic acids with long hydrocarbon tails that can be saturated (no C=C double bonds) or unsaturated (with some C=C double bonds).
- **Fatty acids are activated** through the addition of CoA, which enables them to be transported into the mitochondria.
- **Fatty acids are oxidized** in the mitochondria to create acetyl-CoA, which can then enter the citric acid cycle.

☐ **Metabolism of proteins** occurs only in prolonged fasting states. Usually, proteins are broken down into amino acids and then incorporated in the synthesis of new body proteins. In fasting states, they are broken down into molecules that can enter the citric acid cycle:
- **Amino acids are deaminated**, with the nitrogens ultimately converted to urea.
- **Remaining carbon chains** are converted into pyruvate or acetyl-CoA to enter the citric acid cycle.

☐ **Ketone bodies** are a backup energy source created in states of prolonged fasting.
- **Acetyl-CoA accumulates** in fasting states.
- **The liver** turns acetyl-CoA into ketone bodies.
- Ketone bodies can be used for energy in most body tissues, though they are only used by the brain when they reach an extremely high concentration in the blood.
- **The brain** only uses glucose for energy, except for in extreme fasting states. It switches to ketone bodies in extreme fasting so that it can be powered by stored body fat before it begins breaking down body protein for gluconeogenesis.

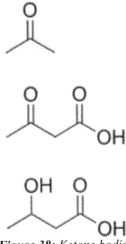

Figure 38: *Ketone bodies.*

- ☐ **Anabolism of fats:** Extra dietary proteins and carbohydrates can be used to make fats for long-term energy storage.
  - **Non-template synthesis**: Biosynthesis of lipids and polysaccharides is called non-template synthesis because these molecules are created without any directions from nucleic acid (unlike protein synthesis).
  - Triacylglycerides are the primary storage molecule for fat. Triacylglycerides are synthesized in the liver and adipose tissue from glycerol and fatty acids.
- ☐ **Metabolic regulation** is essential for maintaining homeostasis, which is a dynamic steady state, integrating the activities of all body systems.
  - **Glycolysis and gluconeogenesis** work in opposite directions, breaking down glucose when it is needed for energy, and synthesizing it when it is scarce. In general, glycolysis inhibits gluconeogenesis and gluconeogenesis inhibits glycogenesis.
  - **Glycogen** is regulated by insulin and glucagon in the pancreas.
    - o Glucagon breaks down glycogen and increases gluconeogenesis, in order to increase blood sugar.
    - o Insulin stimulates glucose uptake and glycogen synthesis.
  - **Glucocorticoids** are hormones involved in stress responses that regulate metabolism. In a fight-or-flight state, you need to mobilize a lot of glucose for quick energy.
    - o Ex: Cortisol inhibits glucose uptake and increases gluconeogenesis.
  - **Thyroid hormones** increase the basal metabolic rate, but levels are essentially stable throughout an individual's lifetime.

- **Body mass** is essentially a high-level manifestation of metabolic regulation. Body mass is influenced by diet, but also by hormones, genetic factors, activity, and metabolic rates.
  - **Ghrelin** is a hormone that increases appetite. It makes you feel hungry.
  - **Leptin** is a hormone that decreases appetite. It makes you feel full.
  - Genetic variations in ghrelin and leptin activity may be involved in differences in body mass.
- ☐ **Metabolism in different tissues**: Different tissues can use different energy sources.
  - **Skeletal** muscle uses glucose. Fatty acids and ketones can be used in fasting states.
  - **Cardiac** muscle uses fatty acids. Ketones can also be used in fasting states.
  - The **brain** uses glucose, except for in extreme fasting states, when ketones can be used.
  - **Red blood cells** use glucose only, because they lack mitochondria.

Cells and Molecules

- ☐ **Eukaryotic cells** can be identified by the presence of a membrane-bound nucleus, organelles, and mitotic division.
- ☐ The **plasma membrane** functions as the boundary of cell contents, as well as controls movement of molecules in and out of a cell, cell protection, and signaling.
  - Structure: **phospholipid bilayer** studded with proteins and cholesterol
    - Phosphorous heads face the cell's interior and exterior (hydrophilic); lipid tails form a hydrophobic central layer.
    - A hydrophobic membrane core means that hydrophilic molecules can't diffuse through the membrane, but hydrophobic molecules can.
    - **Cholesterol** (a steroid) maintains membrane fluidity. At low temperature, more cholesterol makes a membrane more fluid, and at high temperature, more cholesterol makes a membrane less fluid.
    - **Waxes** (alcohol group + long-chain fatty acid) are used by plants to form a waterproof layer on their outer surfaces.
    - **Proteins** carry out a variety of membrane functions, including transport (channels and pumps) and communication (receptors).
    - Carbohydrates on the surface of cells play a role in immunity by enabling our bodies to recognize self vs. non-self cells.

- o The **fluid mosaic model** views the cell membrane as a fluid surface that moves dynamically around proteins and other large molecules contained in it.
- **Solute transport** across membranes depends on permeability, charge, size, hydrophobicity, and intra- and extracellular concentrations.
- **Thermodynamic** considerations:
  - o Passive transport has a negative delta G (spontaneous); active transport has a positive delta G (nonspontaneous).
  - o Entropy: When a molecule is moving down its concentration gradient, it is increasing the entropy of a system.
- **Osmosis** is diffusion of water across semipermeable membrane from a region of high solute concentration to a region of low solute concentration.
  - o Osmotic pressure is a colligative property (dependent on solute concentration) defined as the pressure that you would have to apply to prevent a solvent from moving across the membrane.
- **Passive transport** is the movement of molecules across a membrane without any input of energy. This includes osmosis, diffusion, and facilitated diffusion.
- **Active transport**: is the movement of molecules across a membrane that requires input of energy.
  - o **Sodium/potassium pump**: uses 1 ATP to move 2 K+ into the cell, and 3 Na+ out of the cell.
- **Membrane channels** are transmembrane proteins that allow specific molecules to pass in or out of the cell. Channels can be ungated, voltage-gated, or ligand-gated.
- **Membrane potential** refers to the electric potential created by differences in ion concentrations inside and outside the cell.
- **Membrane receptors** can trigger signaling cascades within a cell. This allows molecules outside the cell to influence the inside of the cell without crossing the membrane.
- **Exocytosis and endocytosis** is the transport of molecules across a membrane by the formation of a pocket in the membrane, which then pinches off to form a phospholipid bilayer vesicle. Exocytosis is the release of molecules out of the cell, endocytosis is the bringing of molecules into the cell.
- ☐ **Intercellular junctions** connect cells to other cells:
  - **Gap junctions** create a protein channel between two cells, so that molecules can move from the cytoplasm of one to the next (ex: Gap junctions enable coordinated contraction of cardiac muscle).
  - **Tight junctions** stick cells together without connecting their cytoplasms. Tight junctions can form impenetrable or waterproof barriers (ex:

Epithelial tissues are made up of sheets of cells connected by tight junctions).

- **Desmosomes** connect cells together by using surface adhesion proteins to connect the cytoskeleton of one cell to another. Provide strong and flexible connections (ex: Desmosomes are found connecting skeletal muscle cells together.)

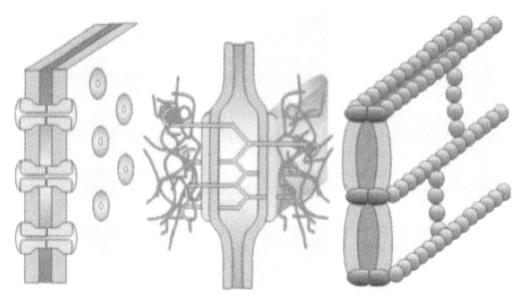

Figure 39: *Intercellular junction types: gap junctions (left), desmosomes (middle), and tight junctions (right).*

- ☐ **Membrane-bound organelles** are characteristic of eukaryotic cells, and perform a variety of specialized functions.
  - The **nucleus** compartmentalizes and stores DNA.
    - o The nucleolus is a section of the nucleus where ribosomes (rRNA) are synthesized. It is visible as a dark spot in the nucleus.
    - o The nuclear envelope is a double membrane regulating what enters and exits the nucleus. Nuclear pores allow molecules to enter and exit the nuclear envelope (ex: mRNA leaves the nucleus via nuclear pores).
  - **Mitochondria** synthesize ATP, the energy currency of the cell.
    - o The inner membrane is highly convoluted, and surrounds the matrix, the innermost compartment of the mitochondria.
    - o The outer membrane surrounds the intermembrane space.
    - o Mitochondria are self-replicating by binary fission.
  - **Lysosomes** are membrane-bound vesicles filled with hydrolytic enzymes that are used to break down a range of waste products and toxins.

- The **endoplasmic reticulum** is a network of flattened membrane pockets continuous with the outer nuclear membrane.
  - Rough ER is covered with membrane-bound ribosomes, and functions in protein synthesis and the delivery of membrane-bound or secreted proteins.
  - Smooth ER lacks ribosomes, and is involved in synthesis of lipids, including new phospholipids for the cell membrane.
- The **Golgi apparatus** a flat stack of vesicles that modifies proteins and/or secretes them via exocytosis.
  - Proteins synthesized in rough ER are transported on vesicles to the Golgi, which then modifies them and sends them out in a new vesicle to their destination.
- **Peroxisomes**: organelles that remove hydrogen peroxide from the cytoplasm and turn it into water and oxygen. They are also involved in breaking down fatty acids and amino acids in some cells, or in removing other harmful species (ex: reactive oxygens).
☐ A **cytoskeleton** provides structural support and sometimes movement to eukaryotic cells.
  - **Microfilaments** are linear polymers of actin. They are thin, strong, and flexible.
    - Microfilaments enable movement through polymerization and depolymerization.
    - Microfilaments form a ring in dividing cells that then contracts, initiating cell cleavage.
  - **Microtubules** are tubulin polymers. They are thicker and less flexible than microfilaments. They are the "train tracks" for secreted vesicles, support cilia and flagella, and form the mitotic spindles.
  - **Intermediate filaments** have characteristics between microfilaments and microtubules, and provide additional structural support.
  - **Cilia and flagella** are supported primarily by microtubules.
  - **Centrioles** are made primarily of tubulin.
  - **Microtubule organizing centers** (MTOC) regulate microtubule systems, including flagella and cilia, as well as the spindle apparatus.
☐ **Tissues** formed from eukaryotic cells:
  - Epithelial cells form into thin layers bound together with tight junctions (ex: epidermis and lining of organs).
  - Connective tissue includes bone, cartilage, adipose, blood, and lymph. It contains cells suspended in a matrix, which is made up of viscous fluid (ground substance) and fibers.

- ☐ **Cell theory** has three tenets:
  - All living organisms are made of one or more cells.
  - The cell is the basic structural and functional unit of organisms.
  - All cells come from other, preexisting cells.
- ☐ **Prokaryotes** ("pro," before, "karyote," nucleus) are a class of organisms that are single-cellular, lack membrane-bound organelles (including a nucleus), and reproduce by binary fission. Prokaryotes are divided into two sub-domains:
  - **Bacteria** have cell walls. Many use flagella for propulsion. They can be classified by shape:
    - o Bacilli: rod-shaped
    - o Spirilli: spiral-shaped
    - o Cocci: sphere-shaped

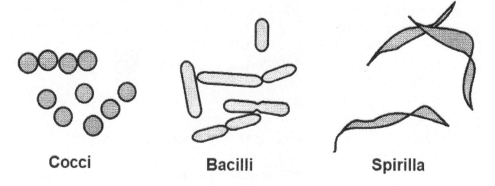

Cocci   **Bacilli**   **Spirilla**

Figure 40: Classes of bacteria.

  - **Archaea** look similar to bacteria, but have significant differences in their genetics, metabolism, and the structure of their cell membranes.
  - **Flagellar propulsion**:
    - o In bacteria, flagella are made of a protein called flagellin, which polymerizes into a helical shape.
    - o Propulsion is driven by a motor protein that spins the end of the flagellin polymer, powered by an ion pump in the cell membrane near the flagellum.
    - o It is very energy-efficient.
- ☐ **Growth and physiology** of prokaryotes:
  - **Reproduction by fission** is asexual reproduction in which one prokaryote divides into two:
    - o Circular DNA is replicated.
    - o One copy moves to each pole of the cell.
    - o The equatorial plate separates the membrane in the middle, forming two identical cells.

o No mitotic apparatus is needed.
- Bacteria can be anaerobic and/or aerobic.
- **Bacterial populations** grow exponentially.
  o Lag phase: delayed growth when bacteria are treated/put into a new environment
  o Exponential growth: rapid population expansion
  o Stationary phase: equal numbers dying and dividing
  o Death phase: if the population gets too big and there are insufficient nutrients, the population will decline
- **Parasitic vs. symbiotic:** Symbiotic bacteria have a relationship with another organism that is non-harmful, or mutually beneficial (ex: gut bacteria). Parasitic bacteria gain benefit by harming another organism.
- **Chemotaxis** ("chemo," chemical, "taxis," arrangement) means movement in response to chemical signals. Many bacteria use this to move toward food or away from toxins. Chemical signals can trigger specific types of flagellar propulsion based on whether the chemical is beneficial or harmful.
☐ **Genetics of prokaryotic cells**: The prokaryote genome is circular double-stranded DNA.
- **Plasmids** are extragenomic DNA in bacteria that contain a small number of genes, and that replicate independent of the genome.
  o Plasmids can be used to synthesize proteins, and to pass genetic material between cells.
  o Antibiotic resistance is typically acquired via a plasmid.
- **Plasmids** can be transferred from one bacterium to another in three ways:
  o **Transformation**: Fragments of DNA from the environment are taken up by the cell and incorporated into the genome.
  o **Transduction**: A plasmid is transferred from one bacterium to another by a viral vector.
  o **Conjugation**: A plasmid is transferred from one bacterium to another through the creation of a pilus, or bridge, between them. Conjugation is analogous to sexual reproduction.

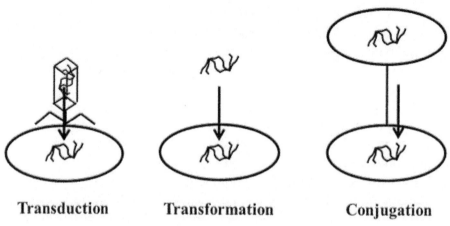

| Transduction | Transformation | Conjugation |

Figure 41: Bacterial conjugation.

- **Transposons** (also present in eukaryotes) are DNA segments that can move around within the genome (exit, enter, or change location). This process can correct a mutation, cause a mutation, or change the size of the genome.
- ☐ **Viruses** have genetic material, but are not considered cells (they are not alive) and cannot reproduce independently.
  - **Structure:** Nucleic acid and protein in a protein coat (capsid). Some viruses also have a lipid layer surrounding the capsid (enveloped virus). A virus has no nucleus or organelles.
    - ○ Viruses are much smaller than bacteria. Bacteria can get viral infections.
    - ○ Genomic content of a virus can be DNA or RNA, double-stranded or single-stranded.
- ☐ **Viral life cycle**: Viruses are self-replicating biological units that must reproduce within a specific host cell.
  - Steps in generalized phage and animal virus life cycles:
    - ○ Virus attaches to host, penetrates cell membrane or wall, and injects its genetic material
    - ○ Uses host synthetic machinery to replicate viral components
    - ○ Self-assembles and releases new viral particles into the environment

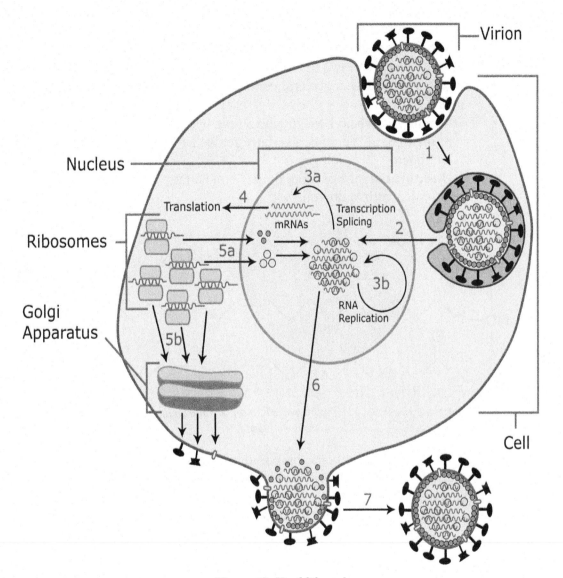

Figure 42: *Viral life cycle.*

- **Retroviruses** are a special class of viruses that have single-stranded RNA genomes, and that replicate through reverse transcription.
  - **Reverse transcriptase** reads mRNA 5'→3' to synthesize cDNA. These cDNA copies hybridize to form double-stranded DNA.
  - **Integrase** integrates the viral DNA into the host's genome.
  - HIV is a retrovirus that damages the immune system.
- **Subviral particles** are infectious agents that are smaller than viruses.

- o **Prions** are made entirely of proteins, and can cause other proteins to fold abnormally (ex: mad cow disease).
- o **Viroids** are circles of single-stranded RNA (no capsid).
- ☐ **Lipids** are a diverse class of hydrophobic molecules. Classes of lipids include:
  - **Triglycerides** (fats): a glycerol connected to three fatty acids by ester bonds
  - **Fatty acids**: a carboxylic acid with a long hydrocarbon tail
    - o **Saturated**: all single bonds; fatty acids that are fully saturated with hydrogen
    - o **Unsaturated**: one or more double bonds; fatty acids that are not fully saturated with hydrogen

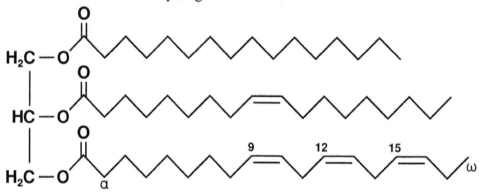

Figure 43: Triglyceride structure: The top hydrocarbon tail is saturated; the middle and bottom tails are unsaturated.

- **Steroids** are hydrocarbons composed of four fused rings.
  - o **Cholesterol** is a steroid, as are some hormones (e.g. testosterone).
- **Terpenes** are aromatic compounds assembled from squalene subunits. Terpenes are the chemical building blocks of steroids.
  - o **Terpenoids** are terpenes modified with non-hydrocarbon functional groups.
- **Phospholipids/phosphatides** comprise two fatty acids and a phosphate group, connected by a glycerol.
- A **sphingolipid** is sphingosine (an amino alcohol with a long hydrocarbon tail) with a polar head group.
  - o **Myelin** has a high concentration of spingolipids.
- **Waxes** consist of a long-chain alcohol ester-bonded to a fatty acid.
- **Fat-soluble vitamins**: D, E, K, and A are soluble in fat. All other vitamins are soluble in water (ex: B and C).
- ☐ **Biological functions** of lipids include energy storage, signaling, and composition of membranes.

- **Storage functions** are generally carried out by hydrolysable lipids:
  - **Triglycerides** cannot be absorbed by the duodenum, and must be broken down by enzymes into monoglycerides and free fatty acids first.
  - Once absorbed into enterocytes, they are reassembled into triglycerides, and then packed together with cholesterol to form chylomicrons.
  - Triglycerides can be both synthesized and stored by the liver.
- **Signals/cofactor functions** are generally carried out by nonhydrolyzable lipids:
  - **Fat-soluble vitamins** function as enzyme co-factors.
  - **Steroid hormones** include progesterone and testosterone.
  - **Prostaglandins** are signaling lipids derived from fatty acids. They act as autocrines or paracrines and are involved in signaling related to inflammation, blood clotting, and vasodilation.
- **Saponification** is the creation of soap from triglycerides treated with a strong base.
- ☐ **Carbohydrates/Saccharides** are a class of molecules, made up of three or more fully hydrated carbon atoms, that play major roles in energy storage, cellular structure, and enzymatic activity. Carbohydrates also form the backbone of nucleic acids.
- ☐ **Nomenclature** and classification:
  - Typical formula: $C_n(H_2O)_n$, or a 1:2:1 ratio of carbon:hydrogen:oxygen
  - Carbohydrates can be linear or cyclic.
  - Suffix "-ose" means carbohydrate
    - Triose: three carbons, $C_3H_6O_3$
    - Tetrose: four carbons, $C_4H_8O_4$
    - Pentose, hexose, etc.
  - Prefix indicates functional group
    - Aldose: contains aldehyde group
    - Ketose: contains ketone group
    - Furanose: five-membered carbohydrate ring
    - Pyranose: six-membered carbohydrate ring
    - Epimers: differ at only one chiral center
    - Anomers: differ only in the configuration around the anomeric carbon
  - All anomers are also epimers; only some epimers are anomers
- ☐ **Glycosidic linkages** are bonds between monosaccharides. They typically form between C1 of one sugar, and C4 of the next.
  - In digestion, humans have enzymes that can break alpha linkages (starch, glycogen) but not beta linkages (cellulose).

- Linkage is called alpha if it forms a linkage that angles downward (think: fish in the sea), or beta if it forms a linkage that angles upward (think: butterfly in the sky).
☐ **Monosaccharides** (know names and structures):
  - **Glucose**: $C_6H_{12}O_6$. Mnemonic: Tell someone to "fuck off" with your right hand (your bird finger is the OH, others are H).
  - **Mannose**: $C_6H_{12}O_6$. Mnemonic: Make a finger gun
  - **Galactose**: $C_6H_{12}O_6$. C-4 epimer of glucose.
  - **Fructose**: $C_6H_{12}O_6$. Like glucose, but one of the hydroxyls is swapped with the carbonyl, forming a ketone. Fructose forms a five-membered ring.
  - **Ribose**: $C_5H_{10}O_5$. Mnemonic: "All right," because all of the hydroxyl groups are on the right.

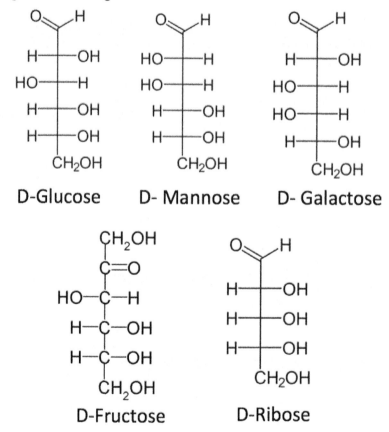

Figure 44: *Common monosaccharides.*

☐ **Disaccharides** (know names and structures) are monosaccharides connected with glycosidic linkages.

- **Sucrose**: glucose + fructose, alpha 1-4 linkage (acetal formed → non-reducing sugar)
- **Lactose**: galactose + glucose, beta 1-4 linkage (hemiacetal formed → reducing sugar)
- **Maltose**: glucose + glucose, alpha 1-4 linkage (hemiacetal formed → reducing sugar)
- **Reducing vs. non-reducing sugar:** Hemiacetals can be further reduced to acetals, so they are called reducing sugars. Acetals cannot be further reduced, so they are called non-reducing sugars.
  - All monosaccharides are reducing sugars.
  - Di- or poly-saccharides with hemiacetal linkages are reducing sugars, while di- or poly-saccharides with acetal linkages are non-reducing sugars.

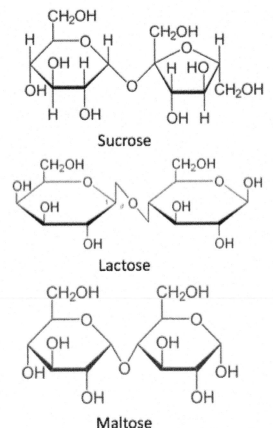

Figure 45: *Common disaccharides.*

☐ **Polysaccharides** (know names and structures) are monosaccharides connected in long, sometimes branching chains with glycosidic linkages.
- **Glycogen**: glucose, alpha 1-4 and 1-6 (branching) linkages

- o Digestible, highly branched for dense energy storage
- **Starch**: glucose, alpha 1-4 and 1-6 (branching) linkages
  - o Digestible, moderately branched for moderate energy storage
- **Cellulose**: glucose, beta 1-4 linkages
  - o Indigestible, unbranched
☐ **Carbohydrates** in nucleic acids:
- RNA = ribose, DNA = deoxyribose (ribose, de-oxygenated)

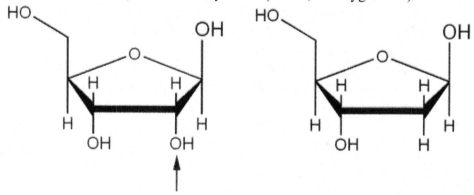

Figure 46: Ribose (left) and deoxyribose (right).

☐ **Absolute configuration** of the last chiral carbon (farthest from the carbonyl) in carbohydrates:
- D carbohydrates are digestible by humans (D for delicious), while L carbohydrates are not. D and L enantiomers differ at every chiral carbon.
☐ **Cyclic structure and conformation of hexoses**: Many carbohydrates can form furanoses or pyranoses via the reaction of the carbonyl group and a hydroxyl group on the opposite end of the molecule.

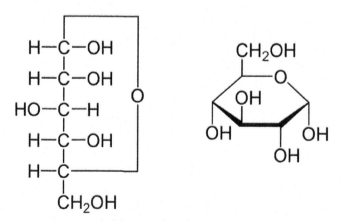

Figure 47: Glucose ring closure.

- ☐ **Hydrolysis of the glycoside linkage**: Di- and polysaccharides can be split into monosaccharides via hydrolysis of glycosidic bonds.
  - Amylase catalyzes the hydrolysis of the glycosidic bonds of starch in the digestive system.
- ☐ **Keto-enol tautomerism**: Some monosaccharides exist in a state of equilibrium between two forms, a keto form (ketone) and an enol form (alcohol), via a transformation of the carbonyl group. In most cases, the carbonyl (keto) form dominates for carbohydrates because it is more stable.
  - **Tautomers** are constitutional isomers that interconvert rapidly and easily. This often involves a double bond switching to an adjacent bond, displacing a hydrogen from one atom to another in the molecule.
  - **Tautomerism** enables conversion between some sugars, with the enol form acting as an intermediate (ex: The keto forms of fructose and glucose exist in equilibrium with the same enol form).

Cell and Organism Reproduction

- ☐ **Mitosis** is cellular reproduction in which two genetically identical daughter cells are generated from the splitting of the nucleus and cytoplasm of a single parent cell.
  - The **mitotic process involves** five stages: prophase, metaphase, anaphase, telophase, interphase (mnemonic: PMATI).
    - **Prophase**: condensation of chromatin into chromosomes; centrioles move to the poles of the cell; nucleolus and nucleus disappear
    - **Metaphase**: chromosomes line up at the equator of the cell, pulled by the centrioles
    - **Anaphase**: sister chromatids split at the centromeres and begin moving toward opposite poles, pulled by the contraction of kinetochore microtubules
    - **Telophase**: nuclear membrane and nucleolus reform; chromosomes become chromatin; cytoplasm is split by pinching/splitting of cell membrane into two separate cells
    - **Interphase**: after the cell has separated into two identical daughter cells, they are said to be in interphase, which is the non-mitotic state in which the cell will spend most of its life
  - **Mitotic structures** include several cytoskeletal components:
    - **Centrioles**: cylindrical structures made of tubulin that organize the mitotic spindle and the process of cytokinesis
    - **Asters**: star-shaped structure that forms around the centriole
    - **Microtubules**: form the polar ends of the spindle apparatus

- o **Spindles**: microtubules that connect chromatids to centrioles in order to split genetic material into two daughter cells
- o **Chromatids**: one copy of a chromosome, connected to an identical copy by a centromere
- o **Centromeres**: groups of proteins that attach sister chromatids together, as well as acting as the site of attachment of spindle fibers via the kinetochore
- o **Kinetochores**: attach microtubules to chromosomes
- **Nuclear membrane breakdown and reorganization**: The nuclear membrane is broken down into small vesicles. These vesicles of the parent cell are reused in the formation of the two new nuclear envelopes of the daughter cells.
- **Chromosome movement** occurs due to attachment of microtubules, which can be polymerized or depolymerized to lengthen or shorten them, pulling the chromosomes along with them.
☐ **Phases of cell cycle**: interphase (G0, G1, S, G2) and mitosis (M)
- **G0**: a period in which the cell is not preparing to divide. Some cells (ex: cardiac muscle, neurons) enter the G0 phase once they are terminally differentiated, because they do not continue dividing once they reach maturity. This stage allows some cells (ex: epithelial) to divide quickly and continuously, while others divide slowly or not at all once they reach maturity.
- **G1**: cell grows and generates needed proteins and organelles. Active RNA and protein synthesis.
  - o G1 checkpoint: If a cell gets large enough, has the proteins it needs for synthesis, and is in favorable conditions, it will pass the G1 checkpoint and enter S phase.
- **S** (synthesis): the cell replicates its DNA. Other RNA/protein synthesis activities are slowed.
- **G2**: cell gets ready to divide. Organelles duplicate. Synthesis of proteins needed for division.
  - o G2 checkpoint: If the level of mitosis promoting factor (MPF) is high enough, mitosis begins.
- **M** (mitosis): cell divides, going through prophase, metaphase, anaphase, and telophase

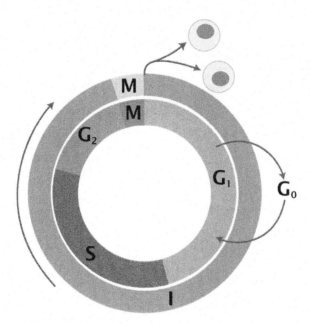

Figure 48: *Cell cycle.*

- **Growth arrest**: Cells may stop dividing because they are terminally differentiated, because their environment is inhospitable (lack of nutrients), because they have gotten large/numerous enough that they are touching each other, or because they have significant genetic damage.
- ☐ **Control of cell cycle**: Checkpoints prevent division of cells that are unhealthy or ill-equipped to reproduce. If damage is bad enough, apoptosis, or programmed cell death, will occur.
- ☐ **Cancer cells** lack checkpoints to control growth, so they proceed through cell division over and over again, while also failing to trigger apoptosis.
- ☐ **Stages of early development** (embryogenesis):
  - **Fertilization:** When a 1n/haploid/23 chromosome sperm penetrates a 1n/haploid/23 chromosome ovum, it yields a 2n/diploid/46 chromosome fertilized egg, or zygote.
  - **Cleavage**: After fertilization, the zygote begins dividing, such that one cell becomes two, two becomes four, four becomes eight, etc.
    - o Around the fourth division (eight cells), the zygote is called a morula. Note that the zygote has not yet grown larger, it has only divided from one large cell into many smaller ones.

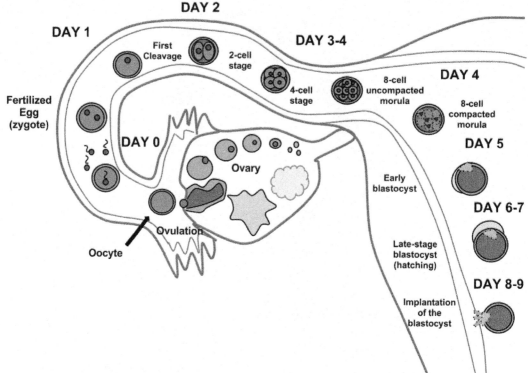

Figure 49: *Ovulation and early embryogenesis.*

- **Blastula formation:** Five to seven days after ovulation, the zygote (morula) becomes a blastula, which consists of a hollow ball of cells called the trophoblast, which will become the placenta, and a small inner cell mass, which will become the fetus.
  - Implantation occurs in the blastula stage.
- **Gastrulation:** Cells begin moving and folding to form a fetus.
  - First cell movements: Invagination, or pinching-in of cells, represents first cell movements. Early cell movements lead to development of primary germ layers.
- **Primary germ layers**: Think of your body as a tube. Endoderm is the lining of the tube, surrounded by mesoderm, surrounded by ectoderm.
  - **Endoderm** is the inner-most layer. It becomes structures that are interior to your body, but in contact with the outside world:
    - Digestive tract linings (including liver and pancreas)
    - Respiratory tract linings
    - Urinary bladder and urethra

- Lining of thyroid and thymus
- **Mesoderm** is the middle layer. It becomes structures associated with movement:
  - Bones
  - Muscle
  - Blood
  - Blood vessels
  - Heart
  - Kidneys
  - Gonads
  - Dermis
- **Ectoderm** is the outer layer. It becomes structures you use to interact with the environment:
  - Epidermis
  - Hair and fingernails
  - Ears, nose, eyeballs
  - Nervous system

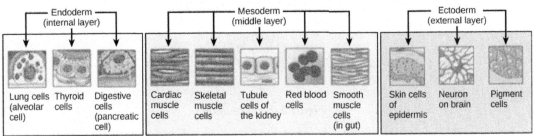

Figure 50: *Primary germ layers and associated tissues.*

- **Neurulation:** The invagination of ectoderm and mesoderm leads to the formation of the neural tube, which gives rise to the central nervous system.
  - **Neural crest**: When the neural tube closes, some ectoderm cells, called neural crest cells, get pinched off, and travel around the body forming a variety of structures, such as melanocytes, facial cartilage, glia, PNS, and adrenal medulla.

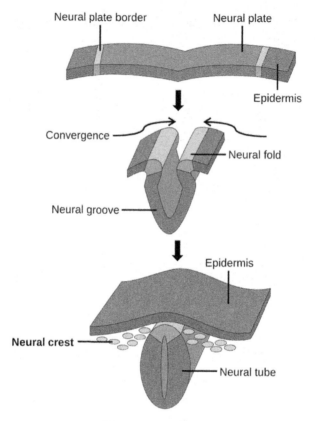

Figure 51: *Neurulation.*

☐ **Environment-gene interactions in development:** Embryogenesis is a sensitive and complicated series of steps and folds to produce a human. Many of these processes can be influenced by environmental factors.
- Ex: fetal alcohol syndrome, when the placenta allows alcohol to cross from maternal blood to fetal blood, can have negative effects on proliferation, migration, and differentiation of cells during development of multiple systems.
- Ex: folate deficiency can lead to improper folding of the neural tube

☐ **Mechanisms of development** concern how the cells of a zygote become the cells of a fully-formed organism.
- **Cell specialization**: In successive generations, cells take on special features that enable them to accomplish specific tasks in the body.
  - **Determination:** Cells are irreversibly committed to becoming a certain type of cell/tissue.

- o **Differentiation:** Different types of cells have different features and abilities (ex: neurons transmit electrochemical messages).
- ☐ **Tissue types:** four main types
  - **Epithelial**: cells connected tightly together in sheets that participate in protecting the body and mediating what can get in and out of it (ex: epidermis)
    - o Epithelial tissue typically has an apical (external) surface and a basal (internal) one, which attaches to connective tissue underneath it.
  - **Connective**: supports and protects the body (ex: fat, cartilage, bone, blood)
  - **Nervous**: specialized cells that send and receive electrochemical signals and make up the nervous system
  - **Muscle**: tissues specialized for movement
    - o **Skeletal**: connected to bones via tendons. Voluntary, striated (made of sarcomeres), multinucleated, cylindrical
    - o **Smooth**: organs and blood vessels. Involuntary, non-striated (no sarcomeres), single nucleus, tapered
    - o **Cardiac**: heart only. Involuntary, striated, single nucleus, branched

Comparing Muscle Cell Types		
Skeletal Muscle	**Smooth Muscle**	**Cardiac Muscle**
Voluntary	Involuntary	Involuntary
Striated	Non-striated	Striated
Multinucleated	Single nucleus	Single nucleus
Cylindrical	Tapered	branched

- ☐ **Cell-cell communication** in development:
  - **Induction** is when one tissue or cell produces a chemical signal that causes another tissue or cell to change the course of its development.
    - o **Autocrine:** a signal that is produced by the same cell that it acts on
    - o **Juxtacrine**: a signal that goes from one cell to an adjacent cell by binding a receptor (no diffusion).
    - o **Paracrine:** a signal that acts on other cells in the immediate area via diffusion
    - o **Endocrine:** a signal (hormone) that acts over long distances via the blood stream.
  - **Pluripotency** refers to cells that are able to differentiate into any of the three germ layers, and therefore into any of the tissues that arise from those layers.

- o **Embryonic stem cells** (isolated from the inner cell mass of blastocysts) are pluripotent.
- o **Adult stem cells** are typically multipotent, meaning they can differentiate into several different cell types, but fewer than pluripotent cells can. They are found in many tissues, and are used for repair and replenishing adult tissues. They undergo mitosis both to replenish undifferentiated cells and to differentiate into needed cells to join tissues.
- o Pluripotent is different from totipotent, which describes a cell that could become any of the germ layers or part of the placenta.
- **Induced pluripotent stem cells** are created when an adult differentiated cell is treated by activation of certain genes and addition of transcription factors to un-differentiate it back to a pluripotent cell.

☐ **Gene regulation in development:** Different cells develop different features through differential gene transcription and translation.
- DNA methylation and modification of histones can turn transcription of certain genes on or off, as can the presence or absence of transcription factors.
- Alternative RNA splicing and post-translational protein modifications can also contribute to differences in how cells develop.

☐ **Apoptosis**, or programmed cell death, plays an important role in development. For example, fingers begin development connected together, but through apoptosis, are separated.

☐ Existence of **regenerative capacity** in various species: Some species can regenerate certain organs or other body parts. For example, starfish can regenerate their legs.
- In humans, the liver can regenerate to its original size if part of it is lost to disease or injury.

☐ **Senescence and aging**: As cells age, their functions can deteriorate, often leading to their destruction. Aging is due to degradation of genetic material over repeated mitotic episodes, but also to accumulation of chemical and/or physical detriments from the environment (ex: UV rays on the skin).
- **Telomeres** are strings of noncoding nucleotides that make up the ends of DNA strands that protect your genetic information from degrading.
  - o A high concentration of C and G make telomeres extra sticky (three bonds).
  - o Each time DNA is replicated, the telomeres get slightly shorter because the ends are destroyed. If the DNA is duplicated enough times, the telomeres get too short to protect the coding DNA, and genetic mutations can occur. This typically happens after around 60 divisions.

- o **Telomerase** is a ribonucleoprotein that mitigates the destruction of telomeres by adding TTAGGG to the end of telomeres. This can be good for healthy cells, but can also aid in the continuous proliferation of cancer cells.
  - o Healthy cells typically stop dividing when their telomeres get too short, to prevent genetic damage. Cells that have stopped dividing in this way are **senescent**.
- ☐ **Female reproductive system** structures:
  - **Ovaries** are the female gonads, and the site for development and maturation of female gametes, called ova (singular: ovum). They produce estrogen and progesterone.
  - **Genitalia**: ovaries, fallopian tubes, uterus, vagina
  - **Primary oocytes** (diploid) are present at birth. Every month, one oocyte completes meiosis I to become a secondary oocyte (haploid). Meiosis II proceeds immediately, but is halted at metaphase II until or unless fertilization occurs.
  - **Follicles** protect and nourish each individual oocyte while it is inside the ovary. At ovulation, the follicle ruptures, releasing the secondary oocyte.
  - The **secondary oocyte** is released from the ovary into the body cavity, where it is then swept into the fallopian tube. It travels down the tube and into the uterus where it is either fertilized and implants into the uterine wall, or exits the body, unfertilized, via the vagina during menses.
  - **Corpus luteum** (the empty follicle) remains in the ovary and continues to produce progesterone. Considered a temporary organ, the corpus luteum decays if fertilization does not occur. If fertilization does occur, it continues producing progesterone to maintain the uterine lining.
- ☐ **Male reproductive system** structures:
  - **Testes** are the male gonads, and the site for development and maturation for male gametes, called spermatozoa. They produce testosterone.
  - **Genitalia**: testes, seminiferous tubules, epididymis, vas deferens, ejaculatory duct, urethra, penis
  - **Spermatozoa** mature in the seminiferous tubules of the testes, then are stored and gain motility in the epididymis. During ejaculation, the sperm travel through the vas deferens to the ejaculatory duct, where they enter the urethra, and then exit via the penis.
- ☐ **Male and female sexual development**: The genes of the sex chromosomes (XX or XY) initiate the development of different gonads in early embryologic development. These gonads then produce different hormones, which lead to additional differences in physiology, as well as differences in behavior and appearance after birth.

☐ The **menstrual cycle** is a repeating pattern of hormonal changes that produce predictable physiological changes, associated with preparing the female reproductive system for potential fertilization and pregnancy. One cycle is approximately 28 days.

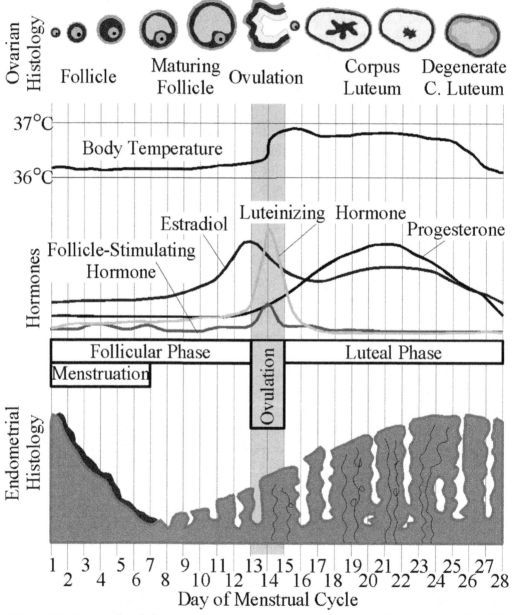

Figure 52: Hormonal and physiological changes of the menstrual cycle (Image credit: Chris73).

- **Follicular phase: Rising FSH levels trigger** maturation of the follicle.
- **Ovulation:** One ovum from one ovary is released from the follicle into the body cavity. Increasing estrogen levels trigger a spike in production of luteinizing hormone. The ovum is swept into the fallopian tube, where it is either fertilized or decays.
- **Luteal phase:** High FSH and LH levels cause the corpus luteum to start secreting progesterone. Progesterone then inhibits FSH and LH production, so those levels fall as progesterone increases. Since FSH and LH are needed to maintain the corpus luteum, it begins to decay, leading to a decline in progesterone levels.
- **If no fertilization, then menstruation:** Falling progesterone levels trigger menstruation, in which the lining of the uterus sloughs off.
- **If fertilization occurs:** The blastocyst secretes hCG, which maintains the corpus luteum so that it can continue producing the progesterone needed to maintain a pregnancy. Eventually, the placenta begins making its own estrogen and progesterone.
  - **Pregnancy tests** typically test for the presence of hCG.
- ☐ **Gestation** (pregnancy) lasts approximately 38 weeks.
  - **First** trimester: corpus luteum supplies estrogen and progesterone
  - **Second** trimester: corpus luteum decays; placenta takes over estrogen and progesterone secretion
  - **Third** trimester: fetus gets bigger and bigger, and moves into position for birth
    - Estrogen levels continually increase throughout pregnancy, both to stimulate fetal growth and to suppress release of FH and LSH.
    - Blood volume and pressure increase.
  - **Parturition** (labor): Progesterone levels, which have been preventing the uterus from contracting, start to drop. Oxytocin triggers uterine contraction.
  - **Lactation**: Falling progesterone levels, as well as increased prolactin levels, stimulates milk production. Oxytocin stimulates milk release.
- ☐ **Gametogenesis** is the production of fully-functional haploid gametes through meiosis.
  - **Sperm:** Meiosis begins at puberty. Gametogenesis occurs in the seminiferous tubules.
    - **Spermatagonium (2n, 46 chromosomes):** undifferentiated cells present at birth; undergoes mitosis, duplicating each chromosome
    - **Primary spermatocyte (4n, 46 chromosomes)** completes meiosis I to form two secondary spermatocytes

- Secondary spermatocyte (2n, 23 chromosomes) completes meiosis II; two secondary spermatocytes become 4 spermatids, each with 23 chromatids
- Spermatids (1n, 23 chromosomes) develop morphologically to become spermatozoa
- Spermatozoa (1n, 23 chromosomes) contribute one half of genetic information to a new zygote
- **Ovum** meiosis begins before birth. Oocytes are arrested in prophase I.
  - Oogonium (2n, 46 chromosomes): undifferentiated cells that undergo mitosis, duplicating each chromosome
  - Primary oocytes (4n, 46 chromosomes) begin meiosis but are arrested at prophase I at birth; each month, one primary oocyte proceeds through the remainder of meiosis I to form a secondary oocyte and a polar body
    - The first polar body divides once into 2 polar bodies, 1n each.
  - Secondary oocyte (2n, 23 chromosomes) proceeds to metaphase II. If fertilized, it will complete meiosis to form an ovum and a polar body.
  - Ovum (1n, 23 chromosomes) contributes half of the genetic information to a new zygote.

Differences Between Spermatogenesis and Oogenesis	
Spermatogenesis	Oogenesis
4 Spermatozoa created from each spermatogonium	1 ovum and 3 polar bodies created from each oocyte
Millions of new spermatozoa are produced daily from puberty until death	One ovum produced every 28 days from menarche until menopause
Meiosis begins at puberty	Meiosis begins before birth
Meiosis is completed before morphological changes	Meiosis is not completed unless fertilization occurs

- **Ova and sperm** have equal genetic content (1n) but unequal cellular content. The ovum has a large cytoplasm with many organelles, while the sperm has almost none.
  - All of the cytoplasm of a zygote comes from the egg. This includes mitochondria.
  - The zygote's mitochondrial DNA will be identical to that of its mother.
  - The ovum destroys any cytoplasmic contribution from the sperm.

☐ **Fertilization** occurs when the genetic information of the sperm enters the egg.
  - The first sperm to reach the egg releases enzymes that eat through the ovum's protective covering, and then the membrane of the sperm fuses with the membrane of the ovum, as a vesicle would, releasing the sperm's cellular content into the ovum.
  - The entrance of the first sperm causes a chemical reaction that hardens the outer layer of the egg, so that no additional sperm can enter.

Human Systems

☐ **The endocrine system** is a group of glands that release hormones into the circulatory system to send signals over long distances in the body. Includes several glands, which secrete different hormones:
  - **Hypothalamus** is the primary link between the nervous system and the endocrine glands. It stimulates the pituitary gland and also produces ADH and oxytocin, which it then transports down axons to the posterior pituitary, which controls their release into the blood.
  - **Pineal gland** is a small gland deep in the brain.
    o Melatonin: modulates sleep cycle and circadian rhythms
  - **Pituitary**: "master gland," sends signals from hypothalamus to each of the other endocrine glands
    o **Posterior pituitary** gland
      ▪ **Antidiuretic hormone** (ADH), or vasopressin, leads to increase in blood pressure by increasing the permeability of the collecting ducts, and therefore the amount of water that is reabsorbed. This increases blood volume.
      ▪ **Oxytocin** stimulates uterine contractions during pregnancy.
    o **Anterior pituitary** gland
      ▪ **Human growth hormone** (hGH) stimulates growth by increasing amino acid transport across cell membrane, which increases translation and transcription, and therefore promotes mitosis and cell growth.
      ▪ **Thyroid-stimulating hormone** (TSH) stimulates release of T3 and T4 from the thyroid via second messenger using cAMP. T3 and T4 form a negative feedback loop with TSH, such that higher T3 and T4 levels in the blood lead to reduced TSH production.
      ▪ **Prolactin**: When progesterone levels fall at the end of pregnancy and suckling begins, the anterior pituitary releases prolactin to stimulate milk production.

- **Luteinizing hormone**: A spike in LH triggers ovulation and corpus luteum development. LH also stimulates testosterone production in males.
- **Adrenocorticotropic hormone** (ACTH): in response to stress, ACTH is secreted by the anterior pituitary to stimulate the adrenal cortex.
- **Follicle-stimulating hormone** (FSH) stimulates the growth of ovarian follicles (females) and sperm production (males).
- **Thyroid** regulates metabolism through T3 (triiodothyronine) and T4 (thyroxine).
  - **T3 and T4** increase basal metabolic rate.
    - Dietary iodide deficiency can lead to goiter. Deficient dietary iodide →decreased T3/T4 production →excess TSH released from anterior pituitary →excessive growth of thyroid
  - **Calcitonin** decreases blood calcium by decreasing the number and activity of osteoclasts. It works in opposition with PTH (parathyroid hormone).
- The **parathyroid** is a set of four small glands on the back of the thyroid.
  - **Parathyroid hormone** (PTH) increases blood calcium levels. It works in opposition with calcitonin.
- **Adrenal gland** ("ad-," next to; "-renal," kidney):
  - The **adrenal cortex is the** outer layer of the adrenal gland.
    - Aldosterone increases reabsorption of ions and water in the distal tubules and collecting ducts, which leads to increased blood volume and pressure.
  - The **adrenal medulla is the** inner core of the adrenal gland.
    - **Catecholamines**: Epinephrine/norepinephrine (adrenaline/nonadrenaline) are stress hormones that produce relatively long-lasting fight-or-flight responses (increase muscle blood flow, decrease organ/skin blood flow, pupil dilation etc.).
    - The catecholamines are also neurotransmitters. The responses they produce as NTs and as hormones are essentially the same, but the NTs produce faster, shorter-duration sympathetic nervous system responses, while as hormones, their effects are slower acting but longer-lasting.
- The **pancreas** is part of both the endocrine system and the digestive system; it acts as both an endocrine and exocrine gland (exocrine in digestive system). Endocrine function is to regulate energy availability/metabolism via antagonistic action of glucagon and insulin.
  - **Glucagon** raises blood glucose levels by stimulating glycogenolysis and gluconeogenesis via cAMP (Cyclic adenosine monophosphate)

second messenger system. It is released by alpha-cells when blood glucose is low.

- At high levels, glucagon breaks down adipose tissue, increasing the availability of fatty acids for energy production.
  - **Insulin** promotes glycogen production and fat production, lowering blood glucose levels. It is released by beta-cells when blood glucose is high.
- Insulin binds membrane receptor proteins, triggering a cascade that makes the membrane more permeable to glucose and amino acids.
- Type I diabetes: Beta-cells don't produce insulin.
- Type II diabetes: Body cells become less sensitive to insulin, leading to high blood sugar. Beta-cells respond by increasing insulin production, leading to high blood insulin levels.

- **Ovary**: both gonad and endocrine gland in females
  - Estrogen: appearance of secondary sex characteristics at puberty
  - Testosterone: same hormone as in males; has a much smaller effect in females
  - Progesterone: prepares the body for pregnancy and lactation
- **Testes**: both gonad and endocrine gland in males
  - Testosterone: appearance of male secondary sex characteristics
- **Peptide and amino acid-derived hormones** are generally water-soluble, while steroid-derived hormones are lipid-soluble.
- **Endocrine system and behavior**: While neurotransmitters enable near-instantaneous reactions to stimuli, hormones create slower responses, but ones that are often longer-lasting. The endocrine and nervous systems work cooperatively in regulating many behaviors.
- Some molecules are used by the body both as neurotransmitters and as hormones, and with similar effects (ex: epinephrine acts as an NT in the ANS and as a stress hormone, in both cases triggering fight-or-flight response).
- In addition to behavior, the nervous and endocrine systems work cooperatively and without conscious intervention to regulate aspects of homeostasis (ex: blood pressure/volume, energy production/use, reproductive activities).
- Cognitive behavioral therapy entails learning to, for example, control your feelings of fear and anxiety, which are ultimately contributing to hormonal changes (reduced stress hormone release).
- Hormonal changes associated with growth and development of secondary sex characteristics are, in part, responsible for behavior changes during puberty.

- Hormonal changes regulate the menstrual cycle, which can also be associated with cyclical behavior changes.

Major Hormones and Their Roles			
Hormone	Type	Released by	Action
T3 and T4	Tyrosine derivative	Thyroid	Increases basal metabolic rate
Calcitonin	Peptide	Thyroid	Decreases blood calcium
PTH	Peptide	Parathyroid	Increases calcium concentration in blood
Glucagon	Peptide	Pancreas	Raises blood glucose levels
Insulin	Peptide	Pancreas	Lowers blood glucose levels
hGH	Peptide	Anterior pituitary	Stimulates growth
TSH	Peptide	Anterior pituitary	Stimulates thyroid to release T3 and T4
Prolactin	Peptide	Anterior pituitary	Promotes lactation
LH	Peptide	Anterior pituitary	Estrogen and testosterone secretion; ovulation
ACTH	Peptide	Anterior pituitary	Stimulates adrenal cortex
FSH	Peptide	Anterior pituitary	Ovarian follicle and sperm growth
Melatonin	Tryptophan derivative	Pineal gland	Regulates sleep patterns
Oxytocin	Peptide	Posterior pituitary	Milk expression and uterine contraction

ADH/ Vasopressin	Peptide	Posterior pituitary	Increases blood pressure
Aldosterone	Steroid, mineral-corticoid	Adrenal cortex	Increases blood pressure by increasing Na+ reabsorption and K+ secretion in collecting tubule
Cortisol	Steroid, gluco-corticoid	Adrenal cortex	Stimulates gluconeogenesis; stress hormone
Catecholamines (epinephrine/ norepinephrine)	Tyrosine derivative	Adrenal medulla	Vasoconstriction in internal organs and skin; vasodilation in skeletal muscle
Estrogen	Steroid	Ovaries	Female secondary sex characteristics
Progesterone	Steroid	Ovaries	Prepares body for pregnancy
Testosterone	Steroid	Testes and ovaries	Male secondary sex characteristics

- ☐ **Respiratory system** primary functions:
  - o Gas exchange: oxygen in, carbon dioxide out
  - o Thermoregulation: breathing out leads to loss of heat
  - o Protection against disease and particulate matter: nostril hair filters out particulate matter; mucus linings trap additional particulate matter and some pathogens; cilia lining respiratory tract sweep pathogens out
- • **Structure** of the respiratory system:
  - o Air enters through nose and mouth, then travels through the pharynx, the larynx, and into the trachea
  - o The **trachea** branches into the **bronchi**, which carry air in and out of the lungs, and then the bronchioles.
    - ▪ No gas exchange occurs in bronchi or bronchioles.
  - o **Bronchioles** continue branching into smaller tubes, eventually terminating in alveoli.
  - o **Alveoli** are microscopic hollow sacs whose outer surfaces are covered with webs of capillaries.

- CO2-rich blood travels to pulmonary capillaries at the alveoli, where CO2 diffuses out of blood into the gas inside the alveoli, and oxygen diffuses into blood from the gas inside the alveoli.
  - ○ The right lung has three lobes (upper, middle, lower); the left lung has two lobes (upper, lower).
- **Cardiac notch:** a deflection of the left lung that makes room for the heart
  - ○ The rib cage protects the lungs and maintains the volume of the chest cavity so that the lungs do not collapse.

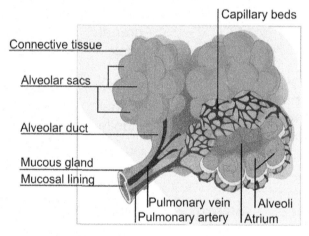

Figure 53: structure of alveoli.

- **Breathing mechanics** in the respiratory system:
  - ○ **Diaphragm:** a "floor" of skeletal muscle under the lungs that drives inflation and deflation by changing the volume of your chest cavity.
    - ▪ When the diaphragm contracts, it increases the volume of your chest cavity, and therefore decreases the pressure, so that air is sucked into your lungs (or pushed into lungs by atmospheric pressure).
  - ○ Intercostal muscles, or the muscles between the ribs, also contract to assist in inhalation. When they contract, they pull each rib up toward the rib above it, further increasing the volume of the chest cavity.
- **Thermoregulation** by the respiratory system:
  - ○ Nasal and tracheal capillary beds bring blood close to the outside world, enabling loss of heat from the blood.
  - ○ Panting is an alternative mechanism for respiratory thermoregulation (ex: dogs). Rapid breathing enables evaporation, and therefore heat loss, from the tongue, in addition to increasing the rate of heat equilibration from breathing in air that is cooler than body temperature.

- **Particulate filtration:** Nasal hairs and mucus and cilia in the lungs trap particulate matter from the air before it reaches the alveoli.
- **Alveolar gas exchange** in the lungs:
  - **Diffusion** is the primary mechanism of gas exchange.
    - Concentration of CO_2 in de-oxygenated blood is high relative to the air; concentration of O_2 in the air is high relative to de-oxygenated blood. Therefore, both O_2 and CO_2 are moving down their concentration gradients.
  - **Differential partial pressure** drives oxygen into tissue and carbon dioxide out of tissue.
    - Partial pressure of oxygen is relatively low in alveoli, so oxygen diffuses into the alveoli and then into capillaries.
    - Partial pressure of CO_2 is relatively high in the capillaries, so CO_2 diffuses into the alveoli and then is exhaled.
  - **Henry's Law:** When a gas is in contact with the surface of a liquid, the amount of gas that will be dissolved into the liquid is proportional to its partial pressure in the gas phase (solubility of a gas into a liquid is directly proportional to partial pressure).
- pH **control** by the respiratory system:
  - Increased CO_2 in blood → increased H+ in the blood → decreased pH. Decreased blood pH signals the medulla oblongata to increase the respiration rate (hyperventilation) to push equilibrium in the opposite direction.
  - Decreased CO_2 in blood → decreased H+ → increased pH. Increased pH signals the medulla oblongata to decrease respiration rate (hypoventilation) to push equilibrium in the opposite direction.
- **Regulation by nervous control** in the respiratory system:
  - The medulla oblongata (in the midbrain) signals diaphragm contraction via the phrenic nerve.
  - CO_2 sensitivity: Ventilation rate is determined primarily by the level of carbon dioxide in the blood, as detected by pH chemoreceptors in the medulla oblongata. Increase in CO_2 concentration → increase in ventilation rate.

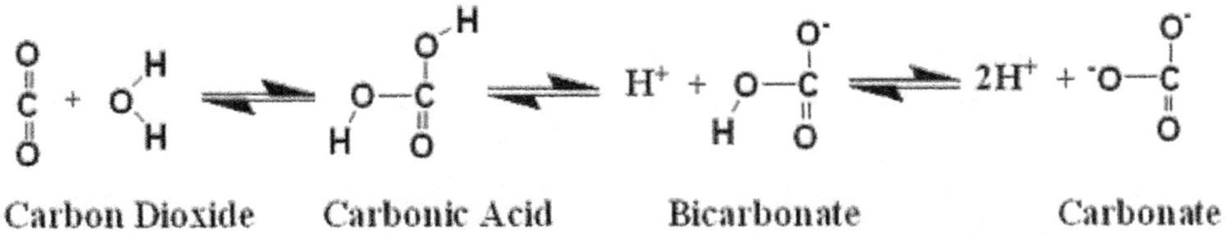

| Carbon Dioxide | Carbonic Acid | Bicarbonate | Carbonate |

Figure 54: pH control in the respiratory system is mediated by the equilibria of carbon dioxide, carbonic acid, and bicarbonate.

- ☐ **Circulatory system** structure, function, and fluid dynamics:
  - Function:
    - o to carry oxygen, nutrients, fluids, hormones, and other molecules to the body's tissues, and to remove metabolic waste from the tissues
    - o To assist in thermoregulation: When blood vessels near the body surface dilate, surface area for heat loss increases. When blood vessels contract, surface area for heat loss decreases, conserving heat.

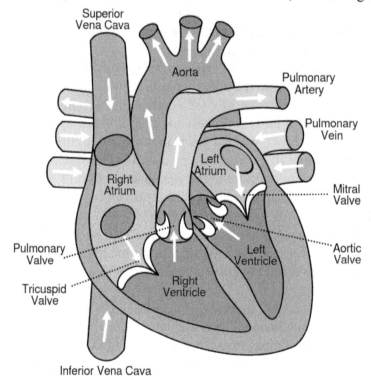

Figure 55: Heart anatomy.

  - Structure of the **heart**:
    - o Deoxygenated blood enters from superior vena cava → R atrium → R ventricle → pulmonary artery→ lungs. Oxygenated blood returns to heart via pulmonary vein → L atrium → L ventricle → aorta → systemic circulation, and finally returns to the heart via the superior vena cava.
  - Structure of the arterial and venous systems:
    - o **Arterial system:** Aorta → arteries → arterioles → capillaries
      - ▪ Thick, muscular, elastic walls without valves
      - ▪ Blood pressure is highest at aorta, and then decreases
      - ▪ Cross-sectional area is lowest at aorta, and then increases
      - ▪ Blood velocity is highest at aorta, and then decreases

- o **Venous system**: Capillaries → venules → veins → vena cava
  - Thin, inelastic walls with valves to prevent backflow
  - Blood pressure decreases throughout, and is lowest in vena cava
  - Cross-sectional area is greatest at capillaries, and then decreases
  - Blood velocity is lowest in capillaries, and then increases
- o **Vasoconstriction** occurs primarily in arterioles.
- o **Capillaries:** One-cell-thick endothelium allows molecules to leave the blood stream and enter tissues, and waste products to exit tissues and enter the blood stream. Capillaries also contribute to thermoregulation when close to surface, as well as to resistance in the circulatory system due to extensive branching. Not involved in vasoconstriction/vasodilation.
- o **Vasoconstriction/vasodilation** is accomplished by contraction or relaxation of smooth muscle in the vessel walls of veins, arteries, and arterioles.
- **Systolic and diastolic pressure** (units: mm Hg)
  - o Systolic: pressure in arteries on contraction of heart
  - o Diastolic: pressure between heart beats (resting pressure)
- **Pulmonary and systemic** circulation:
  - o Pulmonary circulation: deoxygenated blood from heart → lungs → back to heart as oxygenated
  - o Systemic circulation: oxygenated blood from heart → body → back to heart as deoxygenated blood
  - o Blood pressure is higher in systemic circulation, because the systemic vasculature is longer than the pulmonary vasculature, and therefore has higher resistance and higher pressure.
  - o Blood pressure is lower in pulmonary circulation, because the pulmonary vasculature is shorter than systemic circulation, and therefore has lower resistance and lower pressure.
  - o Flow rate is the same in both.
- **Composition of blood**: blood cells suspended in blood plasma
  - o **Plasma**: 90 percent water, 10 percent glucose, ions, hormones, cells, etc.
  - o **Blood cells**: red blood cells, white blood cells, and platelets
  - o **Erythrocytes** (red blood cells)
    - Biconcave disks lacking a nucleus or other organelles, maximizing space available for oxygen transport
    - The **spleen** is an erythrocyte storage space. Erythrocytes are released into circulation in response to stress, in order to increase oxygen-transport capacity (this is true in many mammals, but the effect is minor in humans)

- Erythrocytes develop in bone marrow.
- Erythrocytes circulate for approximately 100 days, and are then recycled by macrophages.
  o Regulation of plasma volume
    - **Osmolarity**: If blood is too concentrated (high osmolarity), water is reabsorbed into blood to increase volume. If blood is insufficiently concentrated (low osmolarity), water is pushed into tissues to reduce volume.
    - **Antidiuretic hormone** (ADH) and aldosterone increases water reabsorption in kidneys.
- **Coagulation** and clotting mechanisms:
  o **Platelets** gather together to plug the opening.
  o **Fibrinogen** circulating in blood is transformed into fibrin by the enzyme thrombin. Fibrin is able to polymerize into strands, which form a net around the platelet plug. This net then catches RBCs and additional platelets, stabilizing the initial clot.
- **Oxygen transport** by blood:
  o Hemoglobin is found in erythrocytes. Each hemoglobin molecule includes four iron molecules capable of bonding four oxygen molecules
  o Hematocrit: the volume percentage of RBCs in blood
- **Oxygen affinity,** or how readily hemoglobin acquires oxygen:
  o Oxygen affinity is increased when:
    - Temperature decreases
    - CO_2 concentration decreases
    - pH increases
  o Oxygen affinity is decreased when:
    - Temperature increases
    - CO_2 concentration increases
    - pH decreases
  o Nervous and endocrine controls
    - ADH and aldosterone increases blood pressure
    - Glucagon increases blood sugar; insulin lowers blood sugar
    - Sympathetic nervous system activation: increases heart rate, increases blood pressure, vasodilation in muscle; vasoconstriction in digestive system
    - Parasympathetic nervous system activation: decreased heart rate, decreased blood pressure, vasoconstriction in muscle, vasodilation in digestive system.
- **Lymphatic system**: collects and recycles interstitial fluid; stores and transports immune cells

- Structure:
  - **Lymph** cycles between bloodstream and lymphatic system via the thoracic duct.
  - Fluid cycle is passive, driven by incidental body movements (no pump)
  - Unidirectional valves prevent backflow
  - System keeps blood pressure up, reduces edema
  - **Lymph nodes**: follicle where B-cells grow
  - **Spleen** filters out dead cells, concentrates immune cells
- Function:
  - **Equalization of fluid distribution**: collects fluid forced into interstitial
  - Transfer of proteins and large glycerides: triglycerides, fats enter bloodstream via lymph
  - Production of **lymphocytes** involved in immune reactions
  - Return of materials to the blood
  - **Process**: blood vessels leak fluid, fluid is collected by lymphatic vessels, vessels collect in thoracic duct, thoracic duct enters into left subclavical vein, lymph returns to blood stream.
- ☐ **Immune system:** protects the body from invaders with two systems: innate immunity and adaptive immunity
  - Innate (non specific) immunity: broad, general protective responses prompted by a variety of toxins and invading organisms
  - Adaptive (specific) immunity: specific response to invading toxins or organisms that have invaded before
- ☐ **Adaptive immune cells**: T-cells and B-cells.
  - **T-lymphocytes are** a class of cells involved in cell-mediated immunity. They are produced in the thymus (T for thymus).
    - **Helper T-cells** assist other WBCs in coordinating immune responses.
      - When they encounter an antigen on an APC, helper T-cells start dividing and secreting chemical signals for recruiting other immune cells to the site of an infection.
      - Activate macrophages cytotoxic T-cells
      - HIV destroys helper T-cells
      - Participate in maturation of plasma and memory B-cells
    - **Cytotoxic/killer T-cells** kill abnormal cells by binding to them, and injecting a toxin that causes apoptosis.
      - No phagocytosis, so killer cells can attack a large number of cells quickly
    - **Regulatory T-cells** (also called suppressor T-cells) reduce the intensity of immune response once an infection has been contained.

They also reduce the proliferation of immune cells, and aid in prevention of autoimmunity.

- o **Memory T-cells are** cells that have encountered certain antigens in the past, and are able to enhance the immune response if the same antigen appears again.
    - When a memory T-cell detects an antigen it has seen before, it starts dividing rapidly.
- **B-lymphocytes are** a class of cells involved in humoral, or antibody-mediated, immunity. They are produced in the bone marrow (B for bone) and mature in the lymph nodes and spleen.
    - o Every B-cell presents one type of antibody (also called immunoglobulin) on its membrane.
    - o When an antibody encounters an antigen (foreign particle), it binds it.
    - o Binding of an antigen triggers the B-lymphocyte to differentiate into plasma cells and memory B-cells.
    - o **Plasma cells** synthesize more of the antibody and release it into the blood to enable identification of additional antigen and associated cells.
    - o **Memory B-cells** proliferate, but do not participate in the immediate immune event. They trigger a faster and stronger response in case of reinfection.
- ☐ **Innate immune cells:** non-specific defense against invaders
    - **Macrophages** are a class of phagocytes that engulf and digest pathogens, and then present antigens on their surfaces to signal other immune cells.
        - o Antigen-presenting cells: Leftover pieces of destroyed pathogens are presented on the cell surface as a signal to other immune cells to locate and destroy the pathogen if they encounter it.
- ☐ **Tissues** of the immune system:
    - **Bone marrow:**
        - o Where lymphocytes and macrophages are born (along with erythrocytes and platelets)
        - o Where B-lymphocytes differentiate
    - **Spleen:**
        - o Removes broken or old RBCs and platelets from the blood, as well as antibody-tagged bacteria
        - o Stores blood cells, including lymphocytes
        - o Similar to a large lymph node
    - **Thymus**: where T-lymphocytes differentiate.
    - **Lymph nodes:**
        - o Remove pathogens from lymph (and therefore from blood)
        - o Where white blood cells proliferate and are stored

o An immune response is triggered when lymphocytes in the lymph nodes detect toxins or invaders.

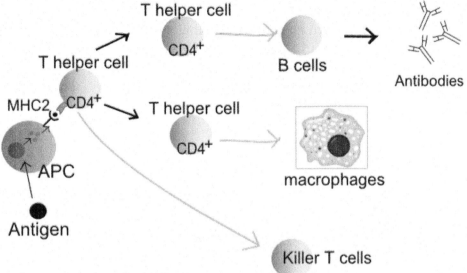

Figure 56: Immune cell types.

☐ **Function** of the immune system:
- **Antigen presentation:** An antigen, or a piece of a foreign cell that has been killed, can be presented on the surface of antigen-presenting immune cells (including macrophages, B-cells) to alert other immune cells.
- **Clonal selection:** a theory to explain how antigen-presenting cells create a diverse array of specific responses
  o Stem cells develop into immature B-cells, each of which presents a different type of antibody. Most of these immature cells will never encounter their matching antigen, and therefore will never mature.
    ▪ Immature cells that bind to self-antigens are destroyed as they appear.
  o When an immature B-cell encounters its matching antigen, it matures, and then clones itself many times, producing offspring that have same antibodies.
- **Antigen-antibody recognition** in the immune system:
  o **Structure of antibody molecule:**
    ▪ Two identical heavy chains, bound by disulfide linkages into a Y shape
    ▪ Two identical light chains, bound to the heavy chains by disulfide linkages, parallel to each of the arms of the Y

- **Variable region:** the tips of the arms of the Y, which includes the tops of all four chains. This region is different for each antibody-producing B-cell.
- **Constant region:** the remainder of the Y, which includes the bottoms of all four chains. This region is constant for broad classes of antibodies.
- **Antigen binding sites:** the tips of the arms of the Y recognize and bind to specific antigens

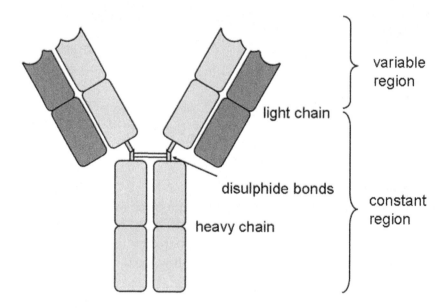

Figure 57: Antibody structure.

- ○ **Function of antibody molecule:**
  - If bound to the surface of a B-cell, they can respond to binding an antigen by recruiting other immune cells as part of an immune response.
  - Unbound, if they bind an antigen, antibodies aggregate into insoluble clumps, which can then be phagocytized.
- **Recognition of self vs. non-self, autoimmune diseases:**
  - ○ Destruction of immature B-cells with self-antibodies ensures that immune responses are not initiated by self-antigens.
  - ○ Autoimmune diseases: When immune cells mistake self-cells for non-self cells, it leads to the destruction of self-cells or molecules perceived as foreign, as well as initiates inflammatory responses.

- **Major histocompatibility complex (MHC):** a group of glycoproteins that binds fragments of destroyed pathogens and transports them to the cell membrane to be displayed and recognized by T-cells
  - o **MHC I:** found on most body cells. Presents viral fragments in response to viral infection of a cell. Initiates cytotoxic T-cell response.
  - o **MHC II:** found only on antigen-presenting cells (B-cells and macrophages). Protein complex that presents digested part of molecule on surface of macrophage. Initiates immune response mediated by helper T-cells.
- ☐ **Digestive system:** Your body is a tube, from mouth to esophagus to stomach to small intestine to large intestine to rectum.
  - Digestion: breakdown of food into smaller pieces
  - Absorption: transport of nutrients out of digestive system for use as energy
- ☐ The **mouth** is the start of digestion:
  - Salivary glands lubricate food and begin digestion by secreting α–amaylase, which breaks α-1, 4-glycosidic linkages, splitting starch into smaller polysaccharides.
  - Chewing increases surface area for enzymatic action.
  - Salivary glands also release lingual lipases as zymogens.
  - Chewed food forms a cylindrical clump, or bolus, to enter the esophagus.
- ☐ **Esophagus:** transports food from mouth to stomach through **peristalsis**, or the unidirectional wave motion of the smooth muscle of the digestive system
  - No digestion occurs in the esophagus.
- ☐ **Stomach:** main site for digestion, no significant absorption
  - Stores and churns food (mechanical digestion), transforming it from bolus into chyme, or a semifluid mass of partially digested food. Protein breakdown (chemical digestion) begins.
  - Low pH (2 to 3) assists in protein denaturation and kills food bacteria.
  - Gastric juice is an acidic fluid secreted by stomach cells, composed of HCl and other acids.
  - **Pepsinogen** is secreted by cells of the stomach, where it switches into its active form (pepsin) in response to the acidic environment of the stomach. Pepsin breaks bonds between amino acids.
  - Mucus lining protects the stomach against self-destruction
  - Structure:
    - o Top: cardiac sphincter
    - o Bottom: pylonic sphincter
  - The gastric mucosa is full of gastric pits, which contain the gastric glands. Gastric glands contain three cell types:
    - o **Mucus cells**: produce bicarbonate mucus coating

- o **Chief cells**: produce pepsinogen (zymogen), protect stomach
- o **Parietal cells**: produce HCl

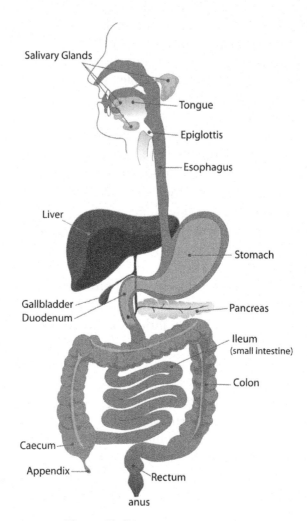

Figure 58: *Digestive system.*

☐ **Small intestine**: majority of chemical digestion and absorption occurs here
- Structure: duodenum → jejunum → ileum
- pH of 6: The pancreas secretes bicarbonate ions to neutralize HCl in the chyme as it enters the duodenum. This disables enzymes that work at low pH (pepsin) and activates enzymes that work at a near-neutral pH.
- The small intestine is lined with **villi**, which increase surface area for absorption in the lumen. Villi themselves are lined with microvilli, increasing surface area even further.

- o Villi also contains membrane-bound digestive enzymes, including peptidases (to digest protein) and nucleosidases (to digest nucleotides)
  - o Villi each contain a network of capillaries close to the surface, as well as a lacteal, which is a lymph vessel.
- **Goblet cells**: secrete mucus to lubricate the intestine and protect the lining of the intestine
- **Digestion** occurs primarily in the **duodenum,** or first section of the small intestine
  - o The pancreas releases digestive enzymes (trypsin, chymotrypsin, pancreatic amylase, lipase) into the duodenum.
  - o The bile duct releases bile, which emulsifies fat to increase surface area for digestive enzymes.

Digestive enzyme	Where it is produced	What it digests	Where it works
α-amylase	Salivary glands, pancreas	Starch, polysaccharides	Mouth, small intestine (neutral pH)
Pepsin	Stomach	Protein	Stomach (acidic pH)
Trypsin	Pancreas	Protein → small polypeptides;	Small intestine (neutral pH)
Chymotrypsin	Pancreas	Protein → polypeptides	Small intestine (neutral pH)
Pancreatic amylase	Pancreas	Polysaccharides →tri/di-saccharides	Small intestine (neutral pH)
lipase	Pancreas, salivary glands	Triglycerides → fatty acids + monoglycerides	Small intestine (neutral pH)

- **Absorption** occurs primarily in the **jejunum** and **ileum.**
  - o Glucose, galactose, fructose, AAs, and small fatty acids are transported (active transport and/or facilitated diffusion) into the epithelial cells of the intestinal tract. From there, they move down their concentration gradients into capillaries.
  - o Fats, glycerol, and cholesterol, in the form of micelles, move into epithelial cells of the intestinal tract (they are nonpolar molecules, so no transporters are needed). There, they are packed into chylomicrons, and then transported into lacteals, or the small vessels of the lymph system. Chylomicrons are then carried by the lymph system to the bloodstream via the thoracic duct. In the bloodstream, chylomicrons are broken down into low-density lipoprotein, which is collected by

the liver, and then turned into high-density lipoprotein (HDL) and very low–density lipoprotein (VLDL).

- ☐ **Large intestine:** absorption of water and electrolytes occurs here; contains E. coli
  - Structure: cecum → colon → rectum
  - Bacterial flora is located in the cecum
  - Appendix is part of the cecum
  - The **rectum** is the last section of the digestive system, continuous with the large intestine, and responsible for storage and elimination of feces.
- ☐ **Liver:** produces bile, processes nutrients, forms urea, synthesizes blood proteins
  - Aids in digestion through production of bile, which emulsifies fat
  - Maintains a constant level of blood glucose under a wide range of conditions
    - o After a meal, glucose concentrations are high. Liver extracts excess glucose and uses it to replenish its glycogen stores.
    - o Any glucose still in the liver is converted to acetyl-CoA and used for fatty acid synthesis, then released into the bloodstream as very low–density lipoproteins (VLDL).
    - o In a well-fed state, the liver gets most of its energy from the oxidation of excess amino acids.
    - o Between meals, the fasting liver releases glucose into the blood.
    - o The liver synthesizes ketones when excess fatty acids are being oxidized.
  - Connected to the gastrointestinal system via the **bile duct**, which empties into the duodenum
    - o The liver is the site of gluconeogenesis, or the formation of glycogen from non-carbohydrates, and glycogenesis, or the synthesis of glycogen.
    - o The hepatic portal vein receives blood from abdominal portion of digestive tract and sends it to the liver for detox. It then enters the vena cava, to the heart, to systemic circulation.
    - o Turns amino acids into ammonia into urea
    - o Synthesizes blood proteins: albumin, which has a role in maintaining oncotic pressure, and clotting factors
- ☐ **Pancreas:** produces enzymes in zymogen form and releases them into the duodenum
  - **Pancreatic amylase** breaks polysaccharides into tri/disaccharides.
  - Trypsin and chymotrypsin break down proteins into small polypeptides.
  - Lipase breaks fat into fatty acids and monoglycerides.
  - The pancreatic duct transports enzymes into the duodenum.

- **Islet of Langerhans**: contain the endocrine cells of the pancreas, including two cell types:
  - o Alpha cells: secrete glucagon
  - o Beta cells: secrete insulin
- **Endocrine control:** hormonal signals regulating digestion; released by the small intestine after a meal
  - o **Gastrin**: stimulates secretion of gastric acid; increases motility of the stomach
  - o **Secretin**: stimulates bicarbonate secretion; triggered by high HCl levels
  - o **Cholecystokinin** (CCK): stimulates gallbladder contraction; triggered by the presence of fat in the duodenum; decreases motility of the stomach

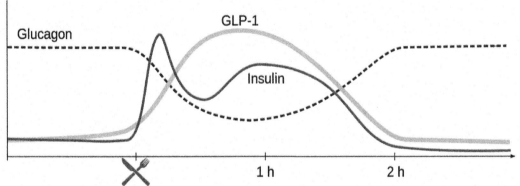

Figure 59: Glucagon, insulin, and GLP-1 levels before and after a meal (Image credit: Pumping Rudi).

- **The enteric nervous system** is a division of the ANS that regulates the digestive system.
  - o **Gastrocolic reflex**: When food enters the stomach, the enteric nervous system triggers the colon to make room by pushing waste further down.
- ☐ **Kidneys** filter blood; secrete waste; and reabsorb useful materials for maintenance of homeostasis
  - **Role in homeostasis:** the kidneys have four roles:
    - o Remove nitrogenous waste products, including urea and ammonia
    - o Maintain blood pressure and volume
    - o Regulate blood osmolarity
    - o Regulate blood pH
  - **Blood pressure:** The kidneys are good at compensating for low blood pressure, but can't do much for high blood pressure.

- o **ADH (Vasopressin)** increases water reabsorption by increasing the permeability of the distal tubule and collecting duct, increasing blood volume and pressure.
  - ▪ Permeability is regulated through addition/removal of water channels (aquaporins) in cell membranes.
- o **Aldosterone** triggers increased reabsorption of sodium ions in the distal tubule and collecting duct, which in turn drives water reabsorption, increasing blood volume and pressure. Aldosterone also increases potassium excretion.
- **Osmoregulation:** Kidneys regulate the concentration of solutes, primarily ions, in blood plasma.
  - o **ADH:** If blood osmolarity is high, ADH increases the permeability of the distal tubule and collecting duct, increasing water reabsorption.
  - o **Aldosterone:** If blood osmolarity is low, aldosterone triggers increased reabsorption of ions from the distal tubule and collecting duct, which in turn drives increased water reabsorption.
- **Acid-base balance:** The kidneys contribute to maintaining constant blood pH of 7.4 through relative excretion and reabsorption of participants in the bicarbonate buffer system.
  - o Increased removal of bicarbonate makes blood more acidic, while increased reabsorption makes blood more basic
  - o Proton (H+) excretion reduces acidity; proton reabsorption increases acidity. Aldosterone increases the removal of excess protons from the blood.
- **Removal of soluble nitrogenous waste:** Ammonia is a major metabolism byproduct, but can be harmful to cells, so it is often converted to urea.
  - o Urea is water-soluble and has a pH near that of blood. This makes it ideal for removing nitrogen from the body.
  - o Urea is secreted into the filtrate from the cells lining the tubules.
- ☐ **Kidney structure:** Each kidney has an outer layer, called the cortex, and an inner core, called the medulla.
  - **Nephron:** the functional unit of the kidney, which produces urine by collecting waste products from the blood. Glomerulus is in the cortex, Loop of Henle descends into medulla.
    - o **Pathway:** Blood flows into glomerulus → Bowman's capsule collects filtrate from blood → filtrate flows into proximal tubule → Loop of Henle → distal tubule → collecting duct → ureter → bladder
  - **Glomerulus:** a bundle of capillaries branching off from an afferent arteriole. The main site for filtration.
    - o Hydrostatic pressure of the blood drives water and small molecules through the capillary walls to be collected in Bowman's capsule. This

fluid is called the filtrate. The rest of the contents of the blood carry on through circulation.

  ▪ Increased blood pressure initially increases glomerular capillary blood pressure, therefore increasing the glomerular filtration rate.
  o Glomerular filtration is based primarily on size. Water, ions, and small molecules are pushed through the capillary walls, while large molecules and cells remain in the blood.
- **Bowman's capsule:** collects the filtrate from the glomerulus. Filtrate moves from Bowman's capsule to the proximal tubule.

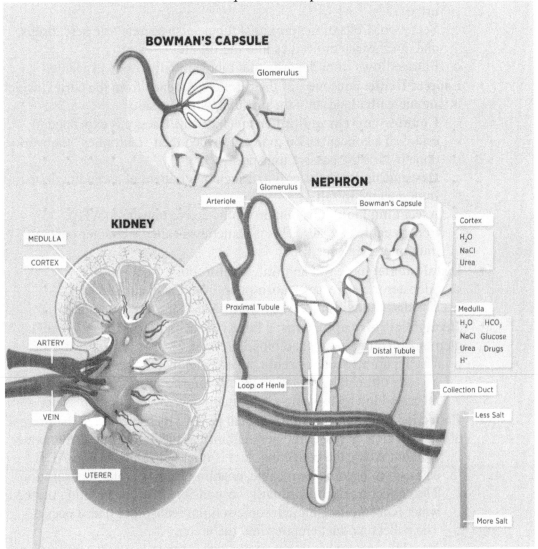

Figure 60: *Kidney structure.*

- **Proximal tubule:** main site of reabsorption, and also a significant site for secretion; reabsorbs salt, glucose, amino acids, vitamins, water
  - Secondary active transport proteins in proximal tubule cells selectively remove glucose and other molecules from the filtrate, returning them to circulation.
  - Water and some other small ions are removed from the filtrate passively via diffusion or passive transport channels
  - When concentrations are high enough to saturate these transporter proteins, excess molecules remain in filtrate and exit the body in the urine.
  - Secretion: Cells of the proximal tubule also secrete uric acid, drugs, and other waste molecules into the filtrate.
  - Filtrate flows from the proximal tubule into the Loop of Henle.
- **Loop of Henle:** concentrates the filtrate. Descends from the cortex, which is isotonic with blood, into the medulla, which is salty.
  - **Counter-current multiplier mechanism:** Energy is expended to establish a concentration gradient, which then "multiplies" the work done by driving passive transport.
  - **Descending loop:** water out, driven by gradient of ascending loop. Impermeable to salt.
  - **Ascending loop:** ions out, driven by active transport (ATP). Impermeable to water. This is sometimes called a counter-current multiplier mechanism.
- **Distal tubule:** more salt and water reabsorption
  - Aldosterone increases reabsorption from the distal tubule.
  - The distal tubule empties its contents into the collecting duct.
- **Juxtaglomerular apparatus**: a bunch of specialized cells that regulate glomerular filtration rate and blood pressure
  - The apparatus secretes **renin**, an enzyme that triggers a chemical cascade ultimately triggering aldosterone secretion, and therefore increased ion reabsorption, and finally increased blood pressure.
- **Collecting duct:** the site of additional passive reabsorption in the presence of ADH, which increases the permeability of the collecting duct to water
  - Without ADH, the collecting duct is impermeable to water. ADH causes it to become permeable, enabling passive water reabsorption.
  - The collecting duct is primarily responsible for concentrating urine via water reabsorption, though some sodium reabsorption also occurs.
  - The collecting duct empties into the ureter.
  - No additional reabsorption occurs once filtrate leaves the collecting duct.

- **Storage and elimination:** Concentrated filtrate exits the kidney via the ureter, which carries urine to the bladder, where it is collected and stored before being released from the body via the urethra.
- **Muscular control of urination:** Two sphincters, the internal and external urethral sphincters, acting individually or together, can keep the urethra sealed.
  - o The internal sphincter is under autonomic control (smooth muscle); the external sphincter is under voluntary control (skeletal muscle).

STRUCTURE	TRANSPORT TYPE	MOLECULES TRANSPORTED
Proximal tubule	Reabsorption by active transport	Glucose, amino acids, vitamins, salt
	Reabsorption by passive transport	Water, Salt
	Secretion into filtrate by active and passive transport	Urea, drugs, toxins, other waste products
Descending loop of Henle	Reabsorption by diffusion driven by concentration gradient	Water
Ascending loop of Henle	Reabsorption by active transport, creating concentration gradient	Salt
Distal tubule / Collecting duct	ADH-driven permeability changes; Aldosterone-driven changes in reabsorption	Water, Salt

- ☐ **The muscle cell** comes in three varieties:
  - **Skeletal muscle** is the muscle you use to move your bones around. It is under voluntary control, and appears striated, unbranched, and has many nuclei. Skeletal muscle comes in two fiber types:
    - o **Type 1 is** slow-twitch fibers. They are red because they have lot of myoglobin for oxygen storage and mitochondria for energy production. They are slow to contract, but also slow to fatigue.
    - o **Type 2 is** fast-twitch fibers. They are white because they have relatively little myoglobin and relatively few mitochondria. They contract fast, and fatigue fast.
    - o Both fiber types are found in most skeletal muscle, but in varying ratios depending on what the muscle is for.
      - Ex: Postural muscles have more type I, because they need to work for a long time and don't need to be fast.
  - **Smooth muscle** is in your blood vessels, your digestive tract, your respiratory tract, the iris of your eye, etc. It is under involuntary control, and appears as single-nucleus, oval-shaped cells without striations.

- **Cardiac muscle** is in your heart. It is under involuntary control, and appears as striated, single-nucleated, branched cells.
- ☐ **Sarcomeres** are the basic functional units of skeletal muscle, composed of thick filaments (myosin) and thin filaments (actin). Sarcomeres consist of five regions:
    - ○ The **I band** is the region of the sarcomere that is only actin (includes the Z line and the sections of actin that extend from it until they begin to overlap with myosin).
    - ○ The **A band** is the region of the sarcomere that contains myosin, including where it overlaps with actin.
    - ○ The **M line** runs perpendicular to the center of the myosin strands, and is part of the cytoskeleton.
    - ○ The **Z line** is the "backbone" of the actin structure.
    - ○ The **H zone** is the myosin-only region between the ends of two actin complexes.

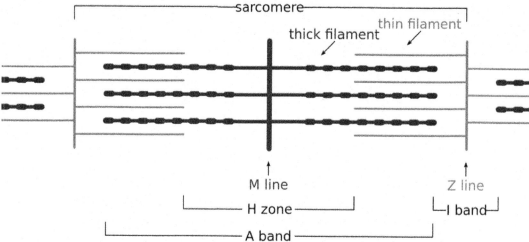

***Figure 61:** Structure of the sarcomere (Image credit: SlothMcCarty).*

- **Troponin and tropomyosin** are located on the ends of each thick myosin filament, and power the contraction of the sarcomere.
- **Muscle Contraction** (sliding filament model) occurs at each sarcomere.
    - ○ **Motor neurons** trigger the release of calcium from the sarcoplasmic reticulum.
    - ○ Calcium binds **troponin,** which causes **tropomyosin** to move, exposing myosin-binding sites on the thin actin filaments.

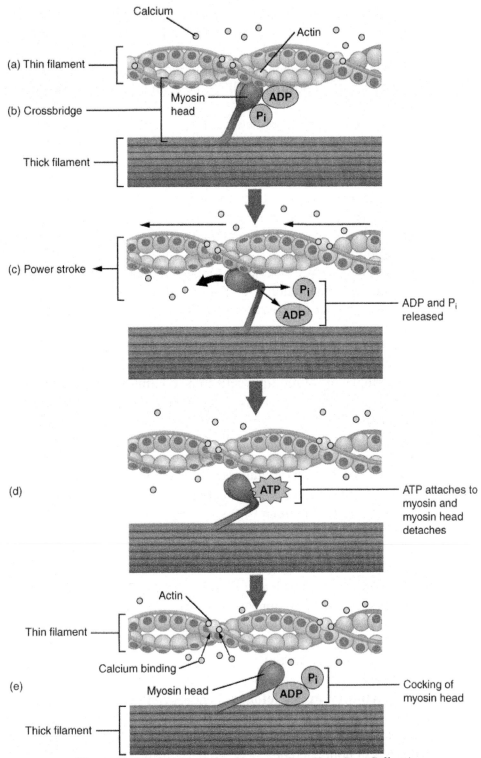

Figure 62*: Mechanics of muscle contraction (OpenStax College).*

- o The **myosin head,** which is in a high-energy "cocked" position and bound to ATP, binds to the myosin binding sites on actin, initiating the power stroke.
  - o **Power stroke:** Myosin uses ATP to move from a high-energy position to a low-energy position, pulling the actin in toward the M-line in the process.
  - o The muscle is now contracted, and actin and myosin overlap fully in the sarcomere (no I band or A band). Myosin is bound to ADP.
  - o **Relaxation**: ATP binds the myosin head, returning it to its "cocked" position. This causes the myosin and actin to decouple and return to their original position. Tropomyosin re-covers the myosin binding site.
- **Muscle fibers** are made up of sarcomeres laid end-to-end in long strands called myofibrils, which are then bundled together and wrapped in a sarcoplasmic reticulum.
  - o **T-tubule system** is a series of tunnels in the membrane of skeletal muscle cells that action potentials can travel through. This enables synchronization of muscle contraction across a large number of sarcomeres.
  - o **Intercalated discs,** which are clusters of gap junctions, enable synchronization of contraction in cardiac muscle. Gap junctions allow the cytoplasms of multiple cells to be continuous with each other, so that depolarization of one cell leads to rapid depolarization of the group of cells.
- ☐ The **skeletal system** provides structural rigidity and support, as well as:
  - o Mineral storage, primarily calcium
  - o Physical protection of vital organs (ex: skull protects brain)
  - **Structure** of the skeletal system includes four types of bones:
    - o Long bones (ex: femur)
    - o Short/cuboidal bones (ex: wrist bones)
    - o Flat bones (ex: ribs, shoulder blades, skull)
    - o Irregular (ex: hipbones, auditory ossicles)
  - **Joint structures** are lubricated by fluid and cartilage, except for immobile joints, in which bone is connected to bone with cartilage:
    - o Ball and socket joint (ex: hip)
    - o Hinge joint (ex: knee)
    - o Gliding joint (ex: ankle)
    - o Immobile joint (ex: skull)
  - **Endoskeleton vs. exoskeleton:** An endoskeleton provides an internal support and protection structure (humans) while an exoskeleton provides external support and protection (cockroach).
  - **Cell types** in bone include:

- o **Osteocytes** are found in lacunae, or pits, in bone, and exchange nutrients and waste in bone.
- o **Osteoblasts** incorporate calcium from the bloodstream into new bone.
- o **Osteoclasts** degrade bone, releasing calcium into the bloodstream.
- **Bone remodeling** is the continuous process by which osteoclasts resorb bone, and osteoblasts build it up again. This mechanism regulates the concentrations of calcium and phosphorous in the bloodstream. This is also the process underlying the growth of bones.
- **Bone** includes cells and a large amount of extracellular matrix. It also contains blood vessels and bone marrow, which makes the cells of our blood.
- **Cartilage** is connective tissue that cushions joints in the skeletal system.
  - o **Chondrocytes** are cartilage cells. Cartilage contains some cells, but is mostly composed of the extracellular matrix that the cells produce.
- **Ligaments** connect bone to bone.
- **Tendons** connect muscle to bone.
- **Endocrine control** of the skeletal system:
  - o **Parathyroid hormone** increases blood calcium levels by increasing activity of osteoclasts and decreasing activity of osteoblasts.
  - o **Calcitonin** decreases blood calcium by increasing activity of osteoblasts and decreasing activity of osteoclasts.
- ☐ **Skin (Integumentary) system**: the largest organ of the body, responsible for protection, thermoregulation, and control of entrance and exit of some molecules
  - **Structure:**
    - o **Epidermis**: outer layer of epithelial cells. No blood vessels. Cells divide relatively rapidly, forming layers of cells of different ages. The outermost cells are dead, glued together with keratin, and slough off throughout the day.
    - o **Dermis**: below the epidermis. Epithelial tissue containing blood and lymph vessels, as well as glands and hair follicles. Cushions the body.
    - o **Hypodermis**: layer below the dermis that connects the skin to underlying muscle and bone. Connective and adipose tissue to cushion and insulate.
      - ▪ Relatively impermeable to water due to hydrophobic keratin binding together dead skin cells of the epidermis.
  - Functions in **thermoregulation and homeostasis:**
    - o **Hair and erectile musculature**: Hair keeps you warm by trapping air close to the skin. When you are cold, an erectile muscle attached to each hair contracts, so that hair stands on end, increasing the amount of air trapped close to your skin.

- o A fat layer provides insulation.
- o **Sweat glands**, located in the dermis, enable cooling by evaporation.
- o **Vasoconstriction** reduces heat loss from capillaries close to the surface of the skin; vasodilation increases heat loss from skin capillaries.
- **Physical protection** against injury, abrasion, and disease organisms:
  - o Nails, calluses, and hair provide increased protection to sensitive or frequently used areas of skin. All are made of keratin.
- Hormonal control:
  - o **Sweating**: Acetylcholine and testosterone increase sweating in response to stress/fear.
  - o **Vasodilation and vasoconstriction** are influenced by epinephrine, norepinephrine, and antidiuretic hormone (ADH).

PART III:
PSYCHOLOGICAL, SOCIAL, AND BIOLOGICAL FOUNDATIONS OF BEHAVIOR

The Senses

- ☐ **Sensory processing and perception:** how signals from the environment (sound waves, light waves, pressure, orientation in space, chemicals, etc.) are translated into neuronal signals
  - General structure and function:
    - ○ **Threshold:** In order to be perceived, stimuli must meet some minimum level of intensity.
    - ○ **Weber's Law:** The just-noticeable difference between two stimuli is proportional to the magnitude of the stimuli (ex: You probably wouldn't notice a difference between a 100 lb weight and a 101 lb weight, but you would notice the difference between a 1 lb weight and a 2 lb weight).
    - ○ **Signal detection theory** is a psychological approach applied to study how people make decisions in conditions of uncertainty. Expectations, past experience, and signal strength, among other factors, can influence how likely people are to perceive a stimuli or a change in stimuli.
    - ○ **Sensory adaptation:** Your senses adapt or adjust to stimuli based on the stimuli they are receiving. (ex: When you first jump into a pool, it's really cold, but you adapt to it. When you first walk into a house, you notice how it smells, but then you stop being able to notice the smell.)
      - ▪ Sensory receptors become saturated or desensitized to stimuli that remain unchanged for an extended period of time, such that sensory receptors don't send the same signal over and over again, and you are able to focus on other, more interesting stimuli.
    - ○ **Psychophysics** is the quantitative study of sensation through experiments that systematically vary or modify physical stimuli and then characterize changes in sensation and response. These techniques are used to identify thresholds, as well as just-noticeable differences and sensory adaptation.
- ☐ **Sensory receptor pathways and types**: For all of the senses, a sensory nerve ending responds to a stimulus that initiates an action potential in the cell. That action potential is then relayed to the central nervous system.
  - **Vision:** Rods and cones detect electromagnetic radiation and transmit signals to the primary visual cortex (occipital lobe).
  - **Hearing:** Hair cells detect mechanical waves and transmit signals to the auditory cortex (temporal lobe).
  - **Taste:** Gustatory receptors detect chemicals in solution and transmit signals to the thalamus and the frontal lobe.

- **Smell:** Odor receptors detect chemicals in the air and transmit signals to the olfactory bulb (inferior forebrain).
- **Touch:** Thermoreceptors and mechanoreceptors detect temperature, pressure, stretch, and vibration, and transmit signals to the primary somatosensory area (parietal lobe).
- **Pain:** Nociceptors detect chemical, mechanical, or thermal damage to tissue and transmit signals to the spinal cord (triggering autonomic responses) and then to the thalamus and somatosensory cortex (parietal lobe).
- ☐ **Perception** is a complex process that integrates both the detection of signals from the outside world and cognitive processes based on past experience, expectation, and other factors.
  - Bottom-up/top-down processing: Perception is driven both by data from the outside world and by our past experiences, expectations, and cognitive short cuts.
    - ○ **Bottom-up processing:** data-driven; information from the outside world is detected by sensory receptors and transmitted to the brain
    - ○ **Top-down processing:** pattern detection; context and past experience are used to interpret new stimuli.
  - Perceptual organization (depth, form, motion, constancy):
    - ○ **Depth:** Slight differences in the image perceived by each eye enable interpretation of depth. Converging/diverging lines can also create a perception of depth, even on a flat surface.
    - ○ **Form:** 2-D images projected onto the retina can be perceived as 3-D through the interpretation of lines, angles, and color changes.
    - ○ **Motion:** Motion sensors in the visual system perceive change in position. Motion can also be perceived by sequential changes in a flat image (think of a row of lights around a sign that are perceived as moving clockwise or counterclockwise, when in fact the lights are just turning on and off).
- ☐ **Constancy:** Familiar objects are perceived as having a constant form, shape, color, etc., even when the actual data received from vision is different (ex: When a car is approaching you from far away, you still perceive it as being the size of a normal car. When you get dressed in the dark, you perceive your jeans as being blue, even though your eyes are not actually receiving any information about color.).
  - **Gestalt principles**: The whole of perception is more than the sum of its parts. Top-down processing of visual cues is used to reach conclusions about visual information that are different from the conclusions that would be made from a strict interpretation of the data.
    - ○ **Similarity:** stimuli that are similar are perceived as a group

- o **Pragnanz:** ambiguous stimuli are resolved in the simplest form
- o **Proximity:** stimuli that are close together are perceived as a group
- o **Continuity:** lines follow the simplest path
- o **Closure:** we tend to ignore gaps in visual forms

Gestalt Principles	Example
Similarity: Black dots are grouped together and white dots are grouped together, so that the field is perceived as alternating lines of black and white dots.	
Pragnanz: Unknown shape is perceived as a circle, a rectangle, and a triangle overlapping each other, the simplest explanation for a complex stimulus.	
Proximity: A field of dots is perceived as three rectangular groups of dots.	
Continuity: A field of dots is perceived as two lines of dots that cross over each other	
Closure: A series of curved dashes are perceived as a circle.	

☐ **Vision** is the transduction of electromagnetic waves into visual information.
- Structure and function of **the eye**:
  - o **Cornea:** transparent covering on the front of the eye. Refracts light. It contributes to the eye's focusing power, but its power is fixed, unlike the lens which can be adjusted.
  - o **Pupil:** an opening beneath the cornea, and bounded by the iris, that allows light to pass through the lens
  - o **Iris:** the colored part of the eye. A ring of smooth muscle controls the size of the pupil. Sphincter muscle contracts to make pupil smaller; dilator muscle contracts to make pupil larger.
  - o **Crystalline lens:** a biconvex, transparent structure that focuses light onto the retina
  - o **Ciliary body:** a ring of smooth muscle that contracts to squish the lens, making it more circular, and relaxes to make the lens more flat
  - o **Optic nerve:** a bundle of nerves from each rod and cone in the retina; carries information from rods and cones to the brain
  - o **Retina:** the lining of the back of the inside of the eye; contains rods and cones for detection of light
  - o **Choroid:** vascular layer of the eye between the retina and the sclera
  - o **Sclera:** outer, protective layer of the eye; appears white; continuous with the cornea

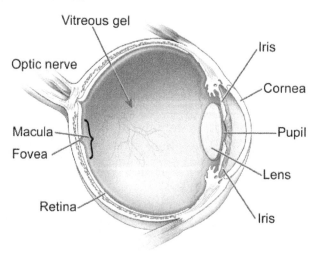

Figure 63: Eye anatomy.

  - o **Optic disc:** the blind spot of the eye; where all of the axons of retinal ganglion cells convene and create the optic nerve. It contains no rods and cones, therefore no visual information is detected when light hits this area.

- o **Fovea:** a small pit in the retina with the highest concentration of cones. This is the region of the retina with the highest visual acuity.
- o **Vitreous:** the gel between the lens and the retina
- o **Aqueous:** the fluid between the lens and the cornea
- □ **Visual pathways in the brain:** how information is transduced from the retina to the brain
  - • **Visual information** from the R visual field is transduced to the L visual cortex, and information from the L visual field is transduced to the R visual cortex.

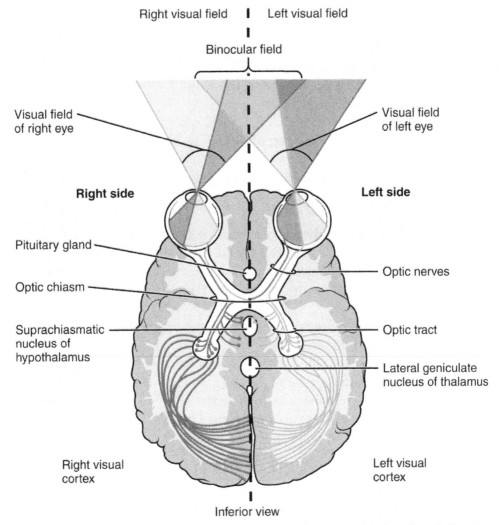

Figure 64: *Projection of visual field to visual cortex (Image credit: OpenStax College.)*

- o The optic nerves cross over each other at the optic chiasm, such that for each eye, some nerves continue into the R hemisphere and some into the L hemisphere.
  - o Information projected on the R side of BOTH retinas (which is information from the L side of each eye's visual field) is transmitted to the L visual cortex.
  - o Information projected on the L side of BOTH retinas (which is information from the R side of each eye's visual field) is transmitted to the R visual cortex.
- **Parallel processing:** In order to interpret visual information, the visual system detects features of visual information separately, and processes them in parallel, while also applying information from the memory to make sense of visual information as quickly as possible.
  - o **Feature detection:** Features detected and processed in parallel include color, line, shape, form, and orientation.
- ☐ **The ear:** structure and function:
  - Outer ear:
    - o **Pinna**: outer, fleshy part of the ear. Its shape helps to collect sound waves.
    - o **Auditory canal**: open to the environment; carries sound waves from the environment to the sensory structure of the ear
  - Middle ear:
    - o **Tympanic membrane**: vibrates when sound waves hit it
    - o These waves are then transferred, and in the process amplified, as they pass from the tympanic membrane to the ossicles (malleus, incus, stapes), which are tiny bones.
  - Inner ear:
    - o **The stapes** causes the oval window to begin vibrating, which transfers vibrations into the cochlea.
    - o **The cochlea** is filled with fluid, and has two "lanes": one for waves moving from the base to the apex, and another for waves making the return trip from the apex to the base.
    - o These two lanes are divided by the Organ of Corti, the basilar membrane of which is lined with auditory receptor cells, called hair cells.
    - o When vibrations reach the far tip of the cochlea, they are bounced back the other direction.
    - o On the return trip, the vibrations are transferred to the round window.
    - o This vibration of the fluid of the cochlea continues back and forth until all of the vibrational energy has been dissipated.

- **Hair cell** depolarization:
    o Hair cells line the basilar membrane of the Organ of Corti, inside the cochlea. Hair cells are surrounded by fluid, like seaweed on the ocean floor.
    o When a wave moves through the fluid, it deflects the stereocilia of hair cells.

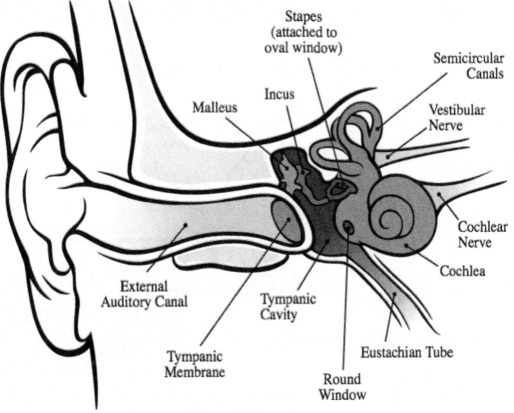

Figure 65: Ear anatomy.

    o **The stereocilia** are connected to one another by spring-like structures called tip links, which act as mechanical gates for ion channels.
    o Deflection pulls the "lid" off of the ion channel, leading to depolarization (K+ influx triggers opening of voltage-gated Ca^{2+} channels, allowing Ca^{2+} influx). This depolarization leads neurotransmitters to be released from vesicles onto the dendrite of an afferent nerve.
    o Unlike most sensory receptors, hair cells do not themselves generate action potentials.

- ☐ **Auditory processing** is the ability to distinguish between different sounds.
  - **Frequency**: Sounds of different frequencies stimulate different areas of the basilar membrane. Hair cells are "tuned" to respond to specific frequencies.
    - o Hair cells toward the base of the cochlea respond to higher frequencies.
    - o Hair cells toward the apex of the cochlea respond to lower frequencies.

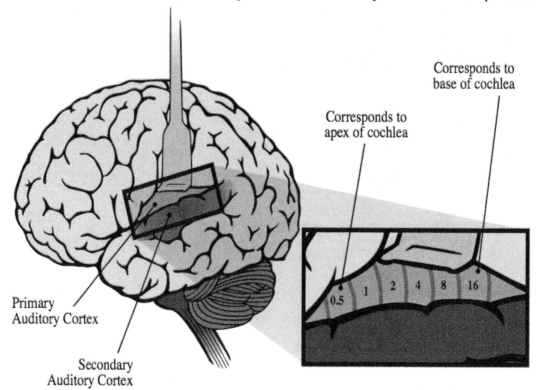

Figure 66: *Auditory cortex.*

- Hair cells transmit signals to auditory nerves, which convene to form the auditory or cochlear nerve.
- The **auditory nerve** carries signals to the primary auditory cortex (temporal lobe), which is mapped in essentially the same way as the cochlea: with the more frontal portion receiving input from the apex of the cochlea, and the distal portion receiving input from the base of the cochlea.
- ☐ **Somatosensation** is sensing your own body and how it interacts with the environment.
  - Types of somatosensation:

- o **Mechanoreception:** perception of pressure. Mechanoreceptors are depolarized due to mechanical stimuli (ex: squeezing your arm).
- o **Thermoreception:** perception of temperature and temperature change that is not causing tissue damage. Very high and very low temperature are detected by nociceptors.
- o **Proprioception** (Kinesthetic sense): perception of your body's position in space, and the relative position of different body parts. It results from sensory receptors for motion and orientation in the ear, as well as stretch receptors in skeletal muscle and tendons involved in posture/stance.
  - ▪ Proprioception may be temporarily impaired during periods of rapid growth (adolescence) or due to intense work to increase strength/flexibility.
- o **Nociception:** perception of pain. Nociceptors in the central and peripheral nervous system selectively respond to tissue damage that can be thermal (extreme hot or cold), mechanical (ex: crushing), or chemical (ex: pepper spray).
  - ▪ When a stimulus reaches a certain threshold of intensity, it initiates an action potential generated in the nociceptor neuron and travels to the spinal cord.
- **Somatosensation is transduced** from receptor → sensory neurons → spinal cord → primary somatosensory area (parietal lobe), which is mapped according to the position in the body from which information is being received (cortical homunculus).

Figure 67: Mapping the body onto the somatosensory cortex.

- o The size of the cortical area devoted to sensation in a particular body part is proportional to the number of sensory receptors, not the size of the body part itself. Therefore structures like the tongue, lips, and fingertips account for much larger areas of the cortex than the legs, back, etc.
- ☐ **Taste:** a form of chemo reception: five tastes; five receptors on your tongue
  - Receptor types:
    - o **Salty**: receptors have Na+ channels, which begins depolarization when they encounter NaCl in solution.
    - o **Sweet**: G-protein coupled receptors begin depolarization when they encounter glucose.
    - o **Bitter**: G-protein coupled receptors begin depolarization when they encounter bitter compounds.
    - o **Sour**: receptors detect acidic compounds (high H+ concentrations); both simple and gated H+ ion channels contribute to depolarization.
    - o **Umami**: a savory taste; people taste umami through receptors specific to glutamate.
  - Each taste bud includes all five receptor types.
  - Each receptor has an axon that reaches all the way to the gustatory cortex.
- ☐ **Smell:** chemoreception of a wide array of molecules in the air
  - **Olfactory neurons** line the olfactory epithelium, and contain membrane-bound receptor proteins.
    - o Olfactory receptor proteins typically have affinity for a wide range of odorants, which contributes to the wide array of smell sensations we can detect (as opposed to gustatory system, which only detects five sensations).
    - o Axons of olfactory neurons convene to form olfactory nerve, which projects into the olfactory bulb. From there, signals are projected to multiple brain areas, including the amygdala.
  - **Pheromones:** secreted chemical signals, detected by the olfactory system, that trigger a social response in other members of the same species. They are especially important in insects and some other non-human animals. While humans have some ability to detect and respond to pheromones, they do not play a significant role in human sensation or behavior.
    - o Animals that communicate with pheromones (ex: mice) typically have two organs involved in pheromone sensation (vomeronasal organ) and perception (accessory olfactory bulb). Humans have a vomeronasal organ, but no accessory olfactory bulb.
- ☐ **Vestibular sense** is a sense of special orientation and balance, which is important for coordination of body movements.
  - Vestibular sense originates in the inner ear:

- **Semicircular canal system** of the ear senses rotation. The three canals are at right angles with each other, and are filled with endolymph (fluid). When the fluid moves, semicircular canals can sense both direction and speed of endolymph movement.
- **Otolithic organs** (utricle and saccule) are calcium carbonate crystals, which are attached to hair cells suspended in fluid. When the otolithic organs move, due to body movement, they pull on the hair cells, triggering action potentials. This enables us to sense gravity and linear acceleration.
    - o Dizziness: When you stop spinning around, the endolymph in your semicircular canal keeps moving, creating a sensation of dizziness.

The Nervous System: Structure, Processes, and Development

- ☐ **Neurons** are the cells of the nervous system.
    - Unidirectional: signals are received by the dendrites, and sent by propagation down the axon.
    - The **myelin sheath** insulates the axon, speeding up propagation so that depolarization spreads from node to node, rather than from point to point all along the axon.
    - When an **action potential** reaches the axon terminal, it causes vesicles containing neurotransmitters to merge with the terminal membrane, spilling neurotransmitters into the synapse.
    - **Synapse**: a small, empty space between the axon of one neuron and the dendrite of the next
    - Once in the synapse, neurotransmitters can be:
        - o Bound to receptors on the postsynaptic neuron, contributing to an excitatory or inhibitory response;
        - o Metabolized by digestive enzymes in and around the synapse; or
        - o Recovered through reuptake, in which neurotransmitters are taken back into the presynaptic neuron by bonding membrane-bound receptors.
- ☐ **Neurotransmitters**: the chemical signals that neurons use to communicate
    - Excitatory: act to encourage the next neuron to produce an AP
        - o **Glutamate** (CNS and PNS): learning and pleasure. Amino acid. Most common neurotransmitter in the body.
    - Inhibitory: act to discourage the next neuron from producing an AP
        - o **GABA** (brain): amino acid
        - o **Glycine** (spinal cord): amino acid

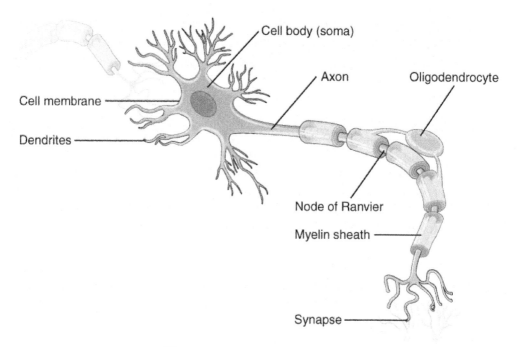

Figure 68: *Structure of the neuron.*

- Movement:
  - **Acetylcholine**: neuromuscular junction, autonomic nervous system. Acetic acid-choline ester. CNS and PNS.
- **Monoamines**: CNS activities including cognition, attention, and regulation of emotion
  - **Serotonin**: also regulates intestinal movements. CNS.
  - **Histamine**: wakefulness, nociception
  - **Catecholamines** (monoamines):
    - **Dopamine**: increases appetite. CNS and PNS.
    - Parkinson's disease results from the destruction of dopamine-secreting neurons in the midbrain that are involved with coordination and smoothing of body movements.
    - **Epinephrine** (adrenaline): promotes fight-or-flight response; produced by adrenal glands
    - **Norepinephrine** (Noradrenaline): promotes fight-or-flight response
- **Endorphins:** endogenous opioid peptides that inhibit pain sensations, promote euphoria.
- ☐ **Peripheral nervous system:** carries messages from the CNS to the body, and from the body to the CNS
  - Made up of **nerves** (bundles of axons) and **ganglion** (somas)

- o Afferent nerves (sensory): carry messages from body to CNS
  - o Efferent nerves (motor/effector): carry messages from CNS to body
- **Schwann cells**: the glial cells of the PNS
- **Autonomic nervous system**: controls involuntary bodily functions (respiration, digestion, circulatory system, excretory system, sexual arousal, etc.)
  - o **Sympathetic nervous system**: fight-or-flight response
    - ▪ Pupils dilate
    - ▪ Blood flow increases in muscles and lungs, decreases in skin and digestive tract; heart rate increases
    - ▪ Digestion inhibited
    - ▪ Orgasm
  - o **Parasympathetic nervous system**: rest and digest
    - ▪ Pupils constrict
    - ▪ Blood flow increases in skin and digestive tract, decreases in muscles and lungs; heart rate decreases
    - ▪ Digestion stimulated
    - ▪ Sexual arousal and genital tissue erection
  - o Sympathetic and parasympathetic work together in **antagonistic control**, meaning that the activation of one deactivates the other.
- ☐ **Central nervous system**: the brain and spinal cord
  - Grey matter: neuron cell bodies, dendrites, and axon terminals
  - White matter: myelinated axons and glial cells
    - o **Glial cells**: produce myelin, provide support functions for neurons
  - Protected by the meninges
  - **Forebrain:** the cerebrum; high-level cognitive processing, speech, decision-making
  - **Midbrain:** connects the hindbrain and forebrain; vision, motor control, sleep/wake behavior, arousal, hearing, temperature regulation
  - **Hindbrain:** the cerebellum, pons, medulla; connects to spinal cord; respiration, cardiac rhythm, blood pressure, autonomic behaviors
  - **Lateralization of cortical functions**: The brain has two hemispheres, left and right, connected by the corpus callosum. Some brain functions, such as language, are lateralized, meaning their function relies primarily on one hemisphere or the other.
- ☐ **Methods** used in studying the brain include:
  - **Lesion studies:** Many major findings in psychology and neuroscience are based on the study of patients who have had damage to specific areas of the brain. Essentially, the cognitive deficits of the patient are attributed to the area of the brain that is damaged in a particular subject (ex: Phineas Gage and HM).

- **fMRI:** Magnetic resonance imaging (MRI) is used to track blood flow in the brain. A typical fMRI study involves exposing subjects to stimuli while they are in an MRI machine (typically images, sounds, or words) and assessing how blood flow in different areas of the brain changes in response to those stimuli. Limitation: subject has to stay extremely still and inside the MRI machine.
- **PET:** Positron emission tomography uses a radioactive tracer injected into a patient's blood stream to assess blood flow in the brain. Limitation: lower resolution than fMRI, but the subject can move; radioactivity risk with repeated use.
- **EEG:** Electroencephalography can be used to measure electrical activity of the brain. This technique is non-invasive (electrodes placed on the scalp), and has high temporal resolution, but low spatial resolution.
- **CT:** Computer tomography is essentially a 3-D X-ray of the brain. CT provides a detailed picture of the structure of the brain, but not the function.

☐ **The spinal cord** relays messages from the peripheral nervous system to the brain, but also can carry out some basic functions without brain involvement.
- **Reflex arc:** the neural structure that enables an automatic response to certain stimuli without involving the brain or consciousness
  - ○ **Monosynaptic:** afferent neuron enters spinal cord, initiates excitatory muscle at synapse with efferent neuron, efferent neuron causes reflex response (ex: patellar reflex)
  - ○ **Polysynaptic:** one or more interneurons participate in passing signal from the sensory neuron to the motor neurons involved in the response (ex: withdrawal from painful stimulus)

☐ **Neuronal communication** and its influence on behavior:
- Neuronal communication is unidirectional, and all-or-none. Either an AP is generated, or it is not. The rate of APs can be increased or decreased, but the intensity of an AP for a given neuron is constant.

☐ **Behavioral genetics:** the field of study considering the interactions between genes and environment in determining behavior
- **Genes, temperament, and heredity:** Temperament, or an individual's baseline social/emotional state, is believed to be in large part determined by your genes, and persistent throughout your lifetime.
- **Adaptive value of traits and behaviors:** Certain behaviors are genetically determined, often traits that confer significant survival advantage (ex: birds flying). Others are learned through observation (ex: riding a bike).

- o **Innate behaviors** are genetically determined, immutable, and generally standardized species-wide. They include reflexes and instincts (ex: birds flying south).
- o A **fixed action pattern** is an instinctive sequence of behaviors that is relatively constant within a species, but is more complex than a simple reflex (ex: mating or courtship dance behaviors in birds).
- o **Learned behaviors** are persistent traits, but based on learning and experience. These are not inherited, and relatively moldable (ex: social skills).
- **Interaction between heredity and environment:** Heritable traits (ex: height, intelligence) influence how we interact with our environment, and our environment and experience can also influence the expression of our genes.
  - o Ex: Siamese cat coat color is influenced by temperature. Colder temperatures leads to darker hair, warmer temperature leads to lighter hair.
- ☐ **Influence of genetic and environmental factors** on the development of behaviors:
  - **Experience** and behavior: Observing and learning from others and the environment can drive the development or change of behavior.
  - **Regulatory genes** and behavior: Environmental factors, including hormones, diet, etc., can lead to upregulation or downregulation of the expression of certain genes, which can in turn influence behavior. This does not change the genetic information; only when, how, and how much it is expressed (epigenetics).
  - Genetically-based behaviors can vary within a population (ex: some people eat more when they're stressed, others eat less).
- ☐ **Human physiological development** is associated with changes in behavior and gene expression.
  - **Prenatal development:** A fetus grows and develops using food, oxygen, and other resources from the mother via the umbilical cord and placenta. Waste is also removed via the placenta.
    - o Some viruses, bacteria, and chemicals, such as alcohol, can cross the placenta and cause damage to a developing fetus. X-rays and environmental contamination can also be deleterious.
  - **Motor development** is indicated by a series of behavioral milestones.
    - o ex: rolling over around 4 months, walking around 12 months
    - o Neonatal/primitive reflexes: innate behaviors seen at birth that disappear with age
      - **Rooting reflex:** turning head when something touches the cheek (breast feeding)

- **Moro reflex:** clutching motion in response to the head being moved downward quickly (preventing a fall if dropped).
- **Developmental changes in adolescence** include development of secondary sex characteristics, associated hormonal changes, and psychological development.
  - Adolescents have underdeveloped prefrontal cortices, which contributes to reduced impulse control and increased behavioral volatility seen in adolescents. The prefrontal cortex continues to develop until age 25.

Cognitive Processes

- **Attention** is the process by which we choose to attend to only a certain subset of the total information that we are receiving, or, the process by which we allocate our limited resources for information processing.
  - **Selective attention:** Processing of visual information involves identifying objects and other visual cues through selectively attending to certain features (ex: At a loud party, you use selective attention to follow one conversation, while blocking out the numerous other conversations going on around you.).
  - **Divided attention:** When we attempt to pay attention to two or more tasks at once, we switch back and forth between attending to one and then the other. Tasks accomplished with divided attention tend to require more mental effort than if the tasks were accomplished in sequence with full information, and often can result in poorer results due to incomplete information and attentional gaps for each task (ex: driving a car while talking on the phone. We think we are attending to both at once, when in fact we are switching between one and the other, leading to information loss and gaps in attention.).
- **Cognition** is the array of mental processes involved in interpreting and responding to the environment, as well as accumulating knowledge and experience.
  - **Information processing model:** Your brain is like a computer. It takes input from the senses, holds it for a short period of time in sensory memory in order to process it, generates a response, and then stores the memory in long-term memory. In this way, we are not just reacting to our environment, we are processing it and storing information so that we get better at responding to stimuli over time. Development is continuously additive, rather than happening in stages.

- **Cognitive development** stages:
  - ○ **Piaget's** stages of cognitive development: Piaget viewed cognitive development as a continual process of developing, and then building upon, capabilities. Stages are identified by the achievement of cognitive milestones:
    - ▪ 0-2 years: **Sensorimotor stage**. Lack object permanence.
    - ▪ 2-7 years: **Preoperational stage**. Pretend play. Use of symbols. Learning to talk. Egocentric. Children of this age think a cake cut in two becomes more cake.
    - ▪ 7-11 years: **Concrete operational stage**. Mathematical reasoning. Conservation.
    - ▪ 12+ years: **Formal operational**. Reasoning about abstract concepts. Consequences of potential actions. Moral reasoning.
    - ▪ *Mnemonic: Suppose Pigs Could Fly?*
  - ○ **Cognitive changes** in late adulthood:
    - ▪ Better: crystallized intelligence, emotional reasoning
    - ▪ Same: recognition, implicit memory
    - ▪ Worse: brain "slows down," due to reduced production of neurotransmitters. Slower walking, thinking, talking, reaction time, recall; worse episodic memory, multitasking ability
  - ○ **Culture** can influence cognitive development (ex: Western cultures are more independent → better at independent tasks; Eastern cultures are more interdependent →better at interdependent tasks).
  - ○ **Genes** and the environment interact to influence cognition and intelligence (The answer to the age-old question, "Nature or nurture?" is "Yes, both.")
    - ▪ Evidence from twin studies: Twins raised separately show both genetic and environmental influences on development.
  - ○ **Biological** factors that affect cognition: Impairment of certain brain areas can reduce cognitive abilities.
    - ▪ Frontal lobe: planning, attention, motivation
    - ▪ Hippocampus: memory
    - ▪ Amygdala: emotional learning
- ☐ **Problem-solving and decision-making** processes and approaches:
  - **Types** of problem solving:
    - ○ **Trial-and-error:** random guesses until something works
    - ○ **Algorithms:** logical procedures that are methodical, rather than random (ex: trying each key in order until you find the one that opens the door).
    - ○ **Heuristic:** a mental shortcut used to simplify complex problems (ex: estimation, rule of thumb).

- **Means-end analysis:** break a big problem into smaller problems, approach smaller problems one at a time, starting with the biggest one
- **Working backwards:** use goal statement to suggest approaches
- **Insight:** sudden realization or conclusion not reached linearly
- **Incubation:** taking time to consider a problem while proceeding with other decisions/activities
- **Barriers** to effective problem-solving:
  - Fixation: getting "stuck" on one strategy or approach that has already been tried unsuccessfully
  - Irrelevant information: creates distraction or influences that can be detrimental to problem solving
  - Constraints: self-imposed decisions or boundaries that limit range of approaches considered
- **Approaches** to problem-solving:
  - Availability heuristic: examples that come to mind
  - Representativeness heuristic: comparing prototypes
- **Heuristics and biases**
  - **Overconfidence**: more confidence than correct
  - **Belief perseverance:** ignore or rationalize disconfirming facts
  - **Confirmation bias**: seeking out only confirming facts
  - **Framing effects:** posing of question influences response
- ☐ **Theories of intelligence:** what it is, how it is formed, and whether it can be changed
  - **General intelligence**: People who score well on one test tend to score well on other types of tests as well. G-factor.
  - **Multiple intelligences:** analytical, creative, practical (IQ is analytical)
  - **Emotional intelligence:** ability to recognize emotions, both yours and other people's
  - **Fluid vs. crystallized intelligence:** fluid intelligence is quick, abstract reasoning; crystallized intelligence is accumulated knowledge. Fluid intelligence decreases with age, crystallized intelligence increases with age.
- ☐ **States of consciousness:** different levels of awareness of stimuli. States of consciousness change naturally throughout the day, and can be altered by drugs.
  - **Alertness:** awareness of yourself, your environment, and ability to respond to stimuli
    - Beta waves are associated with a normal alert state.
  - **Sleep:** a state of consciousness in which you are not aware of the world around you, the passage of time, or your own body

- o Four stages of sleep, in 90-minute cycles (four to five cycles per night)
- o **Non-REM** sleep (stages 1-3):
  - **N1**: drowsiness. Theta waves begin. Hypnagogic hallucinations and hypnic jerks are possible (feeling of falling off a cliff).
  - **N2**: deeper than N1. More theta waves, spikes in activity associated with keeping you asleep (quieting responses to mild, non-threatening stimuli), as well as with memory consolidation and storage.
  - **N3**: deeper than N2. Slow-wave sleep. Delta waves begin. Stage where sleepwalking occurs.
- o **REM** (stage 4): Rapid eye movement. Deepest stage of sleep. Most muscles are paralyzed, but your eyes move rapidly. Dreaming occurs. Similar levels of brain activity to an alert state.
- **Sleep patterns can change with age**: Cycles tend to be longer for younger people; younger people tend to stay up late, older people tend to get up early.
  - o Sleep and circadian rhythms: Wakefulness is cyclical, regulated by circadian rhythms, or our biological 24-hour clock. Influenced by daylight.
- ☐ **Dreaming** occurs primarily in REM cycle. It happens to everyone every night, whether or not you remember.
  - Prefrontal cortex activity (associated with reasoning, planning) is suppressed in REM sleep. As a result, when you remember your dreams, they may seem illogical upon reflection.
  - Example theories of the purpose of dreaming:
    - o Freud: act out/interpret subconscious impulses
    - o Evolutionary psychology: dreams simulate threats, practicing how to deal with them in the real world
- ☐ **Sleep-wake disorders:** Disruption of sleep can lead to psychological and physiological problems, including increased production of stress hormones, weight gain, and risk of depression.
  - Insomnia: difficulty falling asleep and staying asleep
  - Narcolepsy: spontaneous and sudden sleepiness, including rapid entrance into REM sleep
  - Sleep apnea: stopped breathing briefly while asleep; people are often unaware they have sleep apnea
- ☐ **Hypnosis and meditation** are associated with mental state between alertness and sleep, in which you are aware of your surroundings, but are less focused and more relaxed than normal — similar to daydreaming. People are more susceptible to suggestion in this state, enabling hypnosis.

- Alpha waves are associated with daydreaming, light meditation, and relaxation.
☐ **Consciousness-altering drugs** and their effects:
  - Types of consciousness-altering drugs and their effects on the nervous system and behavior:
    - **Depressants** lower basic functions (heart rate, reaction time, processing speed).
      - Alcohol: disrupts REM sleep and therefore memory
      - Barbiturates: induce sleep and/or reduce anxiety; repress CNS activity, reduce memory, and impair judgment and/or concentration
      - Benzodiazepines: enhance brain response to GABA (inhibitory neurotransmitter)
    - **Opiates** are used to treat pain and/or anxiety (ex: heroin, morphine). They act at endorphin receptor sites, reducing pain. High doses lead to euphoria
    - **Stimulants** intensify neural activity.
      - Caffeine: prevents drowsiness; legal, and widely perceived to be safe for regular consumption
      - Nicotine: increases heart rate, blood pressure, suppresses appetite, increases wakefulness; stress-reducing hormones due to stimulus response
      - Cocaine: causes brain to release dopamine, serotonin, and norepinephrine, depleting your brain's supply
      - Methamphetamine: triggers release of dopamine; causes euphoria.
    - **Hallucinogens** lead to altered perceptions of reality.
      - Ecstasy: stimulant and hallucinogen. Includes dopamine, serotonin; stimulates CNS, including BP, can damage cells that produce serotonin. False sense of intimacy.
      - LSD: serotonin transmission disrupted, leading to hallucinations, primarily visual
      - Marijuana: heightened sensitivity to color, sound, taste, smell. Reduces inhibition, relaxes CNS, impairs motor coordination and perceptual skills. Disrupts short-term recall.
      - Medical uses: PTSD treatment; allows for recall of traumatic events in a detached way, without emotional response
  - **Routes of entry** for consciousness-altering drugs: injection, oral, inhalation, transdermal, and intramuscular
    - Quicker response time leads to a higher likelihood of dependence (ex: injection has a faster response time than oral).
  - **Drug addiction** and the reward pathway in the brain:

- Mesolimbic pathway: Dopamine is produced primarily in VTA (ventral tegmental area) in midbrain. It sends dopamine to the amygdala (emotion), nucleus accumbens (motor functions), prefrontal cortex (attention and planning), and hippocampus (memory).
- Continued activation of reward circuit: Dopamine goes up, serotonin goes down. Serotonin is associated with satiety/satisfaction, leading to problems with drugs, other addictions.

☐ **Encoding** of memories is the process by which useful sensory and cognitive information is converted into a storable form (memory) so that it can be accessed for future use. Includes encoding, storage, and retrieval of information.
- Types of encoding:
    - **Visual encoding:** Visual sensory information is stored briefly in iconic and working memory before long-term storage.
        - **Visuospatial sketchpad:** stores visual information (shape, color, form, movement) in the short-term; also involved in planning spatial movements/interacting with the visual information
        - Amygdala: encodes visual sensory info as positive or negative
    - **Acoustic encoding:** auditory sensory information temporarily stored in echoic memory, which repeats auditory info on a loop during processing
        - **Phonological loop:** stores auditory and verbal information in the short-term, repeating it over and over to "rehearse" the order and character of auditory stimuli
        - Lexical and semantic info interact with acoustic info in working memory to enable understanding of language.
    - **Semantic encoding:** process of encoding the meaning of sensory information based on context/significance/preexisting memory
- Processes that aid in encoding memories:
    - **Chunking** reduces the amount of info to be learned by creating groups or categories (ex: thisstringofletters would be easier to encode than this one: xvjklqmo, even though it's shorter).
    - **Mnemonics** improve encoding by organizing information (ex: SOHCAHTOA).
    - **State-dependent learning** relies on being in the same environment and state as when the sensory information was first encoded can aid in recall (ex: the best place to study for the MCAT would be at your MCAT testing center. Too bad they won't let you in!).

☐ **Storage** of memories happens in different ways based on the type and duration of the memory.

- **Sensory:** very short-term (seconds) maintenance of sensory input; modality-dependent (iconic info is stored for less than half a second; echoic for 3 to 4 seconds)
- **Working/short-term:** short-term (minutes) storage, with limited capacity
  - ○ **Magic number:** most people have a working memory capacity of 7 ± 2 items. (think: phone numbers)
  - ○ **Central executive:** integrates and coordinates working memory across modalities, including the visuospatial sketchpad and phonological loop
- **Long-term:** long-term storage with practically infinite capacity in terms of both duration of storage and quantity of stored information
  - ○ **Explicit/declarative:** facts and events
    - ▪ **Semantic memory:** memorized facts, word meanings, and other forms of long-term memory that are dependent on language
    - ▪ **Episodic memory:** sequence and characteristics of life events
  - ○ **Implicit/nondeclarative:** forms of memory that cannot be explicitly articulated, including muscle and sensory recollections
    - ▪ **Procedural memory:** riding a bike, playing the piano
    - ▪ **Priming:** previous experience influences interpretation and response to a new circumstance (ex: You listen to a radio program about bears. Later, when hearing the word "bare," you imagine a bear.)
- ☐ **Retrieval** of memories:
  - **Recall:** conscious and deliberate retrieval of info (ex: taking a test).
  - **Recognition:** identifying information as familiar; much easier than full recall
  - **Relearning:** Relearned information is much more rapidly stored and readily recalled (ex: it takes you less time to learn enzyme mechanics for the MCAT because you already learned it once in class).
  - **Retrieval cues:** processes and signals that aid in retrieval
    - ○ **Context effect:** enhanced retrieval based on surroundings (ex: when you can't remember your password until you start to type it; remembering events from childhood when you visit your elementary school)
    - ○ **False alarm:** when recalling a list of words, reporting a related word that was not originally present
    - ○ **State effect:** enhanced recall when you are in the same state (happy, tired, drunk) that you were in when you encoded the info (ex: when you feel like you're going to cry, you start remembering all the other things that ever made you feel like crying)

- o **Spreading activation**: pieces of information are connected in various ways, such that activation of one locus of the network activates other loci
- **The role of emotion in retrieving memories:** Retrieval cues can be in any sensory modality.
  - o Smell has the strongest link to memory.
  - o Emotionally rich events, facts, or sensory experiences are more likely to be stored, and more easily retrieved.
- ☐ **Forgetting**: when memories are lost, faded, or altered
  - **Aging** and memory:
    - o Implicit memory stays about the same throughout life (bike riding). Recognition memory is stable. Semantic memory improves until age 60 (verbal skills). Crystallized intelligence improves. Emotional reasoning improves. Recall declines. Episodic memory declines (older memories more stable, new memories become more difficult). Processing speed declines. Divided attention becomes more difficult.
  - Memory dysfunctions:
    - o **Alzheimer's disease**: a form of dementia arising from gradual decay and death of neurons and shrinking of the cortex. Initial defects in memory encoding and retrieval, progressing to include cognitive, language, and sensory impairments.
      - ▪ Involves buildup of plaques, or clumps of protein, in the brain.
      - ▪ Terminal
    - o **Korsakoff's syndrome**: caused by thiamine (vitamin B1) deficiency due to malnutrition, especially in conjunction with alcoholism
      - ▪ Typically begins with motor dysfunction
      - ▪ In advanced Korsakoff's, patients confabulate, or make up stories, to fill memory gaps.
      - ▪ Treatable, not terminal
  - **Decay**: Memories decay and can be lost due to insufficient encoding or infrequent recall. Things learned quickly tend to decay more rapidly than things learned over a long period of time.
  - **Interference**: Learning new information can interfere with existing memories, and vice versa.
    - o **Proactive** interference/learning: Past memories interfere with learning new, generally related, information.
    - o **Retroactive** interference/learning: Learning new information interferes with storage or recall of previously-learned information.
  - **Memory construction**: Memories are not static, but rather are modified each time we recall them, and change over time (ex: your favorite

anecdote gets more extreme and embellished with each telling, such that you no longer recall the events accurately).
- **Source monitoring**: process of assigning sources to memories. Not encoded in the same way as the facts and events themselves (ex: you can remember that someone told you they liked a certain restaurant, but can't remember who).

☐ **Changes in synaptic connections** underlie memory and learning.
- **Neural plasticity**: the process by which synapses strengthen or weaken over time. Can include the creation of new connections and/or changes in quantity of neurotransmitters and other chemical factors used. Plasticity is highest in children.
- **Long-term potentiation**: the physiological mechanism by which we learn and remember
  o A neural plasticity process in which neuronal connections are strengthened with repeated use
  o With repeated action potentials from one neuron to a second neuron, the same pre-synaptic signal becomes association with a larger and larger post-synaptic potential. These changes can last for a few minutes, and up to months or years.

☐ **Emotion** and its role in biology and behavior:
- Emotion has three components: physiological, cognitive, and behavioral.
- **The seven universal emotions**: fear, anger, happiness, surprise, joy, disgust, sadness
- **Adaptive role of emotion**: Emotional interpretation also involves cultural, learning factors.
- **Theories** of emotion:
  o **James-Lange theory**: physiological response → emotion (you feel happy because you are smiling)
  o **Cannon-Bard theory:** Physiological response and emotion occur simultaneously; one does not cause the other. Stimulus (cute cat picture) causes simultaneous smiling and feelings of happiness
  o **Schachter-Singer theory**: People interpret physiological arousal. Labeling of an emotion depends on context (ex: drink too much coffee, feel nervous, interpret nervousness as due to work rather than to caffeine alone).
- **Limbic system**: Brain regions involved in generation and experience of emotion:
  o **Hippocampus**: converts short term to long term memory
  o **Hypothalamus**: "below the thalamus" regulates autonomic nervous system (sympathetic and parasympathetic). Adrenaline, epinephrine, norepinephrine. Hunger, thirst, other drives.

- o **Amygdala**: fear, anger, violence, anxiety
- o **Thalamus**: sensory relay station
- Emotions can trigger autonomic nervous system responses (ex: emotion of fear triggers sympathetic nervous system). These ANS responses are the physiological markers of emotion (ex: hyperventilation, dry mouth, flushed face, etc.).
- ☐ **The nature of stress**: a feeling of pressure that can be positive or negative
  - **Appraisal**: first step of generation of stress is a cognitive assessment of a situation for potential threat or challenge
  - Different types of **stressors:**
    - o Significant life change: job loss, going to college, marriage, etc.
    - o Cataclysmic events: unpredictable, large-scale, universally appraised as threatening
    - o Daily hassles: seemingly minor negative events (forgetting keys, car breaking down, etc.), higher for disadvantaged groups
    - o Ambient stressors: pollution, noise, crowding
  - Effects of stress on psychological functions: can lead to anxiety, difficulty concentrating, negative thoughts, and memory problem
- ☐ **Stress outcomes** and responses to stressors:
  - **Physiological** responses:
    - o Autonomic nervous system: Stress can result in temporary or prolonged activation of the sympathetic nervous system, as well as hormonal changes.
      - Sympathetic: fight-or-flight. Increases heart rate, increases respiration, peripheral vasoconstriction, stops digestion, stops immune function, stops ovulation
      - Endocrine system: adrenal medulla releases catecholemines (epinephrine and norepinephrine), major communicators for sympathetic response; adrenal cortex releases cortisol, steroid hormone that redistributes glucose and represses immune system
    - o **General adaptation syndrome** (GAS): a characterization of how the body responds to stress over time
      - Phase 1: alarm phase. Stress reaction kicks in.
      - Phase 2: resistance phase. Body uses up reserves.
      - Phase 3: exhaustion. If there is no recovery, resources get depleted. Tissue damage occurs.
    - o Increased risk of heart disease, depression
  - **Emotional** responses:
    - o **Depression/anhedonia**, which may be associated with dysfunction of the anterior cingulate

- o **Learned helplessness**: loss of ability to identify coping mechanisms and respond to stress due to a perceived inability to influence or control your circumstances.
  - o **Anger** can be a behavioral response to stress
  - o **Anxiety**, including anxiety about relatively minor or typical activities and behaviors.
  - o **Addiction** can also be a response to stress, resulting from an attempt to modulate one's emotional responses to stress by consuming substances such as alcohol and drugs.
- • **Behavioral** responses:
  - o Atrophy in hippocampus and frontal lobe
☐ **Managing stress** with approaches including exercise, relaxation, and spirituality:
  - • **Perceived control:** less control = more stress
  - • Manage stress by taking control in areas of life.
    - o Exercise, meditation, religious beliefs
    - o Cognitive flexibility; reframe approach to stress if its not working
  - • **Optimism** in your perspective can reduce stress.
  - • **Social support** from family, friends, colleagues, etc. can assist in the management of stress.

Behavior

☐ **Theories of personality** are different approaches to explaining the relatively persistent components of our behavior and cognition: motivations, attitudes, identity, etc.
  - • **Psychoanalytic perspective** (Freud): unconscious desires, often rooted in childhood experiences, determine personality
    - o **Fixation** at a particular stage of development influences adult personality.
      - ▪ Ex: "Anal retentive" is a phrase that comes from Freud, who thought that if you as a child resisted the urge to defecate, you were fixated in the "anal" stage of development (toilet training), and would therefore show what some still call "anal" personality characteristics as an adult: fastidious, controlling, and organized.

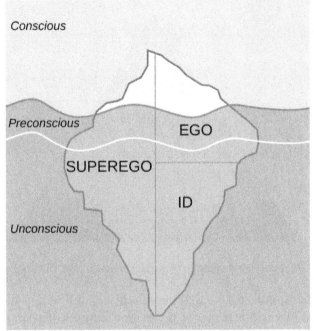

Figure 69: *Freud's theory of mind.*

- o Three components of the mind:
    - ▪ **Id:** Driven to immediately gratify all urges and instincts. Unconscious and largest part of the mind.
    - ▪ **Superego:** Moral compass. Part conscious, part unconscious.
    - ▪ **Ego:** part thoughtful, realistic, and judging. Seeks long-term gratification of more complex desires, and acts as a mediator between the id and the superego. Part conscious, part unconscious.
- • **Humanistic perspective:** people have free will, and can actively work toward achieving their full potential (self-actualizing)
    - o Assumes people are inherently good, and want to improve themselves.
    - o **Maslow's hierarchy of needs**: We fulfill our psychological needs in a series of consecutive steps, starting with basic survival needs, and continuing up to the goal of self-actualization.
        - ▪ From lowest to highest: physiological needs, safety, love and belonging, self-esteem, and self- actualization.

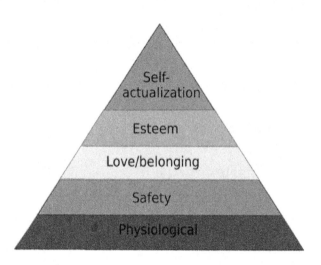

Figure 70*: Maslow's hierarchy of needs (Image credit: FireflySixtySeven).*

- **Trait perspective** says that personality is defined by the presence or absence of various traits, or persistent features of your psychology (conscientiousness, confidence, introversion, etc.).
    - o Ex: The Meyers-Briggs personality test defines personality with four letters that correspond to traits (ex: ENTJ is extroverted, Intuitive, thinking, and judging).
- **Social cognitive perspective** says that your personality is determined by your social environment and experiences.
    - o Ex: If you are raised in a family of loud, argumentative people, you are likely to be loud and argumentative yourself.
- **Biological perspective** says that your personality is inherited from your parents and encoded in your genes.
    - o Ex: You are shy because your parents passed their own "shy" genes to you.
- **Behaviorist perspective** says that your personality is determined by the behaviors that you engage in (as opposed to your internal thoughts or emotional states). Your personality develops like other learned behaviors, from reinforcement of certain behaviors, influenced by rewards and punishments.
- ☐ **Situational approach** to explaining behavior says that your personality is not completely fixed, but rather continuously influenced and molded by the situations you are in. As a result, it is difficult or impossible to generalize a person's behavior in one situation to their behavior in another situation.
    - Ex: You speak and behave differently around your grandmother than you do around your friends.

- **Attribution of behavior** can be either internal (due to a person's intrinsic traits, feelings, etc.) or external (due to a person's situation or environment).
  - o Internal attribution: You got in a fight because you are an aggressive person.
  - o External attribution: You got in a fight because you were in a hostile, threatening environment.
  - o We tend to attribute our own behavior externally, and the behavior of others internally.
    - Ex: I said something awkward at that party because it was an awkward place and the people there were not friendly (external). The guy I met there said something awkward, but that's because he's a weird, awkward person (internal).
- ☐ **Psychological disorders**: classifications, causes, and consequences:
  - **Biomedical approach** treats psychological disorders as purely biological, and therefore caused by abnormalities of structure and/or function of the nervous system. **Biopsychosocial approach** treats psychological disorders as a consequence of multiple factors, including biology, psychology, and social experiences or environment.
  - **Rates of psychological disorders** may be artificially low due to the social stigma associated with them, which may discourage reporting, acknowledgement, and seeking of treatment.
    - o Approximately 25 percent of adults meet criteria for one or more psychological disorders
    - o Approximately 5 percent of adults will have a serious mental illness at some point in their life.
- ☐ **Types of psychological disorders** and their characteristics:
  - **Anxiety disorders** are associated with abnormally pronounced, continuous, and disruptive feelings of worry.
    - o Includes phobias, panic disorders
  - **Obsessive-compulsive disorder** is characterized by:
    - o Obsessions, such as fear of germs or of leaving a door unlocked
    - o Compulsions, or repetitive and ritualistic behaviors (turning lights on and off repetitively, excessive hand washing)
    - o Intrusive, repetitive thoughts or ideas, as well as strong feelings of anxiety and/or guilt
  - **Trauma- and stressor-related disorders** are characterized by a stressful event that leads to pronounced and persistent disturbances of mood, emotion, and/or behavior (ex: post-traumatic stress disorder).
  - **Somatic symptom and related disorders** are characterized by the experience of symptoms suggesting physical illness, but without an

associated physical abnormality or explanation (ex: pain disorder, body dysmorphic disorder).

- **Bipolar** and related disorders are characterized by alternating extremes of mood (depression and mania).
- **Major depressive disorder** is associated with distress or disability due pervasive and persistent low mood, low self-esteem, and loss of ability to experience pleasure from experiences that were previously pleasurable.
  - To be considered a major depressive episode, symptoms must persist for a minimum of two weeks.
- **Personality disorders** are a diverse class of conditions characterized by personality traits that are considered to be outside accepted societal norms (ex: psychopathy).
  - Personality disorders differ across cultures due to different standards for normative behavior.
- ☐ **Biological basis** of nervous system disorders:
  - **Schizophrenia** is characterized by:
    - Positive symptoms, such as hallucinations or delusions
    - Negative symptoms, such as flat affect or reduced pleasure in everyday activities
    - Cognitive symptoms, such as trouble sustaining attentions, disruptions of working memory, or reduced ability to make decisions (executive functioning)
    - Onset in late teens and early twenties
    - There is evidence that schizophrenia runs in families, suggesting genetic and/or social factors.
    - Neuroanatomical differences: Enlargement of brain ventricles, suggesting cerebral atrophy, and thinner-than-normal prefrontal cortex
    - Neurotransmitter differences: abnormal dopamine activity in the ventral tegmental (VT) area of the brain, and the associated mesocorticolimbic pathway
  - **Depression** is associated with:
    - Decreased activity in the frontal lobe and the limbic system
    - Abnormal blood concentrations of stress hormones
    - Abnormal activity of serotonin and dopamine
    - Early-life traumatic experiences and genetic factors may also contribute to depression
  - **Alzheimer's disease** is characterized by progressive memory loss in older adults.
    - Plaques of amyloid beta peptides form and multiply in the brain, leading to destruction of neurons.

- **Parkinson's disease** is a degenerative disorder of the central nervous system, primarily affecting motor functions. Initially, shaking, slowness, and altered gait are observed. The condition advances to include cognitive and behavioral symptoms.
  - o Due to death of dopamine cells in the substantia nigra
- **Stem cell–based therapy** to regenerate neurons in the central nervous system is a potential approach to treatment of psychological disorders, especially degenerative diseases such as Parkinson's and Alzheimer's. Stem cells could replace dysfunctional or atrophied cells to restore critical functions or grow new pathways.
- ☐ **Motivation** is derived from a variety of factors, from satisfying basic needs to achieving long-term goals (like studying for the MCAT).
  - **Instinct** is the most basic motivation. It is biologically determined and difficult or impossible to override.
  - **Arousal** is an optimum level of excitement that we want to reach. Some people seek lower levels of arousal than others (ex: crossword puzzles versus skydiving).
  - **Drives** are biological desires that we are motivated to satisfy.
    - o **Negative feedback systems** are at work in the development and satiation of drives (ex: you are hungry, so you eat, but you only continue eating until you are no longer hungry).
  - **Needs** can range from basic (food, shelter) to complex (becoming a doctor).
- ☐ **Theories of motivation** and its influence on human behavior:
  - **Drive reduction theory** states that we are motivated to reduce various drives (hunger, thirst, self-esteem) through your behavior.
    - o Ex: The hunger drive motivates us to seek food. Once we are full, we are no longer driven to find food (and therefore that drive has been reduced).
  - **Incentive theory** states that we are motivated by the reinforcement of behaviors with rewards.
    - o Ex: You are motivated to do well at work so that you can get promoted and make more money.
    - o Positive reinforcement only; no negative reinforcement
  - **Cognitive theory** states that motivation is the product of conscious cognitive processes, including knowledge, experience, and expectations.
    - o You are motivated to do well at work because you know that this can lead to a promotion. You therefore expect that if you do well, you can get promoted.
  - **Need-based theory** states that you are motivated to satisfy a series of hierarchical needs, starting with the most basic (food, shelter) and

progressing to more complex needs (self-esteem, life satisfaction). You cannot pursue higher needs until the more basic ones are satisfied.

☐ **Attitudes** are learned tendencies. They are less constant/more changeable than personality, broader and less changeable than opinions or preferences. Components of attitudes include:

- **Cognitive**: conscious and logical thought supporting an attitude (ex: You have a negative attitude toward natural supplements because you have read that they are poorly regulated and rarely effective.)
- **Affective**: how you feel about something (ex: You don't like heights because they make you afraid you are going to fall.)
- **Behavioral**: the actions you take due to an attitude (ex: You have a positive attitude toward a political candidate, so you put their campaign sticker on your car.)

☐ **Attitude and behavior** are interdependent.

- **Behavior influences attitudes** because what you do can act to reinforce or change your attitudes.
  - ○ **Foot-in-the-door phenomenon:** You can get people to agree to something big by first getting them to agree to something small. (ex: You are asked first to sign a petition supporting a cause. If you sign, you will be more likely to say "yes" later when asked to make a donation.)
  - ○ **Role-playing effects:** If you act out a behavior associated with a certain attitude, you may start to take on that attitude for yourself. Also called, "drinking the Kool-Aid."
- **Attitudes influence behavior** because you may choose to act or not act based on your attitude toward something.
  - ○ Ex: Two political candidates knock on your door, one Democrat and one Republican. If you have a pro-Democrat attitude, you are likely to behave more positively toward the Democrat than the Republican.
- **Cognitive dissonance** is a state of mental discomfort that arises from holding two or more contradictory beliefs or attitudes at the same time, or from being presented with new information that contradicts a belief or attitude that you already hold.
  - ○ Humans tend to act to resolve cognitive dissonance in various ways, such as by denying the veracity of conflicting information, or changing a belief or attitude to resolve the conflict.

Social Processes

☐ **The presence of others can affect individual behavior** through several mechanisms:

- **Social facilitation:** People tend to behave differently when others are around than when they are alone.
  - o In general, performance is improved by the presence of others for practiced tasks; and worsened for novel tasks.
- **Deindividuation**: People can lose self-awareness in groups, such that their actions are driven by the group rather than by their internal beliefs or drives.
  - o Ex: In the Milgram experiment, people were told by an authority figure to push a button, and that when they did so, they would be administering stronger and stronger electric shocks to someone in the next room. Most people in the experiment continued to do as they were told, even when hearing (fake) screams from the next room, and even when they were told that the shocks were strong enough to kill the person.
- **Bystander effect:** The larger the number of bystanders or observers of a victim in need of help, the less likely it is that anyone will help.
  - o Ex: A homeless man has died on a busy street, but it takes several hours for anyone to notice or call for help, presumably because each individual thinks that someone else is sure to help.
- **Social loafing:** People tend to exert less effort when working on a task as a group.
  - o Ex: That person in every group project who doesn't do anything because they know that they can get a good grade from the work of the others in the group.
- **Social control:** People tend to comply with the accepted norms and values of their social group. Social control can be exerted through means including laws, sanctions, rewards, and other positive and negative reinforcers.
- **Peer pressure:** People tend to conform to behavioral expectations due to the influence of the shared ideas, beliefs, and behaviors of their peers.
- **Conformity**: People tend to match their own attitudes, behaviors, and beliefs to those in their social group. Conformity can result from subconscious influence (when you and your close friend accidentally wear the same outfit on the same day) or overt pressure (bullying).
- **Obedience:** People tend to comply with instructions from those they perceive to be in authority.
  - o Ex: In the Stanford Prison Experiment, a group of college students were assigned roles of either "prisoners" or "guards." The guards obeyed orders to the point that their behavior became violent. The study was shut down.

- ☐ **Group decision-making** is often different from the decision-making of individuals. Factors include:
  - • **Group polarization:** Groups tend to make decisions that are more extreme than the initial perspectives of the individual members. Additionally, if an individual with a moderate belief has a discussion with others who hold the same moderate belief, that belief is likely to become stronger and/or more extreme.
    - ○ If everyone you follow on Facebook has the same views as you, your views are likely to become more entrenched and/or more extreme.
  - • **Groupthink:** When a group of people make suboptimal decisions out of a desire to avoid conflict or maintain conformity.
    - ○ Ex: If the same group of people run a company for a long time, the quality of their decisions may start to decline, as their sense of loyalty to each other can begin to override their willingness to share controversial ideas, challenge their peers, etc.
- ☐ **Social norms** are the values, customs, and behaviors that people do and expect from others that participate in their culture. Norms vary significantly across cultures (ex: In the US, it is a social norm to greet friends with a hug or handshake, while in Southern Europe, it is a social norm to greet friends with a kiss on the cheek.).
  - • **Sanctions** are negative reinforcement behaviors representing social disapproval of a deviation from a norm. Sanctions include shame, criticism, ridicule, etc.
  - • **Folkways** are norms of everyday social interactions. Violation of folkways may inspire mild disapproval from others, but are unlikely to be associated with formal punishments.
    - ○ Ex: greeting an acquaintance you see on the street, dressing appropriately for a meeting, engaging in small talk
  - • **Mores** are social norms that are more significant than folkways, but less significant than taboos. Mores include widely shared ideas about right and wrong. Mores are sometimes associated with formal negative consequences, but not always.
    - ○ Ex: Lying would be a violation of a social more. Some lies (like to the IRS) can result in formal punishment, while others may only result in social disapproval.
  - • **Taboos** are violations of social norm that inspire severe punishment and disgust. Taboos are generally considered to be unacceptable to society at large, transcending cultural variations.
    - ○ Ex: incest, murder

- **Anomie** is a breakdown of social norms in a society, such that individuals do not feel social bonds with others or comply with expectations or social values.
  - Anomie is thought to result from a mismatch between individual's social beliefs and norms and the structure of their social conditions and enforcement mechanisms.
- ☐ **Deviance**, or non-normative behavior, is the violation of social norms.
  - **Differential association theory:** People learn social norms from those around them. Therefore, if someone appears to show deviant behavior, it is likely that they are behaving in a way that they learned from their social group.
    - Ex: People become criminals by learning from other criminals.
    - Deviant behavior could be mediated by moving an individual into a social group that practices normative behaviors.
  - **Labeling theory**: People's behavior is influenced by the language used to describe or classify them.
    - Ex: If people say you are a "criminal," that can become part of your identity and therefore influence your behavior. Therefore, some advocates for criminal justice reform call for an end to the use of such terms.
  - **Strain theory**: Social structure may pressure people into deviant behavior.
    - Ex: People may choose to cheat on tests in response to social pressures they feel to consistently make straight As.
- ☐ **Socialization** is the process by which social norms are learned, taught, inherited, and molded over time.
  - **Agents of socialization** are social structures or devices that work to influence individual's perspectives and behaviors.
    - Family, mass media, peers, workplace, etc.
    - Your political beliefs have developed over time. They may have initially been informed by the views of your family, but were then shaped by the views of your peers, by what you read in various publications, or by the views of those who live or work near you.
  - Other examples of collective behavior include fads, mass hysteria, and riots.

Psychological Change

- ☐ **Learning** is the process through which experience changes our behavior and knowledge
  - Basic mechanism: habituation to repeated stimuli, and dishabituation to stimuli that are not repeated

177

- Stimuli can be in the form of knowledge, behaviors, emotions, preferences, etc.
☐ **Associative learning:** learning through repeated association of two or more stimuli. Includes classical conditioning and operant conditioning.
  - **Classical conditioning** (Pavlov's dog): If you always ring a bell right before feeding your dog, your dog will start salivating when you ring the bell, because he knows that means he's about to get food. The process by which a neutral stimulus becomes a conditioned stimulus.
    - **Neutral stimulus***:* a stimulus with no intrinsic connection to the response of interest (bell-ringing pre-conditioning)
    - **Conditioned stimulus***:* a neutral stimulus that initiates a conditioned response due to associative learning/classical conditioning (bell-ringing post-conditioning)
    - **Unconditioned stimulus:** a stimulus that produces a response because of its intrinsic properties (dog food)
    - **Conditioned response***:* a behavioral response that results from a learned connection (salivating when a bell rings)
    - **Unconditioned response:** a natural behavioral response to some stimulus (salivating for food)
    - **Acquisition:** learning an association between two stimuli
    - **Extinction:** The disappearance of a learned behavior when the association is not reinforced
    - **Generalization and discrimination:** Stimuli that are similar to conditioned stimuli tend to produce a similar response (generalization); dissimilar stimuli produce dissimilar responses (discrimination)
      - Ex: If your cat responds to the sound of you shaking a jar of treats, they might also show some response to similar sounds, like shaking a box of cereal (generalization). However, after responding to the cereal a few times and not getting a treat, your cat will learn to discriminate between the two sounds.
    - **Spontaneous recovery:** Sometimes, conditioning that has gone extinct reappears. Nobody knows why.
☐ **Operant conditioning:** consequences influence behavior. Learning occurs through positive and/or negative reinforcement and/or punishment.
  - **Shaping:** learning by reinforcement of a series of successive steps that lead up to a goal behavior (ex: To teach a dog to sit, you start by rewarding the dog when it sits on it own, and then teach the dog the connection between the word "sit," and the behavior of sitting.)
  - **Reinforcement and punishment:** positive or negative consequences that can lead to behavior change

- o **Positive reinforcement:** a reward is added to increase a desired behavior
  - Ex: You are making bad grades. Your parents say they will increase your allowance (reward) if you start making good grades, so you are motivated to work harder in school (desired behavior).
- o **Negative reinforcement:** a reward is taken away to increase a desired behavior
  - Ex: Your room is a mess. Your parents say that you aren't allowed to watch TV (reward) until you clean your room, so you are motivated to clean more (desired behavior).
- o **Positive punishment:** a punishment is added to decrease an undesired behavior
  - Ex: You drive too fast (undesired behavior). A cop pulls you over and gives you a ticket (punishment), so that you will be discouraged from speeding in the future.
- o **Negative punishment:** a reward is taken away to decrease an undesired behavior
  - Ex: You get in a fight at school (undesired behavior). Your parents say that now you can't go to the prom (reward), so that you will be discouraged from getting into a fight again.
- **Primary vs. conditional reinforcement**: Primary reinforcers have biological value and do not require any learning (ex: food, pleasure), while conditional reinforcers have conditioned, or learned, value (ex: money, grades).
- **Reinforcement** schedules:
  - o **Fixed ratio:** a behavior is reinforced after every x number of occurrence (ex: a salesperson gets a bonus for every ten cars sold)
  - o **Variable ratio:** a behavior is reinforced after an inconsistent and arbitrary number of occurrences (ex: slot machines)
  - o **Fixed interval:** a behavior is reinforced after a fixed amount of time has passed (ex: paid by the hour)
  - o **Variable interval:** a behavior is reinforced after inconsistent and arbitrary lengths of time (ex: fishing)

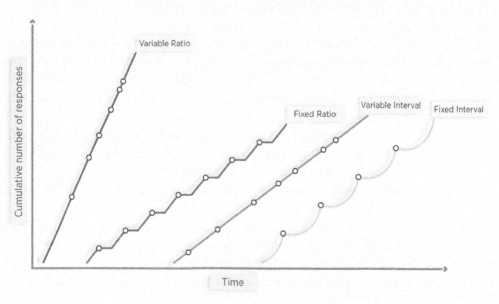

Figure 71*: Comparing reinforcement schedules.*

- **Escape vs. avoidance learning:** Escape learning occurs when a learned, operant behavior is used to escape an ongoing, unpleasant stimulus (ex: quickly leaving a building where a painfully loud alarm is going off, even if it's freezing cold out). Avoidance learning occurs when there is a signal that precedes the onset of an unpleasant stimulus, such that the signal leads to escape behavior before the unpleasant stimulus is actually introduced. Avoidance persists even if the unpleasant stimulus is removed (ex: When you drive by a police car, you slow down, because reducing speed is a behavior to avoid a speeding ticket. You keep doing this, even if you haven't gotten a ticket in years.).
- **Cognitive processes** play a role in associative learning.
  - Motivation, expectation, and experience can influence the quality and/or speed of learning.
- **Biological processes** play a role associative learning.
  - Biological predispositions: Not all organisms can learn the same kinds of things, as most learning has some prerequisite biological tools or predispositions (ex: Cats can't learn to speak English because they lack the vocal structures to do so.).
  - Instinctive drift: A conditioned response that does not align with instinctual responses will not last long, and behavior will drift back to instinct.

- ☐ **Observational learning** is the process by which new behaviors are learned by observing others engaging in that behavior. Monkey see, monkey do.
  - • **Modeling:** Because of observational learning, children's learning is significantly influenced by the behaviors being modeled by other children and adults around them.
    - o Individual behavior may be, in some cases, partly attributable to observational learning (ex: a study showing a link between antisocial television content and antisocial behavior).
  - • **Biological factors** in observational learning:
    - o **Mirror neurons:** neurons that are activated both when you do something, and when you watch someone else doing the same thing
      - ▪ Emotion: Mirror neurons may also underlie empathy, in which you feel an emotion yourself when you observe another experiencing it.
- ☐ **Attitudes and behaviors can change** over time in response to a variety of social, cognitive, and biological forces. Several theories are used to describe this process:
  - • **Elaboration likelihood model** (ELM) is a model for how people are persuaded by the presentation of new information or arguments. It includes two routes for information processing:
    - o **Central route:** People are persuaded through conscious, thoughtful consideration of new information and its impact on a person's attitudes.
      - ▪ Can result in long-lasting behavior change
      - ▪ Used when the recipient of the message is interested and able to engage with the message
      - ▪ Ex: comparing med schools based on the MSAR, which provides impartial information about school's priorities, statistics, etc.
    - o **Peripheral route:** People reach conclusions based on positive or negative cues (credibility, charisma) that are unrelated to the content of the message being received.
      - ▪ Attitude changes are less likely, and fleeting.
      - ▪ Used when the recipient of the message has limited interest and/or ability to actively process the message
      - ▪ Ex: You choose a med school because you heard a presentation about it from an attractive person, and you like attractive people.
  - • **Social cognitive theory** states that people change their attitudes or behaviors based on what they learn by watching the behaviors of others, and the consequences of those behaviors.
    - o Ex: You have a negative attitude toward android phones. Then, a close friend of yours gets an android phone and you see that the phone is

reliable and fun, and that your friend enjoys the phone. This changes your attitude toward android phones.

- Other factors that affect attitude change:
  - **Changing your behavior** can influence your attitudes (drinking the Kool-Aid).
  - **Characteristics of the message** and the target of the message also matter for producing attitude change.
    - Ex: Advertisements targeting men are less effective at influencing women.
  - **Changing social factors** such as moving to a new town, a new school, or meeting a new group of friends can also lead to attitude changes.

The Self

- ☐ **Self-concept/self-identity** comprises a collection of beliefs you have about yourself. It is the answer to the question, "Who am I?"
  - **Existential self:** awareness that you are separate from others
  - **Categorical self:** the categories that you consider yourself to belong to
  - **Self-esteem:** the respect you have for yourself; feeds into self-identity
  - **Self-efficacy:** the confidence you have in your own ability to accomplish your goals; feeds into self-identity
    - People with high self-efficacy tend to view challenges as opportunities, and recover quickly from setbacks. People with low self-efficacy tend to avoid challenges, and are affected more significantly by setbacks.
  - **Locus of control:** your beliefs about the causes of events in your life
    - **Internal locus of control:** You believe that outcomes of events in your life are attributable to yourself (ex: you make good grades because you study a lot).
    - **External locus of control:** You believe the outcomes of events in your life are attributable to forces outside of yourself (ex: you make good grades because the tests you take are easy and professors like you).
- ☐ **Social identity** is the collection of group memberships that define you, and how you identify yourself in relation to various social groups.
- ☐ **Different types of identities**: Identity can be composed of essentially infinite types. It is whatever characteristics or features of self that people believe contribute to their self-identity. Prominent examples include:
  - Race/ethnicity, gender, age, sexual orientation, class, education, culture
- ☐ **Theories of identity development** and characteristics:

- **Gender identity** refers to the gender role that you identify with, as well as the gender that others perceive you to be. Gender identity can be influenced by social and cultural factors (ex: religion, political beliefs, etc.). Gender identity is distinct from biological gender, as some people identify as a different gender than their biological gender.
- **Moral reasoning (Kohlberg):** Moral reasoning depends on your level of cognitive development. As a child, you have a relatively simplistic view of right and wrong, but over time, you develop more nuanced understanding. Not all adults achieve the highest level of moral reasoning.
  - **Kohlberg's theory includes three levels, each with two sub-**levels:
  - **Pre-conventional** (children) is moral reasoning based on your wants and your experiences.
    - Obedience and punishment: interpretation of right and wrong is based on reward or punishment (drawing on the walls is bad because it led to a time-out)
    - Self-interest: interpretation of right and wrong is based on gains and losses for the individual (You scratch my back, and I'll scratch yours)
  - **Conventional** (adolescents) is moral reasoning based on adherence to externally imposed rules or expectations.
    - **Conformity:** interpretation of right and wrong is based on what is acceptable in your social group (it's ok to smoke because my friends are doing it)
    - **Authority:** interpretation of right and wrong based on obedience to laws and social conventions, and the individual's duty to uphold them. This is the highest stage that most of society achieves.
  - **Post-conventional** (some adults) is moral reasoning based on abstract beliefs and principles (ethics).
    - **Social contract:** moral reasoning based on a belief in a social contract (ex: the greatest good for the greatest number of people)
    - **Universal ethics:** moral reasoning based on abstract, universal ethical principles. So few achieve this stage that Kohlberg had difficulty finding people who qualified for this level of reasoning.
- **Psychosexual (Freud):** Early childhood experiences determine aspects of your identity. If you pass through the five stages of development successfully, you will have a healthy, "normal" personality. If you become "fixated" in one stage, you will exhibit a set of "abnormal" personality traits specific to the stage in which fixation occurred.
  - **Oral stage:** (birth to 1 year old): The mouth is the focus of gratification (e.g., breast feeding). You are motivated purely by seeking pleasure.

- o **Anal stage** (1-3 years old): The anus is the focus of gratification (e.g., toilet training). You learn to delay gratification.
- o **Phallic stage** (3-6 years old): genitalia are the focus of gratification. You become aware of your body and the bodies of those around you. You learn the difference between male and female.
- o **Latency stage** (6-onset of puberty): consolidation of identity formed in previous stages. You begin deriving gratification from secondary sources (school, friendship, etc.).
- o **Genital stage** (puberty-adult): genitalia are the focus of gratification, but through consensual adult encounters. Independence from your parents. You derive gratification primarily from secondary sources (intellect, friendship, responsibilities, etc.).
- **Social (Erikson):** The development of your identity is heavily influenced by your culture, language, parents, peers, socioeconomic status, etc., and all influence your identity development.
  - o **Erickson** described social development with a series of psychosocial crises, which, if resolved, result in the development of a particular virtue:
    - **Trust vs. mistrust** (infant): Can I trust anyone? (hope)
    - **Autonomy vs. shame and doubt** (early childhood): Is it ok to act like myself? (free will)
    - **Initiative vs. guilt** (preschool): Is it ok for me to start doing things on my own, without my family? (purpose)
    - **Industry vs. inferiority** (school-going childhood): Will I be able to survive out in the world on my own? (competence)
    - **Identity vs. role-confusion** (adolescence): Who am I and who will I become? (fidelity)
    - **Intimacy vs. isolation** (early adulthood): Can I experience romantic love? (love)
    - **Generativity vs. stagnation** (adulthood): Can I make my life meaningful? (care)
    - **Ego identity vs. despair** (maturity): Did I live a good life? (wisdom)
- ☐ **Cultural and social factors** influence identity formation.
  - • Influence of individuals:
    - o **Imitation:** We experiment with identities by imitating those around us whom we admire or relate to. This is the simplest form of social influence on behavior, and begins soon after birth.
      - Ex: If you stick your tongue out at a baby, they are likely to stick their tongue out at you.

- o **Looking-glass self:** Your identity is influenced by your understanding of how others perceive your identity in interpersonal interactions. You see yourself the way others see you.
- o **Role-taking**: Individuals take on different roles throughout their lifetime, and these roles can become a part of, and influence, our identity.
  - Ex: The oldest child in a family may take on a parental role, caring for their younger siblings, after a divorce.
- Influence of groups:
  - o **Reference group** is a group that an individual belongs to or identifies with (ex: Democrat, Southerner, Red Sox fan). People tend to look to their reference groups when forming new ideas or attitudes, or to reinforce their own views.

Social Thinking

- ☐ **Attributional processes** are those by which we decide (often with mental shortcuts) the underlying cause of our own behavior, and the behavior of those around us.
  - **Fundamental attribution error:** We tend to overemphasize intrinsic characteristics in our assessment of others, rather than considering the influence of others' circumstances.
    - o When assessing negative behaviors in ourselves, we tend to overattribute them to external and environmental factors.
    - o Ex: When someone is rude to you, you are more likely to conclude "That is a rude person," than "that person must be having a stressful day."
  - **Culture** influences how people attribute behaviors.
    - o Fundamental attribution error is more pronounced in individualistic societies (USA).
    - o Collectivist cultures are more likely to attribute behaviors, including their own, to external factors.
  - **Self-serving bias** is the tendency to attribute successes to intrinsic factors (I got into med school because I am smart) and failures to external factors (I didn't get into med school because the process was biased against me).
- ☐ **Self-perceptions** shape our perceptions of others. If we perceive ourselves poorly in one trait, we tend to perceive others as over performing on that same trait. We also evaluate others relative to our values, experiences, knowledge, etc.
  - Ex: If you feel like you are not doing well in school, it can start to seem like everybody else is doing great and you're the only one who is not.

- **Perceptions of the environment** shape our perceptions of others.
  - Ex: If you see a guy in a suit working in a big fancy office, you might conclude that he is important and successful. However, this perception is heavily influenced by the environment in which you saw the guy.
- **Prejudice**, or unfavorable opinions of individuals based solely on their membership in a certain group, arises from several processes:
  - **Power** imbalance among groups can strengthen in-group vs. out-group perceptions, contributing to the development of prejudice.
  - **Prestige**, or the relatively unquantifiable factors that contribute to people's success (ex: social connections, knowing how to play golf) also contribute, because elements of "prestige" can enable social and financial advancement.
  - **Class**, or stratified segments of a society based primarily on income, creates in-group vs. out-group perceptions, contributing to the development of prejudice.
  - **Prejudice includes both social and emotional aspects.** Socially, it can include ideas about the relationships among social groups, their values, and characteristics. Emotionally, prejudice can include feelings of fear, hatred, inferiority, superiority, etc., toward other groups.
- **Stigma** is a particular trait or circumstance that is considered socially undesirable, and can therefore inspire prejudice or negative behaviors from others.
  - Ex: If a certain neighborhood is widely believed to be dangerous and undesirable, the residents of that neighborhood can become stigmatized, such that people falsely assume that they, too, must be dangerous and undesirable.
- **Cultural relativism** is the belief that cultures are different, but no one culture is superior to others. It is therefore inappropriate to assess one culture using the standards or values of another.
  - Ex: Western and Eastern societies show significant cultural differences. For example, Western societies tend to be more individualistic, while eastern societies tend to be more collective. One is not superior to the other, rather, they represent equally valid cultural structures.
- **Ethnocentrism** is the belief that one's culture is superior to other cultures, and therefore other cultures can be assessed using the customs and characteristics of your own as the measuring stick. Ethnocentrism is another process that can lead to prejudice against cultures that are different from your own.
  - Ex: Eastern societies lack the strong individualism that drives Western economies to innovate. In order to progress, Eastern societies must therefore adopt individualistic values.

☐ **Stereotypes** are opinions applied broadly, and often without conscious awareness, to a group of people.
- **Self-fulfilling prophecy:** a cultural expectation or belief that becomes true because people expect it to be true, and behave accordingly
  - Ex: A teacher has one classroom of low-income students and one class of high-income students. If the teacher expects that the low-income students will not perform as well as the high-income students, that can lead to changes in the teacher's behavior toward the two classes, and therefore, could increase the likelihood of the expected outcome.
- **Stereotype threat:** a situation in which an individual becomes anxious when confronted with the possibility of confirming a stereotype about a group that they belong to
  - Ex: Two groups of women are asked to read a scientific article before performing a spatial reasoning task. One group reads an article concluding that women do not perform as well as men on spatial reasoning tasks, while the control group reads an unrelated article. The women who read the spatial reasoning article will not perform as well as the control on the spatial reasoning task due to stereotype threat.

Social Interaction

☐ **Status** is an individual's hierarchical "place" in society. Some types of status are associated with particular obligations, expectations, or rights.
- **Achieved status**: a status that was earned through work, skills, or experience (ex: becoming a doctor is a status that you earn)
- **Ascribed status**: a status that you are born with, or that is assumed by others in your social group (ex: a child born into a wealthy family has ascribed status)

☐ **Role** is an individual's performance of their status, or the characteristic behaviors and traits associated with a particular status.
- **Role conflict** occurs when an individual has two or more roles that are in conflict.
  - Ex: People often feel that their professional role (job) and their family role are in conflict, because devoting more time to one takes time away from the other.
- **Role strain** occurs when there is a mismatch between a role and the person who is expected to take on the role. This can occur because the individual is unable to perform the role, they do not agree with the role, or they receive negative feedback about their performance of the role from those around them.

- **Role exit** occurs when someone abandons a role they have previously held.
  - Ex: A disillusioned New York City banker quits his job to open a bike shop in Portland.
- **Social groups** are the different categories of people that you associate with. There are four types:
  - **Primary groups**: social groups that share strong, enduring relationships (ex: family, lifelong friends)
  - **Secondary groups**: social groups with meaningful, but less intense and lasting relationships. You chose to become a part of these groups (ex: coworkers)
  - **In-group**: a social group with which you identify. People tend to have greater affinity for in-group members.
  - **Out-group**: a social group with which you do not identify. People sometimes perceive out-group individuals unfavorably.
  - **Group size:** as social groups get larger, they tend to become more stable, though the individual relationships that make up the group tend to become less intimate.
    - Dyad: two people. The most basic unit of a social group.
    - Triad: three people. Triads group dynamics differ significantly from dyads, as there is the possibility of uneven splits of opinion (one vs. two, whereas a dyad is always one vs. one).
- **Networks** are a way to look at social groups in terms of the connections among individuals. (ex: An individual Facebook user has a set of "friends," or direct connections, each of whom has their own set of friends, each of whom has their own set of friends.)
- **Organizations** are essentially large, formalized, secondary social groups. As they become larger, divisions of labor tend to emerge, as do hierarchical structures, rules of conduct, etc.
  - The goal of an ideal organization or bureaucracy is to achieve maximum efficiency.
  - **Formal organization** is a fixed set of rules that govern how an organization operates. These rules tend to emphasize coordination, shared objectives, hierarchical structures, and measures to promote efficient operation.
  - **Bureaucracy** is a network of individuals that, together, manage the administration of an organization. While some scholars view bureaucracy as negative, because they can be inflexible and waste resources, others view them as an inevitable consequence of the growth of organization, and one that can be mitigated by efforts to increase efficiency.
    - **Ideal bureaucracies** have five characteristics:

- Division of labor
- Hierarchical organization
- Written rules and regulations
- Impersonality (made of unbiased individuals)
- Employment based on technical qualifications
  - o Perspectives on bureaucracy
    - **Iron law of oligarchy**: All organizations eventually develop oligarchic tendencies, resulting in the concentration of power, money, and resources, in the hands of a few individuals. It is therefore impossible for large groups or organizations to function in a truly democratic manner.
    - **McDonaldization:** a phenomenon by which a culture begins to operate like a fast-food restaurant, meaning that they become highly homogenized, modular, and driven primarily by economic demand rather than shared values, collective social goals, etc.
- ☐ **Expressing and detecting emotion** varies among individuals, based on ability, experience, and characteristics.
  - Gender and culture can influence the expression and detection of emotion.
    - o **Culture**: Some cultures promote the suppression of emotional expression, while others view emotional expression as appropriate or even expected in certain circumstances.
    - o **Gender**: While a male politician expressing anger tends to be viewed more positively (anger indicates strength, confidence), a female politician expressing anger tends to be viewed more negatively (anger indicates aggression and instability).
- ☐ **Presentation of self** is a cognitive and emotional process, which can also be influenced by social and cultural factors.
  - **Impression management** is the process by which we attempt, through our behavior, to influence how other people perceive us. This can occur both consciously and subconsciously.
    - o Ex: Most people behave differently in a job interview than in a casual conversation with their friends. Your desire to be perceived as professional, competent, etc., in the interview. Context causes you to alter your behavior in an attempt to manage the impression that you are making.
  - **Dramaturgical approach** is a sociological perspective that uses theatrical performance as a metaphor for how people present themselves in different contexts.
    - o **Front stage:** the self that you present to others. This can vary based on your social context (the audience) and be influenced by backstage factors.

- **Backstage:** the private self that you are when nobody is looking at you
- ☐ **Verbal and nonverbal communication**: Your presentation of self is not only what you do and say, but also nonverbal elements such as your body language, physical appearance, eye contact, etc.
- ☐ **Animal signals and communication** can seem completely different from human communication, though they tend to be based on some of the same basic principles or instincts that we share, including individual and collective wellbeing, food, shelter, mating, etc.
  - **Animal communication** does not rely on a codified, complex, and endlessly variable language in the same way that human communication does. Communication tends to be driven more directly by evolutionary needs or advantages.
    - Ex: Animals from tigers to honeybees communicate in order to acquire and/or share the location of food.
  - **Interspecies communication** also occurs, and can confer evolutionary advantage.
    - Ex: Some animals avoid brightly-colored insects or frogs, as bright colors often indicate that they are poisonous. This can promote the survival of both the frog and its predator.
- ☐ **Attraction** between individuals can be based on a variety of factors, including physical appearance, status, similarity to you, or dissimilarity to you.
  - What is considered "attractive" is not universal, and varies over time and across cultures.
  - "Attractiveness" signals, which are often associated with good health, can contribute to evolutionary success by promoting mating between healthy individuals, as well as individuals with dissimilar genes or traits, in order to produce offspring with a high probability of survival.
- ☐ **Aggression** is social action intended to intimidate and/or harm others. It can be physical, verbal, or nonverbal.
  - Aggression can provide evolutionary advantage in competition for mates, access to resources, etc.
  - In animals, aggression often takes the form of posturing and display of strength, without actual physical engagement (game theory can be applied to these interactions — it is often more advantageous to both parties to resolve conflicts through display rather than engaging in violence).
- ☐ **Attachment theory** is a model for describing the social, psychological, and emotional characteristics of close interpersonal relationships. This theory focuses especially on attachment formation in infants, positing that successful social-emotional development depends on an infant forming an attachment to one or more primary caregivers.

- **Secure attachment** is considered the "best," and results from a caregiver that is consistently responsive and behaves predictably in social and emotional interactions with the infant. The child will show that they have trust in their caregivers, but are also comfortable being separated from their caregiver for brief periods, have less fear of strangers, etc.
- **Insecure attachment** results from a caregiver that is unpredictable and inconsistently responsive to the infant's social and emotional needs. The child becomes distressed when their caregiver leaves the room, is fearful of others, etc.

☐ **Altruism** is when an individual acts to promote the wellbeing of another.
- Altruistic behavior is seen most often among close relatives.
- Altruism can be evolutionarily advantageous by promoting group survival.
- Altruistic behavior is also more common in interactions with people that you know you will see again in the future (reciprocal altruism).

☐ **Social support** is the personal benefit we derive from being part of a social network. Social support can be emotional (love, trust, affection), companionship (social engagement), informational (advice, even from the internet), or tangible (material assistance).

☐ **Biological explanations** of social behavior in animals:
- **Foraging** refers to a varied array of behaviors directed toward acquiring food. Some animals forage individually, some in groups. A lion forages by hunting zebras, a zebra forages by grazing.
- **Mating behavior** and mate choice varies significantly across species. Types and strategies for mating include:
  - **Random mating**: Mates are selected at random within a species, rather than certain traits resulting in higher frequencies of mating. Enhances genetic diversity.
  - **Associative mating**: Mating occurs more often between individuals that are similar to each other. Inbreeding is an extreme form of associative mating, and can result in genetic disorders.
  - **Non-associative mating**: Mating occurs more often dissimilar individuals.
  - Mating can be monogamous (pair bonding), polygynous (one male mates with multiple females) or polyandrous (one female mates with multiple males).

☐ **Game theory** can be used to model decision making in individual and social interactions contributing to evolutionary success.
- Sometimes, sharing is better for everybody.
- **Hawk and dove** is a classic application of game theory to evolution. There are two types of individuals: hawkish ones, who are prone to fight, and doveish ones, who are more interested in sharing.

- o Hawk vs. hawk: Both will posture, neither will back down. They engage in a physical fight, likely killing one and injuring the other. One wins, but still experiences a risk. Each stands to gain ½ the value, but minus the cost of fighting (V-C)/2, (V-C)/2
  - o Hawk vs. dove: The hawk will posture, the dove will back down. The hawk wins, the dove gets nothing (V,0)
  - o Dove vs. dove: Neither will threaten, so they will cooperate. Each gets ½ of the total value. (V/2, V/2)
- ☐ **Inclusive fitness** is a model used to describe the evolution of social behaviors.
  - • Strategies that promote the survival of the group are sometimes more evolutionarily successful than those that only promote the survival of the individual (ex: If a single antelope in isolation sees a tiger coming to eat him, his best strategy is to run. However, if that antelope is in a group of other antelope, the better strategy is to alert the others and then run, even though this will alert the tiger to the individual's location, as this promotes the long-term survival of the individual, the group, and the species.).

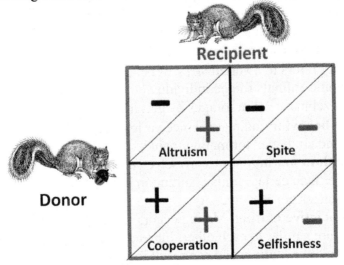

Figure 72: Game theory and cooperation.

- ☐ **Discrimination** occurs when an individual treats another individual in a different, often negative, way, based on perceived membership in a certain group (ex: racism is discrimination based on race).
  - • Discrimination can be carried out by individuals or groups.
    - o **Individuals** may act out discriminatory behaviors based on their prejudices.
      Groups or organizations may act out discriminatory behaviors against many individuals. These discriminatory practices may or may not be formalized in policies.

- Ex: An employer chooses a man for a job over an equally qualified woman because they expect that the woman might get pregnant and take significant leave.
- **Discrimination and prejudice**: Discrimination is the actions taken by an individual or organization based on prejudiced beliefs.
- **Power, prestige, and class** facilitate discrimination by enhancing the perceived differences among groups, as well as the relative advantage and disadvantage between them.

Social Structure

☐ **Theoretical approaches** to understanding social structure. These are not right or wrong, just different lenses through which to view the social world.
- **Microsociology vs. macrosociology:** Micro analyzes the interactions of individuals, and how they generate larger-scale social phenomena. Macro analyzes the interactions and behaviors of social networks or populations, and therefore tends to be more abstract.
  - Ex: Very few people in the U.S. get enough exercise. A microsociologist might look at this as a consequence of individuals not having sufficient incentives for exercise, or of people's peer groups not valuing exercise. A macrosociologist might look at this as a consequence of a food supply chain that prioritizes cheap, high-calorie food; a public education system that doesn't prioritize fitness; and cities and towns that do not provide sufficient recreational opportunities.
☐ **Macrosociology** is more often used to analyze large-scale social issues such as population dynamics, war, poverty, interactions among nations, etc. It tends to focus on institutions and social structures, rather than one-on-one interactions. Macrosociological approaches:
- **Functionalism** views society as a complex network of interdependent components that work together to enable social stability and progress.
  - Ex: Studying the high cost of healthcare as a consequence of a range of interdependent institutions and relationships, such as negotiations between states and pharmaceutical systems, lobbying of political leaders by health systems, declining investment in public health, etc.
- **Conflict theory** (Marxism) is a perspective used to analyze the role and impact of inequality in a society. It emphasizes the importance of power, and imbalances of power, in stabilizing or destabilizing a society.
  - Ex: Many communities have a single employer that employs a large proportion of the population. This employer therefore has significant power over the citizens. If the citizens become dissatisfied with their

working conditions, income, etc., they may rebel against the employer, shifting the balance of power, because while they depend on the employer for income, the employer also depends on the citizens for productivity. This upheaval is inevitable consequence of an imbalance of power.

- **Feminist theory** analyzes the influences of gender inequality on the social world, including discrimination and oppression, as well as the influence of gender inequality on aesthetics, art, and self-expression.
  - o Ex: Inequality of pay between men and women is a consequence of an array of social factors, including socialization of gender norms and differences, women's lack of access to opportunities, differing social expectations, sexual harassment, etc.

☐ **Microsociology** is more often used to analyze social phenomena that revolve around smaller-scale individual interactions, such as family or workplace dynamics, criminality, social customs, etc.

- **Symbolic interactionism** (microsociology): People, places, and things have different kinds of meaning for us, and that meaning determines how we interact or respond to them. That meaning is derived from and shaped by social interaction. This can lead to communication problems.
  - o Ex: Everyone wants to be "healthy," but healthy means different things to different people based on their experiences, values, etc. Imagine that a certain drug can help reduce pain, but also makes your mind foggy. If "healthy" for you means being able to do crossword puzzles, you might not feel healthier taking the drug.
- **Social constructionism** (microsociology): Individuals and groups participate in the creation of reality. Things have meaning because we, as a group or society, have agreed that they do.
  - o Ex: Money is just linen paper with old white men on it, but we have agreed, as a society, that it represents value.
- **Exchange-rational choice theory** (microsociology) is an approach to modeling socioeconomic behavior based on the premise that all large-scale social behavior is an aggregation of the behavior and decisions of individuals. Therefore, social change occurs through influencing the behaviors of individuals.
  - o Ex: If we want people to be healthier, we should have all food prices be based on calorie count, so that it is cheaper to eat healthy. Because people are rational actors, they will change their behavior in response to this change in price, and this will lead to healthy individuals, which in turn will create a healthier society.

☐ **Institutions** are structures within a society that can maintain or influence the behavior of citizens.

- **Education**, particularly public education, is an agent of socialization influencing the development of young people's knowledge and values.
  - **Hidden curriculum** is elements of education that are learned, but not explicitly taught, such as social values learned through interaction with students and teachers, political beliefs held by administrators or political leaders, etc.
  - **Teacher expectancy** is the expectations that a teacher has for individual students may, implicitly, influence their educational outcomes (ex: if a teacher expects minority students to perform poorly, this can alter the way they act toward these students, and by extension, their educational outcomes).
  - **Educational segregation and stratification is when** the quality of education available to different groups, often based on race or income, is different. This can perpetuate inequality in a society.
- **Family** structure, values, and practices influence society.
  - **Kinship and family** are diverse, and include the close relationships of value to an individual, whether or not the individuals are biologically related or contractually obligated.
  - **Marriage and divorce** are formal governmental acknowledgements of the start or end of a contract between individuals. The meaning and value of marriage and divorce varies significantly across cultures and time. Marriage can be considered a primarily economic contract between families. Divorce is relatively routine in the modern U.S., but was once considered shameful.
  - **Violence in the family** (Child abuse, elder abuse, spousal abuse) is a social pattern in which individuals commit physically or psychologically violent acts against family members.
    - Family violence can be viewed as a heritable social trait, as those who are socialized in an environment with family violence may, explicitly or implicitly, view it as acceptable behavior, and therefore perpetuate it through generations.
- **Religion** is a cultural institution that includes beliefs, values, and behaviors practiced by a social group.
  - **Religiosity** is a sociological quantification of the influence of religion on the life of individuals or groups. Religiosity varies widely even within a single religion. Individuals of low religiosity may participate occasionally, casually, or culturally in aspects of religion, while individuals of high religiosity may participate in religious behaviors and make decisions based on religious beliefs every day of their lives.
  - Types of religious organizations can be described on a continuum:

- **Churches** are the most established and dominant forms of organized religious belief and culture.
- **Sects** are subcultures within a religion that typically form in protest to an aspect of a dominant religion, but still maintain significant commonality with a dominant religion. Some sects may develop over time into distinctive denominations or churches.
- **Cults** are characterized by more significant departures from dominant religions than sects, such as wholly new texts or belief systems. The creation of a cult is often initiated by a charismatic leader. Cults can develop over time into denominations or churches.
  - o **Religions can change over time** in response to social forces. This change takes three main forms:
    - **Modernization** refers to changes in religious practice to adapt to social and technological progress (ex: a church starts live-streaming their morning service, so that people can participate over the internet).
    - **Secularization** is the loss of social and cultural significance of a religion over time.
    - **Fundamentalism** occurs when a church reacts to social change by becoming more extreme, strict, or literal in its beliefs and adherence to practices.
- **Government and economy** are cultural institutions that provide structure through the enforcement of laws and maintenance of trade.
  - o **Power and authority** in society are typically concentrated in the government, which creates laws and maintains economic activity.
  - o Comparative economic and political systems is a field at the intersection of sociology and economics, concerned with analyzing the differences among economic and political systems.
    - A comparative economist might study U.S. drug prices by analyzing differences in how drug prices are set across different countries.
  - o **Division of labor** is a cooperative approach to accomplishing work by dividing a complex task into a series of simplified steps, each of which can be accomplished by a single individual.
    - An assembly line uses division of labor to increase efficiency
- ☐ **Health and medicine** are cultural institutions concerned with promoting and maintaining health and wellness.
  - **Medicalization** is a process in which human characteristics come to be viewed as biologically defined and treatable.

- o Ex: Kids that used to be seen as energetic and distractible become kids with ADHD.
- **The sick role** refers to the social behaviors associated with being a sick individual. These behaviors can vary significantly among individuals.
  - o Ex: When you think you are sick, you could have several behavioral responses, which might include asking a doctor, asking the internet, or asking an herbalist or faith healer.
  - o Behaviors associated with the sick role can influence the health of a community by influencing when and if people seek medical advice, and whether they adhere to it.
- **Delivery of health care** refers to the complex system by which individuals receive medical advice, care, products, and devices. These processes can significantly influence the quality of medical care that people receive.
  - o Ex: If a drug supply chain is insecure, it can result in people becoming sick from a treatment that is intended to make them healthier.
- **Illness experience** refers to the process of being ill and how it can affect an individual's perception, values, knowledge, or identity.
  - o Ex: If you have a chronic disease, such as diabetes, that requires continual attention, the experience and behaviors associated with your disease can become part of your identity, as well as influencing your views about health and medicine.
- **Social epidemiology** refers to the study of how social factors, particularly gender, race, and economic disparities, can influence health.
  - o White people tend to be healthier than black people, and rich people tend to be healthier than poor people. A range of medical and social factors contribute to these disparities.
    - Ex: Drug trials are typically conducted with white male subjects. Therefore, much less is known about health effects for women or minority groups. This can result in poorer health and health care for these groups.
    - Ex: Low-income people may have poorer access to health care, as well as less access to healthy food, less knowledge about health, and less social support, all of which may contribute to worse health outcomes.
- ☐ **Culture** is the way of life in a certain community, and the traditions, knowledge, beliefs, and values that you acquire by being part of it.
  - **Elements of culture include: beliefs, language, rituals, symbols, and values**
  - **Material vs. symbolic culture:** Material culture refers to the physical objects associated with a culture, while symbolic culture refers to the ideas, beliefs, and other intangible components of culture.

- o Ex: Archeologists study material culture, learning about cultures of the past through the objects they leave behind. Symbolic culture can include a culture's values, religion, morals, and interpersonal customs.
- **Culture lag:** It takes time for culture to catch up with changes in technology. This can lead to conflict.
  - o Ex: New medical technologies such as stem cells and gene editing are controversial, because they introduce new ethical and practical dilemmas that take time to be resolved by or incorporated into a culture's values and beliefs.
- **Culture shock** occurs when someone moves to or visits a new place and is disoriented or distressed by the differences between cultures.
- **Assimilation** is the process by which an individual or group of one culture begins to resemble another culture.
  - o Ex: Many immigrants experience assimilation, in which they adopt aspects of the culture of a new country.
  - o Assimilation can be viewed as both a positive and negative force. Positive, because it can enable individuals or groups to adapt to a new culture, and negative, because it can erode or even destroy — naturally or by force — the values of a culture, particularly those of a minority group (ex: Native Americans in the U.S.).
- **Multiculturalism** occurs when multiple cultures coexist in a given place, resulting in significant cultural diversity, which can benefit society as a whole.
- **Subcultures** are subgroups of a larger culture that differ in some characteristics. These can be minor characteristics (ex: train enthusiasts could be considered a subculture) or more significant (ex: a radical political party).
  - o **Countercultures** are a type of subculture. They differ significantly from the dominant culture, and are sufficiently large and well defined to influence the dominant culture (ex: the Beat generation).
- **Mass media** refers to media (newspapers, websites, television) that are widely distributed and consumed, and therefore have the potential to transmit, alter, or promote ideas, customs, or values within a culture.
  - o Mass media has significant influence over **popular culture**, which refers to the ideas, objects, language, and values — profound and trivial — that are widely known and discussed in the everyday life of a society.
- **Evolution and human culture** can be viewed as interacting forces in long-term change within the human species.
  - o Ex: Tolerance for lactose is much more common in cultures that were once largely dependent on cattle. For these early cultures, the ability to

digest lactose in adulthood conferred significant survival advantage, and therefore, the culture of cattle farming influenced the biology of a group.

- **Transmission and diffusion:** Ideas, technologies, and values can be transmitted from one culture to another.
  - o Imperialism is an example of cultural transmission through conquering new territory.
  - o The Internet can also be viewed as a mechanism for cultural transmission or diffusion, as it makes ideas and values from one culture more readily available to other cultures.

Demographics

- ☐ **Demographics** refers to statistical analysis of the quantifiable characteristics of a population (age, gender, race and ethnicity, income, etc.)
  - **Age:**
    - o **Aging and the life course**: In addition to the biological and psychological changes associated with age, we experience social changes as we age (ex: when you are a child you are dependent on your parents, but eventually you become independent, and may ultimately have your own dependents).
      - ▪ Social roles, expectations, and healthcare needs change as we age.
    - o **Age cohorts** are groups defined by age that share a set of similar experience (ex: Millennials are an age cohort).
  - **Gender:**
    - o **Sex vs. gender:** Sex is determined by the chromosomes you are born with, while gender refers to how you identify yourself in the social world.
      - ▪ Cisgender: you identify as the gender of your biological sex
      - ▪ Transgender: you identify as a gender that is different than your biological sex
    - o **Sexual orientation** refers to an individual's patterns of romantic and/or sexual attraction. Sexual orientation is generally categorized as heterosexual, homosexual, bisexual, or asexual. Non-heterosexual individuals experience discrimination, including discrimination enforced by law (ex: prohibition of military participation, illegal to marry, etc.).
    - o **Gender is socially constructed,** meaning that it is based on a collection of social ideas and behaviors that we have learned through our social experience.

- o **Gender segregation** refers to the separation of people and social life based on socially constructed ideas about gender. This can be formally enforced by laws (ex: women forbidden to drive or hold public office) or by social norms (ex: girls play with pink toys, boys play with blue toys).
- **Race and ethnicity**:
  - o Race is socially constructed, meaning that it is based on a collection of social ideas and behaviors about our origins that we have learned through our social experience.
  - o **Racialization** is the process by which racial or ethnic identity is applied to a person, a practice, a behavior, or a group that does not claim that identity.
  - o Racial formation theory is an analytical approach to looking at the formation of racial identity through social construction. This approach emphasizes the influence of race on all aspects of social life, and includes both micro- and macrosociological analysis.
- **Immigration** status:
  - o Patterns of **immigration** can impact societies and economies in a variety of ways. They can increase diversity, improve the quality of the workforce, strain capacity and availability of social services, etc. Individuals who immigrate may also experience significant challenges associated with adapting to life in a different country.
  - o Immigrants, especially immigrants who are also of minority racial or ethnic groups, may experience discrimination, stereotyping, and other negative social consequences.
- ☐ **Demographic shifts** and social change:
  - Theories of demographic change attempt to explain how the composition of societies change over time in response to a range of forces.
    - o **Malthusian theory** states that when population growth outpaces a society's ability to produce sufficient food to feed that population, population growth rates will plummet and the society will be returned to subsistence conditions. Essentially, growing populations are doomed to destroy themselves.
    - o **Demographic transition** refers to the transition from pre-industrial societies, which are characterized by small population sizes with high birth and death rates, to industrialized societies, which have large population sizes with low birth and death rates.
  - **Population growth** and decline
    - o **Population projections** are used to model how population demographics will change over time.

- o **Population pyramids** are diagrams used to illustrate the distribution of a population by age and gender. When there are relatively large numbers of young people, the population is expanding, while relatively small numbers of young people indicate that the population is contracting. Equal distributions indicate a population that is stationary.

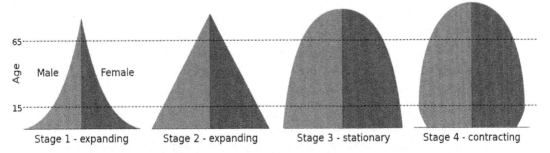

Figure 73: Example population pyramids.

- **Fertility, migration, and mortality**:
  - o **Total fertility rate** is the average number of children born to each woman in a given country, calculated by taking the sum of age-specific fertility rates.
    - ▪ Fertility rate > 2, then population is growing (every two people create more than two new people
    - ▪ Fertility rate <2, then population is shrinking (every two people create fewer than two new people)
    - ▪ **Crude fertility rate** is an alternate (weaker) measure, found by dividing the total number of births in a year by the total population.
    - ▪ Age-specific fertility rate looks at fertility in specific age cohorts.
  - o **Birth rate** is the total number of live births per 1,000 individuals in a population.
  - o **Mortality rate** is the total number of deaths per 1,000 individuals in a population
  - o **Push and pull factors in migration** refer to the reasons that people may choose to emigrate from a country, and to immigrate to a country. These factors may include lack of economic opportunity in one country (push) and availability of opportunity in another (pull), or social upheaval (push) versus social stability (pull).
- **Social movements** are organized efforts to shift the perspectives, behaviors, or values of a society.
  - o **Relative deprivation theory** says that social movements can arise when a disadvantaged group lacks access to resources and rights

enjoyed by the dominant social group (ex: 1960s civil rights movement).
- o Organization of social movements can take many forms. Some are organized around charismatic leaders, others are triggered in reaction to significant social events, and others by the development of ideas or values that run counter to the dominant culture, and others by some combination of factors. Successful social movements have features in common with other social organizations, including bureaucracy.
- o Movement strategies and tactics can include violent or nonviolent protest, political action, social demonstrations, media messaging, etc.
- ☐ **Globalization** refers to the increasing interconnectedness of people and cultures as the exchange of ideas, values, goods, and services becomes technologically easier.
  - Factors contributing to globalization:
    - o Communication technology, such as the internet, contributes to globalization by offering accessible exposure to other cultures online
    - o Economic interdependence, in which nations depend on each other for vital resources
  - Perspectives on globalization:
    - o **World systems theory** views the planet as a single economic system, with three classes of countries participating:
      - ▪ Core countries: fully industrialized, strong central government, strong middle class, diversified
      - ▪ Semi-periphery countries: periphery countries developing into core countries, or core countries that are declining to periphery countries
      - ▪ Periphery countries: weak central government, poor people, dependence on a single type of economic activity
    - o **Modernization theory** states that all countries follow the same path through development, and assumes that all countries can eventually reach the same high level of development.
    - o **Dependency theory** states that poor countries and subjugated to rich countries, because rich countries depend on them for natural resources and other economic contributions. Therefore, poor countries are unlikely to develop into rich countries.
  - **Social changes in globalization**: As people become more aware of other cultures, it can influence their own social views and behaviors.
    - o **Civil unrest**, in which members of a social group become dissatisfied with aspects of their social world and rebel, can occur in response to globalization.

- o **Terrorism**, or an act by one group to erode another group's sense of social and personal security, is often motivated by political unrest, or in response to a perceived cultural threat.
- ☐ **Urbanization** refers to the movement of people from rural or suburban areas into urban areas.
  - **Industrialization** contributes to urban growth, because it is generally dependent on a large workforce in a small geographic area (while agriculture is dependent on a small workforce in a large geographic area).
  - **Suburbanization and urban decline** refers to the outflow of people from urban areas to suburban areas for a variety of reasons, including economic opportunity, health concerns, education, etc.
    - o Suburbanization can contribute to sprawl, in which populations grow quickly but without sufficient urban planning to ensure sustainability.
    - o Urban decline refers to the negative consequences of people leaving a city, such as economic hardship, crumbling infrastructure, unemployment, crime, etc.
  - **Gentrification and urban renewal** refers to the reversal of areas of urban decline. This can result from investment in the redevelopment of urban areas, shifting social preferences for where to live, and migration of social groups. While this process can result in economic growth, it can also be associated with significant challenges and conflicts.
    - o Ex: Low-income residents of a gentrifying neighborhood may be forced to move away because they can no longer afford to live in their community.

Social Inequality

- ☐ **Inequality:** When resources in a society are distributed unevenly, social patterns are created that are used to define categories of people.
- ☐ **Spatial inequality:** disparities based on place
  - **Residential segregation**: People live where they can afford to live. This leads to people being grouped together residentially based on their resources/income.
    - o **Neighborhood safety and violence:** Low-income communities tend to have higher rates of violent crime, which negatively impacts residents in multiple ways, including negative health effects.
    - o **Environmental justice:** Higher-income communities tend to have better environmental health and lower exposure to environmental hazards relative to lower-income communities. This creates an unequal distribution of environmental resources.

- ☐ **Social class and socioeconomic status** (SES): SES is a measure of a person's social and economic position relative to others based on factors including education, income, and occupation. People of similar SES are grouped hierarchically into social classes.
  - **Class consciousness** (Marxist): People hold beliefs about their own social class. Belief that you are of low social rank can be detrimental to your earning ability, motivation, health, etc. In Marxist theory, class consciousness can also inspire organization of lower classes in rebellion against higher classes, in order to take over and control the means of production.
  - **False consciousness** (Marxist): Lower classes do not recognize their own oppression by upper classes due to ideas put forward by upper classes about the reasons and motivations behind class stratification (ex: workers are told, and believe, that by working hard they will be able to move up in social class, when in fact, this is very unlikely).
  - **Cultural and social capital:** the idea that people of higher SES have more cultural and social "wealth" (ex: social connections with employers, familiarity with social conventions and shared interests with those who have higher wealth)
  - **Social reproduction:** the idea that people tend to occupy the same social class as their parents
  - **Power, privilege, prestige:** positive factors associated with individuals and groups with higher SES
    - ○ **Power:** influence on society that contributes to your ability to achieve your own goals
    - ○ **Prestige:** respect that you have from others in society due to your job, your wealth, etc.
    - ○ **Privilege:** access to better education, lack of economic hardship, etc.
  - **Intersectionality:** When you belong to multiple disadvantaged groups based on class, race, gender, religion, sexual orientation, ability, age, etc., these factors intersect and interact with each other in forming an individual or group's experience of oppression or social disadvantage. In order to study these groups, all individual sources of disadvantage should be considered simultaneously.
  - **Socioeconomic gradient in health:** In general, people with higher SES have better health outcomes than those with lower SES (on a continuum).
  - **Global inequalities:** Different countries have different relative wealth. This leads to inequalities in health, wealth, etc., between countries.

- ☐ **Patterns of social mobility** in society:
  - **Intergenerational mobility:** movement of social class from one generation to the next (poor parents send their child to college, their child enters a higher social class)
  - **Intragenerational mobility:** movement of social class within a single generation (a person born into a lower social class rises to a higher one through occupation, gain of wealth, etc.)
  - **Vertical mobility:** moving up or down a social class
  - **Horizontal mobility:** moving position within a single social class (ex: changing job or state of residence without significant change in absolute or relative income)
  - **Meritocracy:** a social structure in which social status is defined only by individuals' skill or ability
- ☐ **Poverty** and its impact on society:
  - **Relative and poverty:** when a person has low income relative to those around them, even if the absolute value of their income is high
  - **Absolute poverty:** (typically defined by the poverty line) when wealth is inadequate to purchase what is needed for survival
  - **Social exclusion:** social disadvantage that results from being systematically blocked from accessing opportunities and resources that are available to others (ex: school segregation). This can result in a feeling of isolation or exclusion from desired resources, activities, experiences, etc., and living on the "fringe" of society.
- ☐ **Health and healthcare** disparities:
  - Health and access to healthcare can be negatively impacted by inequality in class, gender, race, and other factors.
    - o Ex: Low income communities tend to have poorer environmental quality, less access to healthy food, poorer public schools, and fewer recreational opportunities relative to high income communities. All of these factors, and more, can have a negative impact on the health of individuals in low income communities, as well as on the quality of the health care they receive.
    - o Ex: Low income people in rural areas may have poor access to health care because they must travel long distances (which takes time and costs money) to reach health care facilities.
    - o Ex: Some people are more comfortable seeing a health care provider who belongs to their demographic group. When that demographic group is underrepresented in medicine (black men, for example, are currently underrepresented in medicine), this can negatively impact healthcare access and quality for underrepresented groups.

o Ex: Pharmaceutical trial subjects tend to be male and white. As a result, less is known about the effectiveness and side effects of some treatments for women and minority groups. This can lead to poorer health care and/or health outcomes.

INDEX

D

Dalton's Law, 9
Decision-making, 159
Degenerate code, 66
Deindividuation, 175
Delta G, 50
Demographic shifts, 200
Demographic transition, 200
Denaturing, 58
Density, 6, 27
Dependency theory, 202
Depressants, 162
Depression, 172
Dermis, 139
Desmosomes, 90
Destructive interference, 15
Determination, 106
Deviance, 177
Diamagnetism, 25
Diaphragm, 118
Diastereomers, 31, 32
Diatomic elements, 26
Differential association theory, 177
Differentiation, 107
Diffraction grating, 16
Diffusion, 119
Digestive system, 127
Dipole interactions, 34
Dipole moment, 30
Disaccharides, 98
Discrimination, 192
Dispersion, 21, 34
Disproportionation reactions, 28
Distillation, 39
Division of labor, 196
Divorce, 195
DNA, 64
DNA libraries, 71
DNA ligase, 65
DNA polymerase, 64
DNA replication, 64
DNA sequencing, 71
Dopamine, 154
Doppler effect, 14
Dramaturgical approach, 189
Dreaming, 161
Drive reduction theory, 173
Drives, 173
Duodenum, 129
Dynein, 59

E

E and Z notation, 33

Ear anatomy, 148
Eclipsed conformers, 32
Economy, 196
Ectoderm, 105
Education, 195
EEG, 156
Ego, 169
Elaboration likelihood model, 181
Electric field, 9
Electric potential, 9, 10
Electric potential energy, 9
Electrochemistry, 9, 12
Electrolysis, 12
Electrolyte, 12
Electrolytic cell, 12
Electromagnetic Spectrum, 15
Electromotive force, 13
Electron affinity, 27
Electron transport chain, 79, 84
Electronegativity, 27, 30
Electrons, 12, 13, 23, 24, 25
Electrophoresis, 40, 59
Electrostatic force, 24
Electrostatics, 9
Emission line spectra, 24
Emotion, 166
Emotional intelligence, 160
Enamines, 42
Enantiomers, 31, 32
Encoding, 163
Endocrine, 107
Endocrine system, 113
Endocytosis, 89
Endoderm, 104
Endoplasmic reticulum, 91
Endorphins, 154
Enolate, 43, 44
Enteric nervous system, 131
Enthalpy, 50
Environmental justice, 203
Enzyme kinetics, 61
Enzymes, 59
Epidermis, 139
Epinephrine, 154
Episodic memory, 164
Epithelial tissue, 107
Equilibrium, 4
Equilibrium constant, 37, 78
Equivalent protons, 19
Erikson, 184
Erythrocytes, 121
Escape learning, 180
Esophagus, 127
Esters, 46, 47
Ethnicity, 200

N

NADH, 60, 79, 80, 81, 82, 83, 84, 85
NADPH, 82
Natural selection, 77
Need-based theory, 173
Needs, 173
Nephron, 132
Nernst Equation, 13
Nerves, 154
Nervous System, 9, 153
Nervous tissue, 107
Networks, 188
Neural crest, 105
Neural plasticity, 166
Neurons, 11, 153
Neurotransmitters, 153
Neurulation, 105
Neutrons, 23
Newton's 1st Law, 3
Newton's 2nd Law, 3
Newton's 3rd Law, 3
Nickel-cadmium batteries, 13
NMR spectroscopy, 19
Noble gases, 26
Nociception, 151
Nodes of Ranvier, 12
Non-competitive inhibition, 62
Non-metals, 26
Nonsense mutation, 66
Non-template synthesis, 87
Norepinephrine, 154
Nuclear forces, 23
Nucleic acids, 64
Nucleosides, 64
Nucleotides, 64
Nucleus, 90

O

Obedience, 175
Observational learning, 181
Obsessive-compulsive disorder, 171
Ohm's Law, 10
Okazaki fragments, 65
Olfactory neurons, 152
Oncogenes, 70
Oocytes, 109
Operant conditioning, 178
Operon, 69
Opiates, 162
Optical microscope, 22
Optics, 20
Orbital diagrams, 25
Organelles, 90

Organizations, 188
Osmolarity, 122
Osmosis, 89
Osteoblasts, 139
Osteoclasts, 139
Osteocytes, 139
Otolithic organs, 153
Outbreeding, 78
Ovaries, 109
Ovary, 115
Ovulation, 111
Ovum, 112
Oxidation number, 27
Oxidative phosphorylation, 84, 85
Oxidative stress, 86
Oxidizing agents, 28
Oxioreductases, 59
Oxygen affinity, 122
Oxytocin, 113

P

Pancreas, 114, 130
Paper chromatography, 39
Paracrine, 107
Parallel processing, 148
Paramagnetism, 25
Parasympathetic nervous system, 155
Parathyroid, 114
Parathyroid hormone, 139
Parietal cells, 128
Parkinson's disease, 173
Partial pressure, 8
Parturition, 111
Pascal's Law, 7
Pauli exclusion principle, 25
Peer pressure, 175
Penetrance, 74
Pentose phosphate pathway, 82
Pepsinogen, 127
Peptide linkages, 55, 57
Perception, 144
Period, 3
Periodic motion, 3
Periodic Table, 23, 26
Peripheral nervous system, 154
Peripheral route, 181
Peroxisomes, 91
Personality, 168
Personality disorders, 172
PET, 156
pH, 19, 35, 36, 37, 38, 40
Phase change, 51
Phase diagrams, 51
Phenols, 47

Q

R

CPSIA information can be obtained
at www.ICGtesting.com
Printed in the USA
BVOW10s0624230417
482014BV00007B/313/P

9 781634 912600